To Richard.
Thanks for yo
support.
Remember the 1,300
Who never came home

Warmet Best wishes

May 2012.

THE BLOODIEST
YEAR 1972

'In Northern Ireland tonight, another British soldier has been killed.'
The words spoken by Trevor MacDonald on ITV's 'News At Ten' on average three times a week in 1972

This book is dedicated to the following people:

Eddie Atkinson, Green Howards
Dave Hallam, Tim Marsh, Ken Ambrose, Kevin Stevens, Vach and the rest of the
Royal Green Jackets; the finest regiment in the British Army
John Swaine, Mike Sangster, Tim Marsh and Mick Pickford, Royal Artillery
Mick Hill, Steve Norman and Andy Thomas, Royal Anglians
Pete Whittall of the Hampshires
Dave Langston, Army Catering Corps
Dave Von Slaps, Royal Armoured Corps
Phil Winstanley and Steve Horvath, Royal Army Medical Corps
Mike Day, Scots Guards
Arfon Williams and Haydn Davis, Royal Regiment of Wales
Paddy Lenaghan and George Prosser, King's Regiment
Andrew MacDonald, Kings Border Regiment
Ken Anderson, Bob Luke and Tommy Clarke, Royal Corps of Transport
Bill Jones, Royal Electrical and Mechanical Engineers
'Tiny' and June Rose for their combined bravery
Ken Boyd, my UDR comrade
Helen MacDonald, my loving partner
My children Anne-Marie, Anna, Jonathan, Jenny, Robbie, Alex and Nathan; your
dad was never a hero, but he knew lots of them
My grandchildren Sherriden, Kelsey, William and Samuel; may this never happen
again in your lifetimes
To the memory of my late cousin David McGough
To my godson, Jacob Deighton
To my new-found New Zealand and Australian and Jordanian friends who now
not only understand what happened in Northern Ireland but actually know
where it is!
To Jess Hape; you didn't know a thing about the Troubles, but by God, you are my
friend
And to hundreds of others too numerous to mention

THE BLOODIEST YEAR 1972

BRITISH SOLDIERS IN NORTHERN IRELAND
IN THEIR OWN WORDS

KEN WHARTON

SPELLMOUNT

To my late parents, Mark Clifford Wharton and Irene Wharton.
They brought me into this world and made me what I am today.

Photographs have been kindly supplied by various individuals, some
of whom wish to remain anonymous. The author and publishers are
extremely grateful to all contributors, in particular *The Belfast Telegraph*,
the Royal Green Jackets Association, the 94 Locating Regiment, RA,
Alex B, 10 UDR, Ernie Taylor and Terry Friend, RA. Once again, as
he did for the author's previous book, *Bloody Belfast*, Paul Crispin has
provided some memorable images.

The opinions expressed by the individual contributors to this book do
not represent the beliefs or judgements of the Publishers concerning
the tragic events described.

First published 2011 by
Spellmount, an imprint of
The History Press
The Mill, Brimscombe Port
Stroud, Gloucestershire, GL5 2QG
www.thehistorypress.co.uk

British Library Cataloguing in Publication Data.
A catalogue record for this book is available from the British Library.

ISBN 978 0 7524 5906 6

Typesetting and origination by The History Press
Printed in Great Britain

PRAISE FOR THE *THE BLOODIEST YEAR*

Ken Wharton's account of the bloodiest year of the Troubles is as vivid, powerful and moving as its predecessors. This is good, honest history. Soldiers and civilians alike owe him a debt of gratitude for telling it like it was.

Patrick Bishop, author of *Bomber Boys* and *3 Para*

In this new work, Ken Wharton focuses on the worst year of the Troubles: 1972. Once again he brings to life the thoughts and feelings of those in the British armed forces forced to bear the brunt of the Republican's war of terror. An important book.

Adrian Gilbert, author of *POW: Allied Prisoners in Europe, 1939–45*

Lest we forget. Ken Wharton brings to life a period of recent British military history to which attention must be paid.

Damien Lewis, author of *Bloody Heroes* and *Apache Dawn*

Ken has produced a meaty masterpiece from those grim and bleakly savage times … a forensic examination of the bitter and bloody Troubles that defined soldiering for an entire generation of criminally overused, vastly under-appreciated and shamefully ignored unsung heroes. The pages drip with stinging emotion and angry regrets about beloved comrades lost, at the behest of a spineless government and disenchanted public who seemed at a loss as to how to halt the escalating carnage and defeat an enemy that was as cunning as it was ruthless. *The Bloodiest Year* is a book that pierces your conscience like a GPMG 7:62mm round punching through a brick wall. It's noisy, it's messy and I defy any soldier not to be moved by it.

Steven McLaughlin, author of *Squaddie: A Soldier's Story*

'DANNY BOY'

Oh Danny boy, the pipes, the pipes are calling
From glen to glen, and down the mountain side
The summer's gone, and all the flowers are dying
'Tis you, 'tis you must go and I must bide.
But come ye back when summer's in the meadow
Or when the valley's hushed and white with snow
'Tis I'll be here in sunshine or in shadow
Oh Danny boy, oh Danny boy, I love you so.

And if you come, when all the flowers are dying
And I am dead, as dead I well may be
You'll come and find the place where I am lying
And kneel and say an 'Ave' there for me.

And I shall hear, tho' soft you tread above me
And all my dreams will warm and sweeter be
If you'll not fail to tell me that you love me
I'll simply sleep in peace until you come to me.

I'll simply sleep in peace until you come to me.

CONTENTS

One of the things which made me angry about all the mess over there, was the fact that we knew who the IRA were, we knew where they lived and what's worse is that they knew we knew, but the bloody Army wouldn't let us do our jobs!

Soldier, King's Regiment

According to figures, 1972 saw 1,853 bombings in the province. That is an average of over 5 a day. Imagine that happening in England, Scotland or Wales!

Ken Anderson, Royal Corps of Transport

I heard on the television about the soldiers being killed and I just knew that one of them was Eric. I just burst into tears. Later the Army confirmed what I had already guessed; that Eric had been killed.

Widow of a soldier shot in Northern Ireland

One body seemed to be intact apart from the combat jacket being torn, with nothing but dust on it. I still don't know what happened; whether one of them picked up the rifle butt or whether something else triggered a bomb. What was clear was how quickly life could be lost.

Jim, Argyll and Sutherland Highlanders

As soon as the IRA took a hand in things, we were tasked to go in and get them, thus alienating ourselves from the Roman Catholics. And the Protestants hated us for keeping them away from Roman Catholics.

Terry Friend, Royal Artillery

He was deployed to Northern Ireland aged only nineteen and stationed there for two years. During his time there, he experienced incidents of shootings, explosions, riots; searching houses, children crying, looking through personal property. Worst of all having to talk to known terrorists on a daily basis and be civil and cheerful even though they would boast and smile about trying to kill you. He didn't think he would make it through the tour and honestly thought he would be killed before the two years were up.

Michelle Stevenson, former wife of a soldier

She then told me how her mum had taken out a cup of tea to a soldier lying in a fire position behind the wheel of a car. The soldier just looked at her mum, and said in a broad London accent: 'This ain't a good time darling.' Her mum then noticed the gunfire!

Mick 'Benny' Hill, Royal Anglians

Criticisms; too many to mention but all aimed at the government rodents who sent us to do our job. We trained for that job and they never gave a shit about us in any way, shape or form in the whole 38 years of NI. But if you ask me: would I do it all again, as a soldier? Yes I would, just to be at the side of lads like myself who tramped those streets trying to keep the peace. They were caring lads from all backgrounds of life; great mates and priceless and who in the end, were shit all over by our so-called government for all 38 years. I write this with a few tears, Ken; but hey, I'm only human.

John Swaine, Royal Artillery

All my tours were in the 70s and we knew why we were there. But in late 1976, half way through number 5, I was beginning to doubt this. But all it would take would be a quiet 'God bless you son' or a packet of fags or a bar of chocolate pressed furtively into my hand by an old dear, to renew my faith in our job.

Mike Sangster, Royal Artillery

FOREWORD

BY TONY CLARKE

When Ken Wharton asked me to write the foreword for his book, I was surprised and humbled. What could an ageing paratrooper possibly write that could add to the words he has written in his books about the tragedy that is Northern Ireland that we, as British soldiers, experienced?

Our job in the fairly new volunteer British Army – the last National Service soldiers left in 1963 – was to go wherever we were sent and to carry out our duties to the best of our abilities. But how many who joined the Army in 1971, as I did, would have thought they would be fighting British citizens on the streets of British cities for many decades, killing British citizens, and being killed and wounded by British citizens in a war that was never called a war?

In the early 1970s, the Vietnam War was winding down but was still dominating the news and the horrors that played out every day on the streets of Belfast, Derry and in the countryside of South Armagh were a side-show that few, except the families directly affected, paid any attention to. Civil rights, gerrymandered elections, manipulation of city rates and voting irregularities were items that did little to excite us on the mainland.

Surely in the UK there could be no such issues? We were a democratic society, a free society. The sixties had emancipated us with drugs and free love. Everyone could do whatever they wanted; the Beatles, Rolling Stones, The Who and Rod Stewart were our heroes. But in Northern Ireland, 'freedom' was a word only afforded those who embraced Unionism. A large portion of the population were disenfranchised, oppressed, and brutalised and took out their anger and frustration the only way they knew, with extreme violence. It is a common reaction to oppression. It is not an excuse, I do not condone violence as a tool to force a political agenda, or any agenda for that matter; it is simply what happens.

That agenda of violence on all sides of the Northern Ireland conflict is what killed nearly 1,300 soldiers serving in the Province, killed by Unionists and Nationalists alike. That is the tragedy of Northern Ireland, and we the soldiers were caught in the crossfire of religious bigotry, hatred, brutality, criminal acts and political expedience.

On 23 February 1972, I was a Lance Corporal serving in the depot of the Parachute Regiment in Aldershot when a car bomb blasted the Parachute Brigade Officer's Mess killing five women and two men. One of those women was the mother of a Lance Corporal with whom I was serving at the time. The horror of the aftermath is beyond words, and although it was not my first baptism of fire, it made an impact that has stayed with me ever since. I still feel, hear and smell that explosion. It was a retaliatory strike against the Parachute Regiment whose 1st Battalion shot dead fourteen innocent civilians three weeks earlier in the Bogside in Derry.

My own personal journey has spanned 39 years, from the moment I joined the Parachute Regiment as a Private in 1971, until now. If, in 1972, anyone had told me I would walk into the Bogside in 2010 and meet family members of those killed on Bloody Sunday, I would have laughed in their faces. If anyone had said I would write an article in the *Derry Journal* on 16 June 2010 on the day after the Saville Report was published, I would have thought them completely insane. If anyone had said I would be visiting Northern Ireland and Derry in particular, as part of a Peace Organisation I would have demanded euthanasia immediately. Such was the anger and hatred I felt for the IRA, UDA and UVF, indeed anyone that screamed obscenities and spat in our faces as we tried to do our job.

Times have changed, and so have I. The future demands it.

There is a peace agreement and no matter what we think about some of the principal players that are a part of that agreement, our responsibility now is to support those that fervently pray for this to succeed in Northern Ireland, so that their young families may grow up in peace and not suffer the kind of atrocities that occurred in the early 1970s. The Saville Inquiry eclipsed the suffering and sacrifice that thousands of military families in England, Scotland and Wales have endured over the 38 years since Bloody Sunday. The anonymous coffins laid to rest in nondescript graves on grey rainy days. The pain etched on the faces of parents, sisters, brothers, children and wives, ignored by a society too self-centred to care. The veterans of the Northern Ireland conflict and their families are, for the most part, forgotten.

When I was serving we could not apply for War Disablement Pensions because we were told that Northern Ireland was not a war. Many of us endured multiple surgeries, disablement, combat stress disorder and were cast aside as being no longer useful, left to fend for ourselves in a society that didn't care. But those of us who served, fought, suffered injuries and died, know that we fought a shadowy dangerous war against an enemy determined to annihilate us. We fought and we died as the politicians debated the finer points of policy, constitutional anomalies and ancient insanities of which they understood little. Historically, the British soldier has simply fought when asked to, and suffered a violent, ignominious death for some paragraph on a sheet of paper in a parliamentary library.

In his extraordinary books, Ken Wharton has ensured that the veterans of the war in Northern Ireland are not forgotten. He shows that they served with courage, honour, dignity and distinction, and that many paid the ultimate sacrifice, something that cannot be fully appreciated unless you read their experiences contained between the covers of this book.

A.F.N. Clarke
Marina del Rey, California

AUTHOR'S NOTE

I had no real knowledge of Northern Ireland or conceptions of that land other than the words of the hauntingly lyrical songs of that 'Emerald Isle'. My late mother's favourite songs were 'Danny Boy' and the beautiful 'Mountains of Mourne' and listening to them overmuch as a young boy clearly influenced my visions of the country.

> There's beautiful girls here; oh, never you mind.
> With beautiful shapes nature never designed.
> And lovely complexions, all roses and cream.
> But O'Loughlin remarked with regard to the same;
> that if at those roses you venture to sip,
> the colours might all come away on your lip.
> So I'll wait for the wild rose that's waiting for me,
> where the mountains of Mourne sweep down to the sea.

If I thought that it was always green and that friendly little leprechauns and frightening banshees populated it, I was in for a rude awakening.

At the time of writing, the outrageously named 'Real IRA' and the 'Continuity IRA' continue to cause grave tensions in Northern Ireland. There was a car bomb in Newry, Co Down, policemen injured by booby traps, hoax bombs in Londonderry and countless more defused before they could detonate. The three killings at Masserene Barracks in March 2009 and at Craigavon are still seared fresh in the memory as what can only be described as 'men of evil' are intent on throwing away the hard-won peace dividend. That they can so easily forget the 4,500 plus deaths over those agonising 38 years is testament to their crass stupidity, selfishness and loses them their self-appointed crown of defenders of their 'communities'. The murder of Catholic police officer Ronan Kerr in Omagh in April 2011 meant that the terrible list is still not closed.

I am told by Republicans and members of Catholic communities in Northern Ireland, that there is no appetite for further prolonged and ultimately unsuccessful violence. There can be so few people inside that small country who want a return to the days of the Troubles and yet the men of anger, the men of violence and the men of hatred have taken it upon themselves to commence their 'struggle' all over again.

As was once famously said by Oliver Cromwell when addressing the Rump Parliament and centuries later by his own Conservative colleagues to Neville Chamberlain, following the debacle in Norway in 1940: 'In the name of God, go!'

For you Dave McGough; RIP, cuz.

ACKNOWLEGEMENTS

Where on earth does one begin when confronted with the task of writing a fairly comprehensive list which will acknowledge in full – and name every single person or institution – all those who helped me and without whom, I would still be typing out page one? There is nowhere that one can logically start, so simply, I will recall all that I can on this list but crave the reader's indulgence when I state the blindingly obvious; it is by no means exhaustive!

None of my achievements would have ever happened, nor would the writing of these oral histories of the Northern Ireland Troubles have ever come to pass without the magnificent help from new and old comrades from every regiment and corps of the British Army. I must acknowledge Ken Ambrose, David Hallam, Tim Marsh and Darren Ware of the Royal Green Jackets; has there ever been a finer regiment in the Army? Eddie Atkinson (Green Howards); Tommy Clarke, Ken Anderson and Kevin Wright (RCT); Alex 'B' and Jim Henderson (UDR); Mike Sangster (Royal Artillery); David Mitchell (Gordon Highlanders); Mick 'Benny' Hill and Steve Norman (Royal Anglians); Pete Whittall (Staffs); John Swaine (Royal Artillery); Haydn and Roy Davies and Arfon Williams (RRW); David Langston (ACC); Von Slaps (RTR); and Andrew MacDonald (Kings Border Regiment). Then there is Paddy Lenaghan and George Prosser (Kings) who also became my friends.

My profound thanks to journalist/author Kevin Myers for permission to use quotations from his quite excellent *Watching The Door: Cheating Death In Belfast In the 70s* and for his contribution to Chapter Nine under the title 'Para Shoot Out'. Thanks also to the *Sunday Observer* and *The Guardian*.

There is one organisation to whom I am forever indebted: NIVA, the Northern Ireland Veterans Association. If you served in Northern Ireland and are not yet a member, please contact them at http://www.nivets.org.uk/forums/content.php.

I am grateful to James, co-webmaster from Britain's Small Wars for his invaluable assistance in bringing together some excellent contributions from his site: http://britains-smallwars.com/ni/index.html.

I owe much to my partner, Helen MacDonald with whom, as we say in Yorkshire, I live 'over t'broom' who, over the last four years has been my biggest confidante, my human spell checker and the lady who has guided my life. No mere words could ever express the emotional debt that I owe this woman.

I have seven wonderful children who, at the time of writing range from 16–40 and three beautiful grandkids with a fourth pending. All of you have been my inspiration.

Finally, I would like to acknowledge those wonderful people of Northern Ireland who never supported the men of violence and who only wanted peace for their beautiful country.

INTRODUCTION

On the morning of 16 August, 2009, I awoke on the Gold Coast of Australia and heard the news that the 200th British serviceman had been killed in Afghanistan. Even 12,000 miles away, I could imagine the gasps of anguish and pain in the household of the man's loved ones and I could hear the disbelief in the voices of the great British public. I could also imagine the opprobrium of the British tabloid editors as they prepared vitriolic headlines to condemn the handling of the war by the Labour Prime Minister, Gordon Brown. In truth, it could have been any prime minister of any of the major political parties; the colour of the man's party was not of any consequence. Then I cast my mind back to 1972, the year that 172 British soldiers perished in many different ways in a small part of the United Kingdom and I do not recall the gentlemen of the fourth estate sharpening their knives for the PM of the day, Edward Heath.

It wasn't Afghanistan or Iraq, the Falklands or even a foreign country; it was part of Britain. It wasn't the muddy trenches of the Somme or the steamy jungles of Burma; instead, it was the blackened terraced housing, the modern housing estates and quaint rural villages of Northern Ireland. In that year of 1972, the 172 British families were visited, to be informed by a nervous but professional CVO (Casualty Visiting Officer) that their son, husband, father or brother would not be coming home again; a victim in a myriad ways of the Troubles.

I applaud from the bottom of my heart the good folk of Wootton Bassett in Wiltshire who have turned out in their hundreds, caps doffed, children and women, tradesmen and medalled veterans alike, to greet the Union Jack-draped coffins of Britain's fallen from Afghanistan. But who turned out to greet the homecoming of Trooper Ian Caie's coffin after his death at the hands of the IRA in Crossmaglen, other than his grieving family? Which newspaper editor condemned the British government as the body of Lance Corporal Peter Deacon Sime, killed on the Ballymurphy estate, was borne home to his native Scotland? Who but Private Tommy Stoker's family and friends welcomed his coffin back to Yorkshire? Which member of the general public spoke up when the 172nd coffin was returned to these shores as that terrible year, that *annus horriblis* of 1972, came to a bloody close? There is of course no answer; we know that Britain's forgotten war attracted the grief of only a fallen soldier's immediate family, his circle of friends and his stoical but saddened comrades.

This is not intended to be a definitive, quintessential or comprehensive account of that terrible year, but my objective is to deal with as much of what happened as possible. I have tried to cover every death and as many of the major incidents as possible; I apologise for any omissions. This brief oral and factual history of one year in a long, long war will deal with the insanity of 1972, although, how many people would notice one particular year of insanity in the whole 28 years of madness?

Ken Wharton, Gold Coast, Australia

PROLOGUE

DECEMBER, 1971

4 December 1971 dawned; it was a cold Saturday morning. For those in work it was the start of a weekend. For the thousands of Ulster's unemployed it was a day like any other day; but for fifteen people living in north Belfast, it was to become the last day of their lives.

As the third Christmas of the Troubles approached, the past eleven months had seen a shocking rise in the number of deaths and already 61 members of the British Army and eleven members of the RUC had been killed. A further six soldiers or former soldiers would lose their lives that month as a consequence of the Troubles and a further 38 names would be added to the death toll for the final 27 days of December.

On that Saturday, fifteen Catholic civilians were killed when Loyalist paramilitaries exploded a bomb at the Tramore Bar, better known as McGurk's, in North Queen Street, Belfast. The bomb had been planted by the Ulster Volunteer Force (UVF). Four of those killed were women (including the owner's wife and fourteen-year-old daughter) and this attack was one of the worst single incidents during the Northern Ireland conflict. Only one of the bombers, the driver of the getaway car, was ever convicted. Immediately after the bombing, and for some time later, there was some speculation amongst the security forces and other official sources about the culprits. They maintained that the bomb had gone off inside the bar, implying that it was being prepared by the IRA and thus represented an 'own goal'. The atrocity would only be outdone by the slaughter of the Paras at Warrenpoint in 1979 and by the outrage at Omagh in 1998.

It was an ordinary Saturday night, insofar as any day or night in Northern Ireland during the period of the Troubles could be described as ordinary. McGurk's was busy and the revellers enjoyed their drink, conversation and music. At exactly 20.47 what a survivor described as a 'large bulbous cloud of light' appeared and the bar collapsed. Another eyewitness said that he had observed a man with a parcel wrapped in plastic get out of a car and carry it towards the doorway of the bar. The young man stated that he saw the bomber strike a match and then run back to the car which he described as having a Union Jack – the hallmark of Loyalists – in the back. As it drove off the young man walked over, merely out of curiosity, to see what it was. However, having observed that it was a bomb he had just enough time to run and warn another passer-by before it exploded and both were blown off their feet.

The dead were the eponymous Philomena McGurk (46), mother of four and wife of the bar owner; her daughter Maria (14); James Cromie (13); Edward Keenan (69); his wife Sarah (58); John Colton (49); Thomas McLoughlin (55); David Milligan (52); James Smyth (55); Francis Bradley (61); Thomas Kane (45); Philip Garry (73) the local 'Lollipop Man'; Kathleen Irvine (45) ; Edward Kane (25) and Robert Spotswood (38). The slaughter, as previously stated, was thought to have been an IRA 'own goal' but the author, through other sources, has never been convinced and a UVF man was later convicted of the murders.

Initial speculation after the bombing was to lay the blame at the door of the Republicans; indeed, adopting a purely cynical viewpoint it could have well suited the British government and senior Army officers to make the Provisionals scapegoats. It was suggested that it was an IRA bomb being transported to another location which had exploded prematurely. It would take a further seven years before UVF member Robert Campbell actually admitted that it was the Loyalists who had planned and planted the no-warning bomb; the no-warning bomb was their hallmark.

Shortly after the explosion, an IRA gunman using renewed rioting in the North Queen Street area as cover, shot and seriously wounded Major Jeremy Snow (36) of the Royal Regiment of Fusiliers; he died of those wounds four days later. A married father of two, his family were living in the garrison town of Catterick in North Yorkshire; two RUC officers were also injured in the shootings. On the same night (8 December), the first Catholic member of the UDR, Sean Russell (30), father of five, was murdered at his home in New Barnsley on the edge of the Ballymurphy estate in Belfast by IRA gunmen. Two other UDR men were murdered two days later by the IRA at a border farmhouse near Strabane; Sergeant Kenneth Smyth (28) and former UDR soldier Daniel McCormick (29) were ambushed and killed by masked gunmen as they drove to work.

A bloody weekend followed and, in an apparent tit-for-tat bombing, the IRA carried out a no-warning attack at a furniture shop on the Shankill Road. In the explosion, two men and two young children were killed. Harold King (20) and Hugh Bruce (50) died and the two other innocents were Tracey Munn (2) and Colin Nicholl (17 months). Both were in prams outside the shop and stood no chance; the IRA clearly were not fussy as to who they killed just as long as they were seen to be the 'protectors' of their community. The deaths of the other side were always cheered – irrespective of age or sex, just so long as they were just that: the other side.

On the Sunday, John Barnhill, then an Ulster Unionist Party member of the Northern Ireland Senate, was shot dead by the Official IRA at his home in Strabane. To the neutral observer – if, during the Troubles there could be such a thing – Barnhill, known also as 'Jack' was simply a man who disagreed with the IRA; to them, he was a sworn enemy and that alone 'justified' the death sentence. The Provisionals were judge, jury and executioner; to the terrorist, life was that simple.

The IRA had other festive gifts for the people of Northern Ireland in the run-up to Christmas 1971 and amongst them was a device planted at Lavery's Bar on the Lisburn Road in south Belfast on the 21st. On the same day, two EOD (bomb disposal) personnel had a miraculous escape from one planted at Gass's cycle shop in the city centre. But bar-owner John Lavery (60) would not be so lucky. Enraged at the IRA's attempt to blow up his premises, he waited until the bombers had left and attempted to carry it outside, something he'd successfully accomplished on a previous occasion. It detonated, killing him instantly. An employee, Brendan Morgan described what happened next:

> As soon as I saw the gun, I knew he [the gunman] was planting a bomb. Another barman and myself ran over to the side door and rushed out. I had just reached the shop opposite when the bomb went off. Mr Lavery was still inside. He may have been trying to carry the bomb outside. He did it once before, but on that occasion it turned out to be a hoax. A local journalist was among the first on the scene and he described his nausea at stepping across hundreds of pieces of Mr Lavery's body.

The killings continued until the 31st and included another British soldier, Anthony Aspinwall (22), a Somerset soldier of the Gloucestershire Regiment and father of three young children, fatally wounded by an IRA sniper in a Falls Road side-street on the 16th, dying in the Royal Victoria Hospital the following day with his family at his bedside.

On 30th December, the IRA ushered out the old year as their somewhat grandiosely titled Director of Engineering Jack McCabe (55) was killed when explosives which he was mixing detonated at a safe house in the Santry district of Dublin. He was a former gun runner from earlier conflicts with both the British and Irish governments. Having ignored the basic rule that sparks and gunpowder don't mix – at least not safely – he used a spade to mix the explosives on a concrete floor.

A Royal Artillery man, Richard Ham was also killed on the 29th (see Chapter One) and thus the path was paved for the worst single year of the Troubles. Over 180 people had died during 1971 and 1972 was to bloodily outdo that total. The seconds ticked down towards the New Year and the Grim Reaper would be busy; the IRA and the Loyalist murder gangs would see to that.

Belfast city centre was completely dead at night. Its only population was that of unfortunate soldiers fruitlessly walking the deserted streets in the rain, their hands cold and wet on their rifle stocks.

Kevin Myers, author and journalist

My late mother would often hear on the news that another soldier had been killed in Belfast, or somewhere else in Northern Ireland. Because we, like a lot of working class families, didn't have a phone, she would stay up all night, waiting for the dawn in case there was a knock at the door and it was my Regimental Welfare Officer giving her the news that she dreaded the most.

Ken Wharton, former soldier

Patrolling was up and down the streets, always one man walking backwards and then alternating. Every 20 metres, you'd do a complete 360 and then start counting off the paces in your head, 'One, two, three' trying not to lose count, trying not to trip over, trying not to get shot. Another 20, and then a 360, and so on. Every street corner, one man down on his haunches, watching through his sights whilst the others dash across. Hard target everywhere, bob and weave, always moving, always trying to stay alive. See some kids, stand near them, hope that some IRA bastard would think twice about shooting; try to stay alive another day.

Rifleman, Royal Green Jackets

Belfast, I live and breathe you. Belfast, you are etched deep within my soul. Belfast, I have become you and carry the stink of your corpse like a cause.

Tony Clarke, Parachute Regiment

CHAPTER ONE

JANUARY

[This chapter was written some months before the findings of the Saville Inquiry into Bloody Sunday were published. All comments stand as written and were not influenced by the report. Comments on the Inquiry appear in this book's Epilogue.]

1971 had ended badly for the British Army on December 29 with the shooting of Gunner Richard Ham (20) of the Royal Artillery in Foyle Road, Londonderry. His worried mother had tried several times to purchase his discharge from the Army but he had refused, preferring to stay with his friends and comrades in the 22nd Light Air Defence Regiment.

On the first Monday of the New Year, an IRA car bomb was detonated in Callender Street, Belfast, only several score yards from Belfast City Council's offices; 60 people were injured, but thankfully none were killed. The 'economic war' so favoured by the Provisional IRA was on; this year it would only grow in intensity. The avowed intention of the Provos was to make the North ungovernable.

The first CVO (Casualty Visiting Officer) or regimental officer as they were then known, to be dispatched from his regiment's home depot received his orders on Wednesday 5 January. He was ordered to report to a household in the Bristol area. Earlier in the day, a foot patrol of the Gloucestershire Regiment – the 'Glorious Glosters' – came under fire from IRA gunmen in Ardmoulin Street in the vicinity of Divis Road. Private Keith Bryan (18) was hit by one of two shots fired from a position close to St Peter's. He was immediately rushed to the nearby Royal Victoria Hospital (RVH) but succumbed to his wounds less than an hour later. He was the first British soldier to die that year.

Not long after Private Bryan had been taken away in an ambulance, local Catholic women were seen on the spot where he fell, laughing and joking. 'The death of a soldier was almost enough to make one of the Falls hags drop a stitch when knitting' as one former squaddie told the author.

The pattern of IRA attacks on the security forces during those first two years was tragically unpredictable. Although foot patrols and mobile patrols became less regular in their planning, the IRA with its growing army of 'dickers' could increasingly predict where an Army patrol might be, and was becoming more and more emboldened. Generally, as one journalist observed, it might involve a stolen car with typically three or four men inside. It would stop at the end of a street with excellent cover and with the route of an approaching patrol in plain sight. The boot would be popped open and a weapon or weapons would be passed out by pre-arrangement. As the lead man came into range one gunman would either spray indiscriminate automatic fire in his direction or go for the carefully aimed head or chest shot.

If he went down, the gunman or gunmen would rely on the other soldiers to be either too shocked to move or to rush to aid their stricken comrade; it would be like shooting fish in a barrel. The locals would have a grandstand view of the shooting and would cheer each hit on a soldier. Often the soldiers, uncertain of a target, might not even return fire and the gunmen would throw their weapons back into the boot of their car and melt away into the heart of nationalist territory. The bolt holes and safe houses were legendary amongst the rabbit warrens of the 'Murph, Turf Lodge and Andersonstown.

Kevin Myers in *Watching The Door* wrote of the bloody aftermath of a shooting incident in which two soldiers were wounded in such an ambush on Shaw's Road, west Belfast.

On the ground, sitting in a pool of blood, lay a soldier's helmet. Children rushed over to examine it. One boy of about twelve scooped it up with a long stick, whirling it above his head as he pranced in the blood. Then, like an Orange band-leader, he yanked the stick upwards, sending the helmet even higher [which] he caught expertly on his head ... still dancing in the blood of a stranger from England.

The IRA's stated aim was to kill a British soldier every day, and leading Provisional Brendan Hughes said that he simply wanted to get out and 'shoot Brits'. The Provisional IRA saw themselves as an army, organising themselves into brigades, battalions and even companies. The very worst of the lot was 'D' company – the 'dogs' – which largely controlled west Belfast. They saw themselves as an army at war, something the soldiers of the British Army recognised but the British government singularly and spectacularly failed to do.

ARMAGH AMBUSH

Mike Pinchen, 42 Commando, Royal Marines

In the early hours, just after Christmas, we were patrolling in two vehicles between Armagh and Blackwatertown. We had just passed through the latter when we were ambushed. I was in the leading vehicle, a Land Rover, which also carried the C42 radio and signaller. I remember a loud bang and a flash, and then what seemed slow motion, a series of sparks flying off the roof of the armoured PIG following behind. It must have only been a split second but it seemed ages before I reacted. It was pitch black and we were driving along a country road that had a raised embankment on one side. The terrorists were lucky they caught us, as we had never been this route before. Anyway, I returned fire in the direction of the flashes that came from the top of the bank. At first the driver braked, as if to carry out an anti-ambush drill but we were in a sort of gully so he put his foot down, and with the other vehicle closing from behind, we drove out of it. I suppose they could have mined the road or set up a 'stop group', but we were in the 'killing ground' and had little option. Further on the road turned sharp left, at right angles to their position.

We de-bussed and took up all round defence. The section commander then let off a flare in the direction of the terrorists' position and the GPMG was readied to 'get to work' but there were no targets of opportunity, and it would be irresponsible to just blast the area. Meanwhile, the radio operator had sent a Sit-Rep and we were ordered not to penetrate the field until a cordon had been established by other patrols in the area. A sweep of the area revealed the terrorists' position, where a combat jacket and some spent cartridge cases were found, but our birds had flown. Back at Gough Barracks seven bullet marks were found on the PIG, which wasn't much considering they were using at least one automatic weapon. It had been a close shave and, as with most people who have come under fire for the first time, it sort of changes you. You come of age so to speak, and one becomes a better soldier for the experience.

'K' Company was re-deployed to Bessbrook, which at that time was not established as a base. It had an RUC station but little else, so we were housed in a primary school and it took a lot of hard work to establish this as a base of operations. Sangars were built and the playing field was set up as a heli-pad, with positions to cover take-off and landings. A marquee tent and some pipe-work were erected as a shower room, complete with wooden pallets as duck boards. The most amusing part was the ablutions. Designed for infant school children it was now being used by hairy-arsed 'bootnecks'. One could have a conversation, face to face with an oppo when sitting on the 'throne', because the partitions between the traps were so low. During the time at Bessbrook patrols on the border continued, through Newtownhamilton and on as far as Forkhill.

42 Cdo completed its first of fourteen tours on 18 January 1972, being relieved by the Devon & Dorset Regiment, who sadly, within a few weeks, lost three of their people. On the plus side we did not lose anyone, although 5 Marines were wounded. On the down side was the thought that people with whom we had made friends were still there, facing intimidation, injury and sometimes death, whilst we were able to go home and forget it; well for a while at least, until the next time, which would not be long in coming.

Belfast was becoming 'Berlinised' and Royal Engineers had long ago sealed off all of the streets leading from the Crumlin Road, into both the Protestant and the Catholic areas, with corrugated barricades the height of the houses. Flax Street in the Ardoyne used to empty into the Crumlin Road, but the Army closed off the road permanently with a huge brick wall and turned that end of Flax Street into a cul-de-sac. Everywhere, the walls were beginning to spring up and none more noticeably than the 'peace line' along North Howard Street and Cupar Way; the 'Berlin Wall' had come to Belfast.

The day before Keith Bryan's killing, the Army had shot and fatally wounded IRA member Daniel O'Neil (20) during an exchange of shots in the Leeson Street area. A patrol had come under fire from a car and they fired back and hit O'Neil; he died in hospital on the 7th. A day later, a Catholic pub owner was shot and killed and robbed by gunmen believed to be Ulster Volunteer Force (UVF) as he returned home after closing for the night. Peter Woods (29) had no political connections and whether he was targeted for being a Catholic or simply for his night's takings is unknown.

On the 11th, proving that not only the British Army had NDs (negligent discharges) the IRA managed to shoot and kill one of their own at 'weapons training'. Michael Sloan (15) was accidentally shot at a house in New Barnsley, on the edge of the Ballymurphy estate. The following day, masked IRA gunmen entered printers' premises in Waterford Street, opposite Dunville Park and close to Springfield Road. They singled out Raymond Denham (42) a part-time policeman in the RUCR (Royal Ulster Constabulary Reserve) and forced him to lie on the floor, before cold-bloodedly shooting him in the head at close range. One of the IRA gunmen (Tony Lewis) was later killed in an 'own-goal' explosion.

A day later, the IRA demonstrated its callous ruthlessness by continuing its tactic of attacking soft targets as they shot and killed an off-duty Ulster Defence Regiment (UDR) man. At around

16:00 hours on Thursday 13 January, Maynard Crawford (38) from Lambeg, Co Antrim, a Sergeant in the UDR was sitting in a van outside a building site in Newtownabbey where he was employed as a foreman. The married father of two was well known throughout the then-fledgling UDR and was noted for his size – over sixteen stone and well over six feet tall – and his incredible shooting prowess. Whether or not he was targeted for these reasons is a question perhaps only Ulster politicians such as Gerry Adams or Martin McGuinness can answer. What is more likely is that he was in all probability unarmed and easy prey to the IRA. Whatever the reason, he became the second British soldier to die with the New Year less than two weeks old.

As Sergeant Crawford of the 9th Battalion sat in the van, a hijacked vehicle containing four masked men pulled up alongside and fired two rounds at him, killing him instantly, making him the fourth UDR man killed whilst off duty in the previous seven weeks. *Lost Lives* (p141) reports that he was a former 'B' Special, having served over seventeen years and that his distraught widow received 98 wreaths and over 150 letters of condolence. The measure of the man was that his funeral was the largest seen for several years in the Lisburn area. One of the few growth industries in Ulster during the years of the Troubles, thanks to the paramilitary killers – both Republican and Loyalist – was that of the undertaker.

On the 17th, the IRA pulled off a remarkable propaganda coup and scored a stunning success against the British government. Seven of its members who were internees staged an escape from the prison ship, HMS *Maidstone* moored in Belfast Lough. *Maidstone*'s deck was surrounded by ten-foot-high barbed wire and was moored 20 feet from the land, with entry to the jetty guarded by sand-bagged sangars. The men swam close to 300 yards through icy water and evaded Army and police only to later poke fun at the authorities with a hastily arranged but nonetheless triumphant press conference.

The men were Jim Bryson, Tommy Tolan (killed by the Official IRA in 1977), Thomas Kane (killed in a car crash in 1976), Martin Taylor, Tommy Gorman, Peter Rodgers and Seán Convery. Bryson was later re-arrested but then was 'sprung' by the IRA again from Crumlin Road Jail – the second such escape from this institution, involving the IRA – shortly before he was killed. He was shot on the Ballymurphy estate on 31 August 1973, dying in hospital a little over three weeks later on 22 September.

The *Maidstone* escape had been conceived after the prisoners had noticed a seal swimming through the ring of barbed wire which surrounded the ship, and reasoned that the gap was also sufficient to allow a human through. They had also been tossing tin cans overboard to monitor the movements of the tide. There was barbed wire ringing the ship some ten to fifteen yards out from the hull so the men thought they would have to swing out and jump into the water, but the splash would have given them away. Fortunately for the IRA men, a day before the planned escape another ship moored alongside the *Maidstone* and when it departed it left a thick mooring cable which had held the two boats together. It hung down from the top deck and out into the water beyond the barbed wire. Waiting for the right moment, having previously sawn through the iron bars in their cell, one by one, they jumped over the side, slid down the cable into the water and made good their escape.

A waiting car driven by accomplices drove off, forcing the men instead to hijack a bus and drive through security gates before heading into Belfast. In a pub in Andersonstown, drinkers took off their own clothes to allow the semi-naked men to look 'respectable'. They then had to dodge UDR patrols out searching for them before escaping across the border. They were feted as a *cause celebre* by IRA/Sinn Féin for some time, leaving a deeply embarrassed HMS *Maidstone* commander to hastily review security. As noted, three of the escapees were killed over the course of the next five years and at least one of the others was involved in continued terrorist activity. It was a humiliating experience for the security forces, especially in view of the Crumlin Road Jail breakout the previous year; it wouldn't be the last one. In that incident, nine IRA prisoners – known later as the 'Crumlin Kangaroos' – escaped over the wall of the jail. The break-out from the *Maidstone*, allied to the earlier Crumlin Road escape, was a massive shot in the arm for the IRA and within days the men were being paraded in front of the world's media in Dublin.

I WON'T…

Terry Friend, Royal Artillery

When we arrived in Belfast, we were first sent to the Royal Victoria Hospital to guard it and carry out vehicle patrols. On my very first day, I ended up in the main road, outside the hospital entrance, directing traffic. At one side of the entrance, armed and behind a sandbagged sangar, my mate Frank Halfpenny kept a beady eye on me. It took some getting used to, seeing buildings protected by walls of sandbags. It created the impression that we were all playing extras in a Second World War film! Every day after breakfast, as we filed out of our billet to carry out our duties, we passed a message board up on the corridor wall.

There was a large photo pinned up on it, which was from the *Daily Express*, and was half the size of one of that paper's pages. It showed a line of squaddies in riot gear, one of whom was completely engulfed in flames over twelve feet high, from an exploding petrol bomb. The caption above the photo read: 'Stay alert; do not let this happen to you!' It made me shudder every time I walked past it!

The previous October, in an attack on soldiers on the Ballymurphy estate, IRA gunman Eamonn McCormick (17) had been shot and fatally wounded; he died on 16 January. On the 18th, after agreeing to give evidence against two men who had hijacked his bus at gunpoint, Sydney Agnew (46) was targeted at his home in east Belfast and shot dead. The IRA were clearly involved in this cowardly murder – carried out in front the man's terrified children – and was one more piece of evidence that they considered themselves above not only the rule of law but also the law of human decency. Mr Agnew's killing was cited as justification for the introduction of the non-jury Diplock Courts, established later that year to try terrorist-related cases.

On the very same day, Prime Minister Brian Faulkner banned all parades and marches in Northern Ireland until the end of the year. Belatedly waking up to the provocation caused to both communities by the other's marches, he acted some three or four years too late.

Only a few more days would pass before another CVO would be dispatched to an unsuspecting family; this time it would be to the Exeter area. On a winter's Thursday, a detachment from the 'drunk and disorderlies' the Devon and Dorsets was giving close protection to a Royal Engineers party who were investigating a suspect device at Derrynoose, South Armagh, very close to the border with the Irish Republic. Three landmines, planted by the IRA on a roadside with the obvious intention of hitting an Army vehicle patrol, exploded. Private Charles Stentiford (18) from the village of Cheriton Fitzpaine was killed instantly by one of the explosions which were detonated by an IRA unit skulking across the protection of the border. Private

Stentiford, who was engaged to be married, had only been in the Province a matter of days. He is buried at the English Cemetery in Crediton, Devon. That the carnage could have been much worse was of course no consolation to the young man's distraught family and fiancé.

FLAX STREET MILL

Jock 2413, Royal Artillery

We were shaken awake by my mate, Ned at about 0900 hours. I was as stiff as hell having slept on the bare floor and it was freezing into the bargain. My first thought was: 'Where the hell are we?' I then vaguely remember somebody saying earlier on that we were going to Flax Street Mill. As we had no 'small kit' a proper wash and shave was out of the question, but one of the lads found a discarded bit of soap in the washroom and we did our best to clean off some of the grime, using the tail of our shirts as a towel. A shave would have to wait again and our 5 o'clock shadows had grown to two days growth. I also found that the black marks round my eyes wasn't dirt. I looked like a panda. I realised I was starving and we were happy to hear that the Queens' had kindly arranged a late breakfast for us. Trouble was there was not an eating iron or plate in sight so it was 'banjos' all round. Mine consisted of a slice of bread, three sausages, bread, bacon, more bread, two fried eggs garnished with beans and a final slice of bread. Never before, or after can I remember a tastier or more welcome scoff.

Some of us went in search of other Battery mates greeting them with 'Got any fags' as we had ran out. Sadly this was the case all round. We were also told that we couldn't purchase any from the Queens' shop as they only had a few packets left and that was for their own lads. Happily, Ned indirectly solved this problem by getting me spammed as radio op on a foot patrol down the Crumlin. I found the Queens' radio room and one of our Battery NCOs; a mate handed me the radio and gave me the frequency to use. Led by the boss, with me humping a bloody great A41 as well as my rifle, we took a quick swan around the area.

It was fairly quiet but the whole place stank of burnt rubber and there were wrecked cars and rubble everywhere. The boss got my attention when he pointed out some strike marks on the wall at the junction of Butler Street. You could also see nails and scorch marks where blast bombs had exploded. A bit further down, some of the locals started to acknowledge our good afternoons so I asked the boss if I could pop into one of the shops to buy fags for the lads. A couple of the lads joined me. At first, the shopkeeper was a bit anti but I think the sight of our still dirty and unshaven appearance caused him to have a change of heart and we virtually cleaned him out of fags and chocolate. As we got back outside, there was a radio call for the boss telling him to return to base asap. We quickly legged it back where I was ambushed by my nicotine starved mates. I didn't even make a profit; honestly lads!

***

January was not over yet and the grim reaper had more work to do at the behest of the emboldened IRA and on 25 January, the Royal Regiment of Fusiliers lost Fusilier Terry N. Thomas (21) in circumstances as yet unknown. The young soldier was born on Guy Fawkes Night in 1951; the author cannot find any details of the cause of his death nor where he was from or where his funeral took place. That the highly respected National Armed Forces memorial placed his name on their roll of honour is sufficient cause for the author to accord him the same recognition.

The IRA, still to perfect the art of bomb making completely, lost one of their members when Peter McNulty (47) was killed during a premature detonation as he planted a device outside the RUC station at Castlewellan, Co Down. The following day, the IRA ambushed an RUC vehicle with five officers inside as it drove along Creggan Road, Londonderry. The car was en-route for Rosemount RUC station when gunmen opened fire and, as the car accelerated away from danger, a further two gunmen opened fire from about 50 yards away. All five policemen were hit, but Sergeant Peter Gilgunn (26) the father of a small baby and Constable David Montgomery (20) were both killed. A day later, the IRA shot and killed Constable Raymond Carroll (22) at a petrol station in Oldpark Road, Belfast; he was the fourth RUC/RUCR officer killed in sixteen days.

Three days before the events at Free Derry Corner, the Army came up against the IRA in a toe-to-toe armed confrontation at Forkhill, South Armagh. During a fire fight which raged for several hours the Army was forced to expend over 1,000 rounds as they fought to subdue several IRA teams.

The IRA, especially the Provisionals, were utterly ruthless, showing the same mercy to their 'touts' and informers as they did to members of the security forces (SF) or anyone who opposed them. For, once a volunteer had been arrested, even if only for the maximum permitted four hours, they were immediately under suspicion and would be 'debriefed', often in a most violent manner. If, even for a single second, the commanders felt that the volunteer had been 'turned', the interrogation methods would be become even more violent and torture was used. If the case were 'proven' the sentence was summary execution, with a hood over the head and a round or two fired at the base of the suspect's skull. And if he were innocent a six-month 'sabbatical' was normally imposed so that they could keep a low profile before returning to the fray in order to duck under the Intelligence radar.

'JUSTICE'

Jock 2413, Royal Artillery

When the IRA executed one of their own members for touting, they usually used two weapons and both shots were fired through the back of the head so that the exit wounds meant that the victims' family could not have an open coffin wake. Plus, there were quite a few occasions when the family of the so-called tout were prominent Republicans and the bodies just disappeared without the usual execution announcement. This enabled the families to claim compensation from the government. Another indignity which the dead informers suffered was the fact that when the body was discovered, a rope was tied around their legs and it was dragged by an armoured PIG several yards in case it was booby trapped. I actually witnessed that happen in the Bogside. The lad was nineteen years old and a paid informer. He must have been so scared because his hair was literally standing on end.

———◦◦◦◦———

There were some men who became touts or 'sources' and were employed and run by Military Intelligence, Garda Special Branch or the RUC Special Branch. Other, shadowy organisations such as E4 emerged later, but this book deals only with 1972 and the precursors to that year. Some of these men were principled, some were men who gave in to pressure from their 'handlers' or to family or simply did it for the money. George Clarke's superb *Border Crossing* deals with the art of informing and the stories of those who risked a violent death at the hands of their IRA masters.

Just two of these individuals were Marty McGartland (author of *Fifty Dead Men Walking*) and Sean O'Callaghan (*The Informer*) although this list is not exhaustive. Sean O'Callaghan showed some valour in deciding to work against an intrinsically evil organisation, something he'd recognised with each successive atrocity. Others gave their services under duress, trapped in an interview room following arrest on serious charges and faced with the choice between fifteen or twenty years inside HM's 'hotel system' or a hood job if their undercover role was discovered by erstwhile colleagues. O'Callaghan wasn't even known to the authorities and, I believe, his decision to accept the latter risk was motivated solely by common decency and humanity. That too is noteworthy courage although, by his own admission, he has at least two murders on his conscience, having shot RUC Special Branch Inspector Peter Flanagan in an Omagh pub on 23 August 1974 and being part of the IRA unit involved in the gun and RPG attack on the UDR base at the Deanery in Clogher. During that earlier raid, on 2 May 1974, UDR Greenfinch Eva Martin became the first female member of the security forces to die in the Troubles.

THE AMERICAN CONNECTION

The IRA received much of their funding from Irish-Americans, generally from six generations back, spurred on by over-emotive feelings of injustice fuelled by the notion that their ancestors were forced out of their homeland and compelled to flee to the New World across the Atlantic. Many of the people who poured funds into the NORAID collection boxes, and then indirectly into the coffers of the Provisional IRA, were misguided and naive in the extreme.

To these people, being Irish meant donning green wigs, drinking green beer in an Irish bar in Boston, Detroit, Chicago, New York or Philadelphia on St Paddy's Day. Watching the marching bands of Irish-Americans, everywhere a sea of green, feeling a nostalgia for a place they'd never been. They had vague notions of potato famines, despicable English landlords evicting helpless women and children or of Cromwell's troops slaughtering Catholics. That there were injustices by the English in Cromwell's day, that the famine killed thousands and that Britain has a history of heavy handedness is not in doubt. No British person of fair mind can deny that we, as a nation, have much to answer for in terms of how we treated the Irish. The trouble was that the Americans, rather like the Loyalists who lived for the memory of 1690 and the Battle of the Boyne, seemed unable to accept that times and governments had moved on.

A close friend of the author was in an Irish bar in Philadelphia on 27 August 1979 when there was a huge cheer and drinks were handed out free of charge. When the young Englishman enquired as to why, he was met with: 'The lads have just offed a dozen fuckin' Brits!' At Warrenpoint, Co Down earlier that day, sixteen paratroopers and two members of the Queen's Own Highlanders were killed by IRA landmines, the worst day of the Troubles for the security forces. The sheer, blind hatred of those Americans, comfortable, well removed from danger, could in no way be justified by their total isolation from the scene or the on-going situation in Northern Ireland.

Thus it was against this ill-informed background that NORAID flourished and money collected 'for the families back home' was used to purchase arms and explosives for a terrorist grouping with an apparently insane blood-lust. One of the leading members of NORAID – remotely controlled by the IRA's Dublin leadership – was Martin Lyons. Through Lyons or under him, NORAID's primary function was fund raising and in general terms its propaganda differed little from that of the Provisional Republican movement in Northern Ireland. However, it was also an organisation founded and rooted in a section of Irish America, subject to quite different political and cultural pressures than the Republican movement in Ireland.

Furthermore, as Ed Maloney claims through his interviews with Brendan 'The Dark' Hughes, it was Lyons, at the bidding and through the personal negotiating skills of Hughes, who supplied the first Armalites to PIRA. Previously the Republicans had had to make do with old M1 and M2 carbines, Garands and even older .303s. The Armalite was a lightweight, high-velocity rifle of various calibres, capable of automatic and semi-automatic operation. It was lightweight and highly corrosion-resistant, small, accurate, and could fire a high velocity round with a muzzle velocity of 925 metres or 3,250 feet per second. It was a formidable weapon and in the hands of a dedicated and determined terrorist even more so. The semi-automatic Armalite AR-7 was noteworthy in that it could be disassembled and the components stored in the butt. Primarily made of alloys, the AR-7 would float, whether assembled or stored, due to the design of the butt, which was filled with plastic foam.

PIRA dubbed the rifle the 'widow maker' and smuggled significant quantities of AR-18s into Northern Ireland during the early 1970s. It became a symbol of their later 'Armalite and ballot box' campaign, as defined by national director of publicity for Sinn Féin and alleged former IRA member Danny Morrison in his address to the party's 1981 *Ard Fheis* (annual conference): 'Who here really believes we can win the war through the ballot box? But will anyone here object if, with a ballot paper in this hand and an Armalite in the other, we take power in Ireland?' As *Belfast News Letter* columnist Alex Kane wrote in June 2010, 'it was an early admission that they knew that terror alone was never going to be enough.'

Morrison was later arrested, jailed and subsequently cleared of the false imprisonment of a 'tout', Special Branch agent Sandy Lynch, himself believed to have been one of the gunmen responsible for the deaths of IPLO leader Gerard 'Dr Death' Steenson and Tony McCarthy, shot in a west-Belfast inter-faction ambush in March 1987.

Once the IRA had begun to receive regular supplies of Armalites, the balance on the streets in terms of arms began to shift a little more in their direction. Gone were the days when the IRA had to take rusting weapons and even wet ammunition and clean and dry them before use; now they were being equipped professionally.

It wasn't just the Americans who misunderstood the terrorists. A common misconception amongst the general public on the British mainland was the view, certainly in the early days, that the IRA was some sort of picture book, country bumpkin, rag-tag army of 'freedom fighters'. Ireland has for many years been perceived as a romantic green island, full of poets, leprechauns and thatch-roofed cottages. Britons dismissed the IRA as quaint, jovial, red-haired types, armed with old German First World War Mauser rifles or stolen and obsolete Lee Enfields which had been donated to the Cadets and TA.

Jokes abounded such as the one about the IRA member who was about to aim a grenade at a soldier. He pulled out the pin and threw it whilst the live grenade exploded in his hand! The reality was that the IRA was armed with Armalites, courtesy of some crooked US Army quartermaster or wealthy donor in Massachusetts, or via NORAID and other top-of-the-range, state-of-the art weaponry. They had RPG7s, commercial explosives and later on in the conflict, surface-to-air missiles. All of this had to be sourced, paid for and shipped into some quiet, shadowy cove on the coast of Ireland.

Arms were smuggled in and sold by members of the US Forces in the UK and by 'sympathisers' – Irish or otherwise – amongst crew members of passenger liners and merchant ships. There were many merchant seamen serving on the cross-Atlantic run on the QE2 for example and many of these were from Northern Ireland and indeed, IRA sympathisers. It is known that Irish-American longshoremen smuggled the first shipment of Armalites into UK-bound passenger ships in New York harbour at the dead of night. The Falls Road area of Belfast was a popular recruiting ground for seamen and it was inevitable that some of those recruits would also support the aims of the Provisionals. It need only be a handgun or two here, a grenade or two there and given the ease with which weapons could be picked up, the arms could be smuggled in 'penny packets'. Similarly Armalites with their folding butt could be hidden under a jacket or in the bags of the Belfast dockers and taken ashore

The USSR was also a prime supplier, either directly or indirectly, to the IRA as part of their plans to destabilise the West. Gaddafi, the Libyan leader was a great supporter of the IRA and was a major supplier of their weapons, as were both the PLO (Palestine Liberation Organisation) and the Basque separatists, ETA. Although the following incident – the seizure of the ship, *Claudia*, a Cypriot-registered coaster – took place in 1973 and as such is outside the scope of this book, it is worth recounting as one wonders just how many ships got through before and after that setback for the Republicans.

Carelessness on the part of the IRA led to the seizure of one of the biggest ever illegal arms caches in the history of Ireland aboard that merchant ship in March 1973. The haul of almost 1,000 rifles and anti-tank guns, 100 cases of landmines, 5,000lbs of explosives and 500 hand-grenades sent from Libya on the *Claudia*, was intercepted off Helvick Harbour in Waterford by the Irish Navy.

A leaked Irish Army memo in Department of Defence files that year points to the rashness of the IRA in not taking elementary security measures and failing to react to information available to them. These, it says, were among the main factors contributing to the success of the Defence Forces operation. The memo describes the IRA decision to send 'such a well known person on the mission in the first place; a person in fact who has no particular talents in this field.' The man in question, IRA Chief of Staff Joe Cahill, was sentenced to three years in jail. He later told the Special Criminal Court his only crime was in 'not getting the contents of the *Claudia* into the hands of the freedom fighters'. He was convicted along with four other men.

The Army memo said bringing the ship into territorial waters when they could have off-loaded out to sea, out of sight, contributed to the IRA's failure. They had also neglected security surveillance on shore to detect Army and Garda movements and they failed to react when a submarine was spotted close by and when the captain picked up three ships on his radar.

This was not only a major setback but it was also incredibly embarrassing for the Provisionals. However, weapons continued to pour in from their Irish-American well-wishers as well as the more conventional of Britain's enemies. That supply chain although occasionally interrupted by SF successes was to continue until the very end of the Troubles.

One prominent American who was seen as an apologist for the IRA was that doyen of the Irish-Americans, the late, and in the opinion of this author, unlamented Senator Edward Kennedy. His honorary knighthood given by the Labour Prime Minister Gordon Brown was in my opinion an affront to decency and an insult to all those killed by Kennedy's heroes in the IRA. Arguably, his legacy was to completely poison Anglo-American relations on this side of the Atlantic. For many years, he was the leading Irish-American supporter of the IRA and was seen as the cheerleader for the naive and misguided in his own country who believed all that they heard about the 'home country'. These were the people who believed the British Army was also occupying Dublin; the same people who sang 'Merry Ploughboy' and 'Bonfire on the Border' and 'The Men Behind the Wire' from the comfort of their bars, resplendent with Irish tricolours and little statues of leprechauns.

The very fact that they applauded the ethnic cleansing of what the Irish Republicans called the 'Scots Irish' speaks volumes about their misguided and ill-informed opinions about the British. Kennedy himself said that Ulster Protestants should 'be given a decent opportunity to go back to Britain!' Did this largesse also mean that he was prepared to give back Manhattan Island to the Native Americans or grant the Sioux and Cheyenne their traditional hunting grounds once more? He compared Britain's presence in Ulster with America's in Vietnam, and later put great political pressure on President Jimmy Carter in order to stop him selling arms to the RUC. Kennedy spoke out against violence in Northern Ireland whilst sponsoring and nurturing relations with the likes of Gerry Adams and Martin McGuinness and personally, it is alleged, convinced the US State Department to grant Adams a visa to the US in 1996.

Members of PIRA, wanting to go to the United States to raise money, used Senator Kennedy to clear their path and ensure there were no immigration difficulties, according to Maria McGuire's book *To Take Arms* (she was a leading member of PIRA until she left the organisation). She claims that it was Kennedy who got former commander of the provisional wing in Belfast, Joe Cahill, into the US after the immigration department had refused him entry.

> We knew that Edward Kennedy would be quite ready to play Ireland for all it was worth; if he was going to use us, we might as well as use him … we enlisted the help of the prominent civil rights lawyer Paul O'Dwyer. Whenever there seemed to be any difficulty over obtaining a visa for a member of the Provisionals intending to go to the U.S. to raise funds, we would phone an official of one of the New York Irish American Associations, Jack MacCarthy; MacCarthy would contact O'Dwyer, a phone call from Kennedy's office to the American Embassy in Dublin would result in all difficulties disappearing.

She also claims that fund-raising in America was 'very easy' and that 'I also agreed with the Provisionals' methods. I remember the occasions when we heard late at night at night that a British soldier had been shot and seriously wounded in Belfast or Derry, and we would hope that by morning he would be dead.'

BLOODY SUNDAY

On 30 January an event occurred in the Bogside which, nearly 40 years later, still reverberates around the world and not merely amongst the Republican community in Northern Ireland. On that Sunday, soldiers from 1st Battalion, the Parachute Regiment opened fire on civil rights marchers in what has become known as Bloody Sunday, killing thirteen protestors and fatally wounding a fourteenth.

This book deals with the year from the perspective of the ordinary British soldier and it is not in its remit to apportion blame or responsibility for the deaths. This is also not intended as an exhaustive account of the events of that day but rather a simple analysis of sorts. That the tragedy was a turning point and hardened Republican opinions for decades is a moot point. One side

claims that the soldiers opened fire without cause or justification whilst the other claims that they came under fire from an IRA gunman or gunmen. Whatever the rights and wrongs, no matter who did what and to whom, the march at Free Derry Corner seemed doomed from the very off; as one RTE journalist wrote, 'The march meant blood on the streets as assuredly as December 25 means presents under the tree.'

There are several schools of thought and I choose to believe the following, taken from my sources in the military. They assure me that there was an initial shot or shots, probably fired from the Catholic Rossville Flats at members of the Parachute Regiment in Great James Street. This was followed by a burst from what was, unmistakably, a Thompson sub machine gun, a known and trusted favourite of the IRA. There are allegations that one or more Paras fired either individually or between them, three rounds from an SLR, before the first rounds from the IRA. Both the Provisionals and the Officials had members in and around the march as 'contingencies', but have always claimed that the Paras fired first before they 'retaliated'. It was stated that both wings of the IRA would not have a presence at the march, but instead, their 'volunteers' would keep their weapons inside their cars and patrol the Creggan and Bogside, ready for action if necessary. On a purely personal note, I did not and do not trust anything that the IRA said or says about Bloody Sunday and it was in their power and their intention to cause trouble that day. Interestingly, the Deputy First Minister of the Northern Ireland Assembly, Martin McGuinness has allegedly admitted that he was there but has always refused to answer probing questions about his presence.

Even before the main incident when the bulk of the shots were fired at the demonstrators, Paratroopers had already opened fire on protestors after coming under nail bomb attack at 'Aggro corner'. This was so named by soldiers after they were regularly attacked at the entrance to the Bogside. Two rioters were wounded, but then the Paras opened fire on the crowd. Without a doubt, of the 20,000 marchers, many were in an ugly, violent and confrontational mood as they stoned the soldiers who retaliated with CS gas and water cannon. Their aim was to reach the symbolic Guildhall and also damage the already struggling businesses in the city centre. The stewards did their best to marshal the crowd but mobs broke away intending to injure the soldiers on the barricades. I blame the mob for precipitating the violence, but it is also the author's belief that the Paras' officers totally lost control of their men on that day.

Their CO, Lieutenant-Colonel Derek Wilford (38 at the time) a well respected and very experienced officer has always defended his men and has never believed that they were in the wrong. Some twenty years after the event he said: 'There might have been things wrong in the sense that some innocent people, people who were not carrying a weapon, were wounded or even killed. But that was not done as a deliberate malicious act. It was done as an act of war.'

Derek Wilford was exonerated by the Widgery Tribunal and has, in my opinion, been unfairly blamed for all of the events of that day. Whilst I still maintain that the Paras' officers had virtually no control, their CO is clearly seen and heard shouting 'cease fire' and words to the effect of

Left, top: An image that went round the world as Father Edward Daly shepherds the group carrying Jack Duddy away from Rossville Flats and the Bogside, flanked by a paratrooper. The tension is visible in this photograph of Bloody Sunday. (Stanley Matchett/Belfast Telegraph)

Left, below: A protester is 'doubled' away by a serious looking paratrooper as the disaster of Bloody Sunday unfolds. (Fred Hoare/Belfast Telegraph)

'Do not fire back for the moment unless you identify a positive target,' as the Paras appear to be firing indiscriminately; clearly they did not heed his instructions. In the immediate aftermath of the shootings, a blackened-faced Wilford is asked by a TV interviewer if he had any worries about the shootings. He replied that he had 'none at all.' In a 1992 BBC interview he added 'If you get into an enormous crowd which is out to make mischief you are in the first instance a party to it. If you are on the receiving end, as we were, then you have to assume that they are all out to make mischief.'

If any portion of blame is directed at Wilford it would be to say that, if he was aware of their mood prior to the march then he was guilty. Guilty that is of gross naivety for believing that they were the right people for the day and at worst, he is guilty of not listening to the barrack room murmurings. If it was the British government's intention to give the rioters a 'bloody nose' and used the Paras as an instrument to do the job, then Heath's cabinet is ultimately culpable.

Those killed that day were Jack Duddy (17); Paddy Doherty (31); Hugh Gilmore (17); Bernard McGuigan (41); James Wray (22); Michael Kelly (17); William McKinney (27); Gerard McKinney (35) (no relation); Kevin McElhinney (17); John Young (17); William Nash (19); and Michael McDaid (17). Also killed was IRA member Gerald Donaghy (17) and John Johnston (59) who died of his wounds on 16 June.

The real 'truth' about Bloody Sunday will probably never emerge and there will be conjecture from now until the end of time. Despite the millions and millions of pounds spent on tribunals, the men who know the answers will take them to their graves. The soldiers have always maintained that all of their shots were 'aimed' and that their targets were armed. There is however, disturbing evidence that several of those killed were actually prostrate on the ground at the time and were trying to escape the flying 7.62mm rounds. At least one of the dead was shot in the back as he crawled away, already wounded. Photographic evidence also suggests that one of the protestors walked out into the firing, waving a white handkerchief in order to try and stop the soldiers from shooting. As posterity has recorded, he was shot and killed.

In informal discussions with military eyewitnesses, whose names and stories were given to me on the strict basis that they are not for publication, I have learned more. The Paras have a fearsome reputation as soldiers, quite rightly earned at the Second World War battlefields of Tunisia, Crete, Normandy, Arnhem and the Rhine Crossing in 1945. Without a doubt they are a first class fighting elite, superbly trained, fit and professional. However, my sources tell me that in the days and weeks leading up to the tragedy, the Paras had two of their number maimed by explosions and were in the mood 'for blood'. Whether or not this was true, it might have been expedient for the GOC Northern Ireland to have withdrawn the Paras from policing the march. A platoon of the King's Own Border Regiment was at nearby Bligh's Lane and 2RGJ and a Guards' company as well as others were also in the city at the time.

The Paras were not equipped nor suited for the 'policing' role which was required of them on the day of the NICRA march. It is alleged that their officers were aware of the fact that their men felt frustrated and wanted 'kills' in order to give the IRA/marchers a 'bloody nose'. If this was indeed the case, why did this information not filter its way through to HQNI (Head Quarters Northern Ireland)? At the very least, why did it not filter through to their commanding officer? If it did so, why was preventative action not taken?

HQNI were cognisant of the reputation which preceded the regiment and by allowing them to take part in the operation are at least partially culpable. Peter Pringle and Philip Jacobson in their work *Those Are Real Bullets Aren't They?* speculate that an unidentified Para officer actually warned civilian friends to stay away from the march. If this was the case – and here the author is making no claims as to the veracity of the accusations against the soldiers – and the regiment's own officers were aware of their men's feelings, why were they not pulled out of the operation? 2RGJ were at nearby Magillian Army camp prior to Bloody Sunday and peacefully policed an anti-internment demonstration, even offering the marchers cups of tea and refreshments. That demonstration was later aggressively broken up by the Parachute Regiment; a portent of things to come?

Pringle and Jacobson talk about the improper requests from the Chamber of Commerce and Council types who wanted ring leaders shot as an example and even of senior British government officials who were also advocating what in effect were summary executions. If these sentiments were influencing the thoughts of the red tabs in HQNI then that at least provides some sort of rationale behind bringing in a regiment clearly unsuitable for the type of 'policing' required for the fateful NICRA march.

If HQNI is not culpable, who is? Was it the Heath government who decided to take off the 'velvet gloves' and show the Provisionals who was boss, or did the top echelons of the Army wish to prove a point? Was it the intention to deliberately let the Paras 'off the leash?' The Paras are shock troops and are trained to act aggressively and 'not take prisoners'. It was very obvious to senior Army commanders that the troops from other regiments were fighting a losing battle in Londonderry. The shooting of two rioting youths the previous year had driven a major and perhaps irrevocable wedge between the residents of both the Bogside and the housing estate of the Creggan and the soldiers who had initially been welcomed as liberators. The city centre was gradually being closed down by a lethal combination of IRA bombs and the perhaps contrived weekly, sometimes daily, rioting, which had a major effect on the mainly Protestant businesses.

The Paras have always maintained that their shots were 'aimed' and if that is indeed the case, given the nature of the shootings and the people who they hit, then those were the actions of undisciplined soldiers, not the hallmark of a professional unit. Sad to say, but whatever the provocation on the day – and here one has to point the finger of blame also at the Provisionals who set the scene for the tragedy – the Paras behaved in an unprofessional and dangerous manner. The accusation of being totally beyond the control of their officers must therefore stand. In any conflict there is a right way and a wrong way to behave. Those soldiers on the day chose the latter.

At approximately 16:15 the first of over 100 rounds was fired by the 1st Battalion, Parachute Regiment; precisely 20 minutes later, the final round was fired. One former member of the regiment who was serving with 'C' Company on the day of the shootings said that he and other soldiers were convinced that they were under IRA attack. The former soldier, who gave evidence to the Saville Inquiry, said:

> I saw a gunmen; I am convinced of it. I brought my rifle up into the aim but he disappeared so I didn't engage. I saw some soldiers firing aimed shots but I also saw another soldier firing from the hip. He must have fired off half a magazine, around 10 rounds and I remember thinking: what are you doing, because you would not hit anything like that. In the debrief afterwards I mentioned it because it was so obviously unprofessional.

Another soldier who joined the regiment a few months after Bloody Sunday said that there was no sense within the battalion that the soldiers had committed a terrible crime.

It had been a very busy tour and Bloody Sunday was one of a series of bloody events the Paras had been involved in.

It wasn't something which was openly talked about but it would come up in conversation, there was no sense it was being covered up. The feeling of those who took part, mostly guys from the anti-tank platoon, was that they were under fire and so they responded. Another member of the anti-tank platoon told me that the rounds were splashing around his feet when he got out of the PIG. I think part of the problem for the IRA on that day was they thought that the Army would never try and cross the barricades in the Bogside because up until that day they hadn't.

The IRA had been saying 'The British Army will never enter the Bogside again'. So when the two 1 Para Companies went in, the IRA was not ready or in positions to properly defend. They weren't at prepared positions and reacted late by firing off a few shots and that is when the shooting began. The view at the time is that most of the deaths were probably caused by about three or four soldiers, who had been in the Army for some time, so they were experienced, who genuinely thought they were involved in a major battle with the IRA.

A soldier from the King's Own Border Regiment, who admittedly was not at 'Free Derry Corner' but nearby at Bligh's Lane, made the following comments to me about the aftermath of the shooting.

Their officers had no control at all and when I saw them, after the shooting, they [the Paras] were cock-a-hoop and laughing and gloating. They seemed like they were celebrating a football match or an FA Cup Final or something. Of course, I only saw the aftermath, but they were behaving in an unprofessional manner and even if they were fired on first, which I do actually believe, then their response was unjustified and way out of proportion; they were unprofessional. Even if they were caught up in all the adrenaline and emotion, there is still no excuse. I blame their officers, because, as I said, they totally lost control of their men and the situation. There were other units in the vicinity, including Jackets [Royal Green Jackets], Drop Shorts [Royal Artillery] and Cold creamers [Coldstream Guards]; why didn't they use them?

A former Scots Guardsman told the author: 'I've always thought the Paras were gung ho to the extent that it got in the way; a complete contrast to the Royal Marines, who when I first worked with them, blew me away with their professionalism.' Again, the comment is from a former soldier who was in Belfast during Bloody Sunday and therefore didn't witness the events, but his experience and knowledge mean that his comments carry weight. They are not untypical of many Northern Ireland veterans.

38 YEARS ON

Gunner, Royal Artillery

Your comments on Bloody Sunday reflects what most of the rest of us felt about the actions of the Paras that day. There were too many witnesses from other units who backed up the claim that they came under fire first for this to be denied. What is not in doubt is that they were totally out of control, which places the blame directly on the shoulders of the officers present. Their actions that day resulted, indirectly, in the deaths of several members of my regiment as the Royal Artillery basically had a permanent presence in Londonderry throughout the 70s and suffered the highest casualty rate of any unit deployed there. Whilst I cannot bring myself to personally blame the lads on the ground for what happened, I hold their officers totally responsible.

One geographical point is that you could not see Rossville flats from Great James Street. You would have to be in Little James Street almost up to the junction of William Street before you could see the flats. All the buildings in Great James Street were at least four floors high. How that street looks is firmly embedded in my mind as it was at the checkpoint there that Gunner Mark Ashford was murdered, 17 January 1976. I was first at the scene about 30 seconds after it happened. Even the next street up, which was Sackville Street, could not be seen from Rossville.

If memory serves, there was a temporary barrier erected at the junction of William Street and Little James Street and this was the sally point of the initial assault. From there, if you crossed William Street it leads to Rossville Street and it was this junction that was called 'Aggro Corner'. The flats and the car park where the Paras debussed would then be on your left. The main body of rioters were attacking the barrier at Waterloo place and the idea was that the snatch groups would co-ordinate their assaults so as to trap the rioters in William Street. The timings went a bit awry and the Little James Street group was delayed by the barrier allowing the rioters to escape towards Rossville. This was told to me over a pint several years after the fact by a couple of lads who were there. They also said that there was no proper plan to proceed into the Rossville car park. The problem is that over the years, the truth has been distorted so much by both sides that it is difficult to know who to believe.

If you continued up Rossville Street for about 50–70 yards, you had Kells Walk on your right which led to Glenfada Park where a lot of the civilians were shot. Of course, you've only my memory to trust for this as I've recently looked at a map of the area and it's all changed. What used to be Aggro Corner is now a roundabout, and of course the flats have gone, although Glenfada Park looks the same.

It is still a mystery why the powers that be used the Belfast resident unit when there were three other battalions available. The King's Own Borderers were the Ballykinler Province reserve, 1 Royal Anglians were the Londonderry resident unit and 2 RGJ were at Ballykelly.

The history of the Troubles has proved time and again that a highly aggressive unit like the Paras was totally unsuitable to the softly, softly approach to urban IS [Internal Security] duties. The way they went about things just stirred things up and it was usually other units who suffered the backlash.

<hr />

Colour Sergeant Ken Ambrose of the Royal Green Jackets steered me in the right direction of a quotation from Bert Henshaw, late of 1 RGJ who sadly passed away in 2008 and to whom this author has previously paid tribute. Bert was discussing 'hard targeting' which, in its simplest form, is the art of making oneself as difficult a target as possible in order to stay alive on the battlefield, or in this case, the streets of Northern Ireland. Bert wrote: 'On routine patrols they [the Paras] would bang off live rounds just to get across the street, They'd call it hard targeting, but I'd call it bad soldiering; if you fire a shot at night, you don't know where it's going.' Clearly the troops were the wrong regiment. The author on a 2008 visit to Londonderry, whilst walking in the Creggan estate, experienced at first hand the absolute hatred the people of the Nationalist community hold for the men who wear the maroon beret.

While it certainly was already open season on soldiers as far as the Republicans were concerned, Bloody Sunday gave a fresh impetus to their 'shoot as many British soldiers as possible' campaign. The Provisionals benefited the most from that day's tragedy in terms of a boost to recruitment and there was an inevitable knee-jerk response from the Irish-American lobby whose collection tins were jangling for months afterwards. They cannot have expected such carnage and would have settled for one or two 'martyrs' for the cause in order to bring in recruits. The scale of the slaughter no doubt both shocked and pleased them.

Towards the end of that terrible day, some Provisionals came out in small numbers and engaged the Royal Anglians at one of the barricades which had hitherto barred the way to the Guildhall. Shots were returned and a lone Anglian who had ventured into the area beyond, reported engaging a gunman who was hit twice and seen to fall. There are no reports of an IRA death and it will be recorded in Army lore as a 'possible hit.'

Whatever the personal feelings of this writer, fourteen people still lie dead, some under monuments proclaiming that they were 'murdered by Crown Forces' in a cemetery near the Creggan Estate. As the bloodstains were washed away from Free Derry Corner, so too was the Catholic community's belief in the impartiality of the British Army. It was not only the Paratroopers' reputation that was sullied. The UDR had been set up around 1970 with the intention of being a non-sectarian organisation. Catholic members felt that they could no longer belong to an army that was no longer perceived – regardless of how well most individual soldiers conducted themselves – as non-sectarian or fair minded when it came to the treatment of their religion. According to John Potter's 2001 history of the regiment, *A Testimony To Courage*, during the year some 108 Catholics resigned and from a community which made up 33 per cent of the population, their members represented less than four per cent of the UDR.

BLOODY SUNDAY: FROM A DIFFERENT ANGLE

Jock 2413, Royal Artillery

Like many other soldiers who served during Operation *Banner*, I married a local girl. She was from that 'friendly' tourist resort called the 'Murph. I stayed at the Seamen's Mission with her and my early morning view was Divis Flats and reveille was usually played by a rifle or machine gun. I had hired a car and it wasn't half a strange experience getting pulled in at VCPs. The lads used to look at my driving licence, suss that I was a soldier, call me a mad bastard, and send me on my way. Towards the end of my leave, we arranged to be married and the service was carried out in the Sacristy of St John's Chapel on the Falls Road at 8 o'clock at night.

I had to leave for the UK, first week in January and my wife point blank refused to stay in Germany during my absence so, as we had Xmas leave, silly me decided to spend it in Belfast, staying with the sister-in-law who lived in Moyard Parade, just up from the Vere Foster barracks. As we walked up from the bus stop on the Springfield Road, I joked that it would be interesting if we were stopped and searched by a patrol as one of my cases was full of army kit for my course. There was a Christmas truce at the time so it was fairly quiet with just the odd incident. I actually started to feel bulletproof walking around the area with my short sleeves and shorter hair as nobody seemed to pay me much attention except the Scots Guards who were the unit

Thought to be smashed windows at the Vere Foster School on the Ballymurphy Estate which was used as a security base by the Army.

in the area. I lost count of the times I was stopped and questioned by foot patrols. It all seemed a bit of a game at the time.

First week in January 1972 I left Belfast for my course at Larkhill. All went fine for the first three weeks until I received a letter from my wife saying that she had been given a bit of a rough time from some locals as she had married a soldier. There were no telephones available in those days, and as we had just been paid and had been given a long weekend, silly bollocks here decided to go to Belfast. I flew in and caught a bus up to Ballymurphy. I did feel a little nervous, but at the time, being a typical squaddie, I think my mind was more on a dirty weekend than the dangers of the area. It was shocks all round when the sister-in-law answered the door to me.

'What the fuck ya doing here, ya stupid wee bastard?' she said as she dragged me indoors and slammed the door. 'Fine welcome' I thought; I soon found out why.

Unbeknownst to me, just before New Year, two other soldiers were on leave, staying with a family in Springhill, right next to Ballymurphy. As they sat in the living room watching TV, three gunmen burst in and shot and wounded both of them. There had been nothing on the news about this and the local jungle telegraph didn't pick up on it till much later. I was also told that, two weeks earlier, an off duty UDR soldier had been shot dead in his house in New Barnsley. [Private Sean Russell who was murdered by the IRA in his home.]

The Greater Ballymurphy area is a cluster of housing estates based at the foot and lower slopes of both the Divis and Black Mountains, to the west of Belfast's city centre. The area is approximately one square mile in size and it consists of housing estates such as Ballymurphy, Dermott Hill, New Barnsley, Moyard, Springfield Park, Sliabh Dubh, Springhill, Westrock and Whiterock. Within this is the Ballymurphy estate, the centrepiece of the larger area. It is sometimes known as 'God's Little Acre.'

The Orange Order marches which begin on 12 July every year used to march to the Whiterock Orange Lodge close to the 'Murph in their usual provocative manner. In the early days of the Troubles, the estate, although predominantly Catholic, did contain Protestant families and was considered by most observers as 'mixed'.

Kevin Myers wrote of it: 'Ballymurphy was built just after the war and was a miracle of forward thinking. Intended to be a slum from its first day, it had instantly realised this heroic ambition ... it imitated in meanness and misery the conditions in the horrific Victorian slums its new residents had come from.' (*Watching The Door* p17.)

The worst bit of news was that the local IRA had known that I had been there and had planned to take me out just after the New Year. As they were preparing their weapons, one of them had an ND which seriously wounded one of the bastards. An army escorted RUC unit had been in the vicinity serving a summons and was on the spot almost immediately and arrested three with weapons as well as the one who was shot, who was all of seventeen years old.

And here I was right in the middle of it again. To make things worse, the problem the wife got involved in had been something minor caused by the family of one of the internees. The mother-in-law, who was a well known and popular lady in the area, had sorted that out by the simple process of visiting the local Official IRA boss. It was there that she was told about the botched attempt against me but he blamed the 'provies' who were trying to move in on the area. He also told her to warn me not to come back. 'Too bloody late now' I thought.

It was decided that the best thing was for me to stay indoors over the weekend, and do a runner early Monday morning. I'd had enough of the wife being exposed to this. I was also a bit worried that the 'provies' would at some time take it out on her for losing their little band of murderers and so we spent all of Saturday and most of Sunday arguing about her coming with me. So much for my dirty weekend!

Everybody was aware that there was a massive civil rights march taking place in Londonderry on Sunday afternoon, but where I hid it was quiet. At about 5.30pm I was watching something on TV when the programme was interrupted by a news flash. It said that serious trouble had broken out during the march and several people had been shot. I sat there watching it all unfold in front of me less than an hour after it had all happened. First it was six people shot, then ten, and then it could be as many as twenty with several of them dead. By 6pm it was confirmed that thirteen were dead with a further fourteen wounded; none of the casualties were army. It's quite difficult for me to describe how I felt. Although pleased that no soldiers had been injured, the fact that 27 people had been shot in a short space of time made me wonder if we'd declared war on the Bogside. I also knew that it was a dead certainty that the shit was going to well and truly hit the fan. Even as I sat there, I could hear a right racket going on outside with shouting and bin lids and knew that the lads in Vere Foster were in for it.

For the next hour or so, I had a ringside seat to a fair old bit of trouble right outside the flats and I heard the unmistakable bang of rubber bullets being fired. I should explain that the entrance doors to the flats were at the rear with the living room facing towards Ballymurphy and we were on the ground floor. The plan was that if I was targeted, it would be something heavy through the window followed by me and don't stop running till I reached Vere Foster barracks hoping that there wasn't some trigger-happy sod on sentry.

At about 7pm there was a loud knock on the door. The sister-in-law went to answer it while I adopted the 'ready' position. The door closed and it had been an IRA messenger going from door to door telling everyone to be indoors by 8pm and not to come out till given the OK. Immediate frustration built up inside me and I wanted to go down and warn the lads but the rest of the family ganged up on me. Then fate took a hand, and there was a bit of a commotion at the rear of the flats with lots of shouting and screaming. Naturally everyone went to have a look. It turned out to be a fairly large number of soldiers, Kings Own Scottish Borderers, who had made their way behind the flats to try and outflank the rioters.

They were now getting a hard time from the local occupants, and, to this day, I don't know what I was thinking, but I took the opportunity to warn them. On the living room floor was a piece of brown paper and a crayon where the kids had been playing earlier on. I tore off a piece and crayoned a warning to the effect that we had been told to stay indoors. I can't remember the exact wording but I deliberately used 2000hrs instead of 8pm. The problem of passing this on was solved for as soon as I got to the door, this evil looking git grabbed me by the shirt and pushed me against the wall screaming abuse in a broad accent. I took the chance and using my strongest brogue, I shouted 'Fuck off ya bastard,' and got eye contact with him and pushed the bit of paper into the hand that had hold of my shirt. He looked at the paper, then back at me and I was nodding my head like hell. He let me go and thankfully disappeared with my message. I prayed that he was switched on enough not to go waving it about till he got back to camp. The ruckus at the back of the flats had spoiled the KOSB's ambush plan as the crowd out front disappeared and I watched the lads make their way down to the school. I was shaking that much I must have smoked five fags in ten minutes.

For some squaddies, weary of being used as fairground 'Aunt Sallies' and tired of being bricked and bottled and petrol bombed, the events of that day were seen as payback. For others, there was the dread that this was just the excuse that PIRA and the others had been waiting for. A Lieutenant said to no-one in particular but within my own earshot: 'That's just opened up a whole can of worms!' One Guardsman commented to me: 'The way I felt at the time, is the same way I feel now – the Paras weren't in the same army as me on that day. I felt shame.' The next contributor was not there at the time but his emotions sum up what many military men feared would happen as soon as the final echoes of those 7.62mm rounds had died away on William Street.

CAMP DEBATE

Pete Whittall, Infantry Junior Leaders Battalion, Later Staffords

The audio recordings and visual images that captured the military operation in Londonderry on 30 January 1972, in and around the Bogside area of William Street and Rossville flats was a real eye opener to the escalating dangers and civil unrest across the province as a whole. As a young junior soldier I was very aware of the Troubles across the water from mainland Britain as many of our adult instructors had served tours of duty in the province since 1969 and had shared first hand graphic images of their experiences with us. The sounds and pictures now beaming from our NAFFI TV were those of the civil rights march and disorder forming the never-to-be forgotten Bloody Sunday. Thirteen unarmed civilians were killed and many others seriously wounded as a result of the action taken by 1 Para.

As a young fifteen-year-old these images would bring the soldier's experience out in the province right into our hearts, minds and psyche forever. I can remember seeing marchers running everywhere trying to get away from the gunfire of the Paras and using anything that seemed solid enough to take cover behind to protect themselves. I can vividly remember hearing the CO of the Paras instructing his men to cease firing and to control their shots, or words to that effect; the sounds and images shown on television were awful and depicted mayhem, disorder and sheer panic amongst civilians as well as the soldiers. For me it was the most disturbing reality of the anger and lawlessness that existed at the time which had built up over centuries but created by the modern troubles and tensions from 1969 onwards. I can remember talking to a number of lads from different regiments who were watching the TV and we all realised that in a little over eighteen months or so many of us would be posted to Northern Ireland to face similar circumstances, not a welcome thought.

It was difficult to gauge who was right and who was wrong in dealing with the situation, as there we were, in our barracks at Park Hall Camp in Oswestry, hearing and seeing these surreal images of which we could hear the screams, the gunshots and the officer's commands; we could see bodies lying still, lifeless, and soldiers opening fire with the mayhem happening all around them. Our first reaction was to say 'what were the Paras doing; they are out of control.' We couldn't believe that the British Army, one of the best trained and highly disciplined military forces in the world, was acting so irrationally. I do recall one soldier saying 'Typical bloody Paras!' I said 'It's easy for us sitting here making judgement, when our lads are in a very violent situation and having to make snap on-the-spot decisions to protect themselves and the community.' This created a hot debate amongst the fifteen or so junior soldiers watching the news reel at the time. I said 'that may, or may not be us guys in eighteen months, two years time.' The room went silent and a colleague said something like 'You're bloody right Pete; we are in no position to criticise or otherwise. God forbid it could be us or worse to come in the not too distant future.'

My heart went out to both the civilians and the SF that day as the circumstances were so violent and changing that the reality of what was happening must have been so difficult to gauge.

Four months earlier, at the end of the British summer and long before the events of Bloody Sunday, an officer in the Royal Green Jackets second Battalion was shot and badly wounded by the IRA. Major Robin Alers-Hankey (35) had been in charge of a Jackets unit protecting firemen from rioters whilst they fought a blaze at a timber yard near Abbey Street, Londonderry.

The married father of two from Winchester – the home of the Rifle Depot and spiritual home of the Jackets – was hit in the stomach by a gunman and treated for several weeks in a hospital in the Londonderry area. On 3 January, having been sent home to convalesce, he was returned to hospital where, 27 days later, on the same day as the tragedy of the Bogside took place, he died from complications caused by his initial wound. On the day that the whole world watched the events of Bloody Sunday unfold who else, other than his loved ones and comrades, noticed the death of this popular officer?

On the last day of the month, an IRA car bomb exploded outside BHS (British Home Stores) in the centre of Belfast. Paul McFadden (30) was terribly injured and he died of his wounds five days later; in the same attack, an RUC officer lost a leg and others were badly injured.

BLOODY SUNDAY: PART 2

Jock 2413, Royal Artillery

I got the family to close all the windows and curtains and told them to sit on the kitchen floor to put as many walls as possible between them and the front wall. Moyard used to be a mixed area until the ethnic cleansing of August 1971 so there were a lot of empty flats. [The Moyards were a small collection of streets to the north-east of New Barnsley and only a few hundred yards north of the 'Murph itself.] It didn't take a genius to work out that they were ideal fire positions to shoot down at Vere Foster School and a 7.62 round would go through the walls like they were made of paper. Of course, me being 'bullet proof' I made myself comfortable by a corner of the front window. I started clock watching. Five past; ten past; quart...' and then something like two thunder flashes went off right near the front gate of the barracks, and this was followed by an outbreak of shooting coming from New Barnsley. It sounded like three different weapons as the noise was like 'boom; crack; pop' all mixed up. It must have been at least twenty shots. There was no return fire from the school. Then, sounding like it came from the room I was in, shooting erupted from what I think was upstairs next door.

It was definite rifle fire but I didn't hang about to count the shots as I was on my hands and knees making a rapid exit from the front room: I knew what was coming. The SLR sounds like a howitzer when it's fired in a built-up area, but the noise of rapid fire rounds passing through paper thin walls is something else. On top of this, the women in the kitchen started screaming, but thankfully it was from fear only. The shooting had stopped, so, trying to be Mr Cool, I asked the sister-in-law to put the kettle on. The poor cow was shaking so much she dropped a cup on the floor breaking it, the noise setting off another few screams. As it seemed to quieten down a bit, I resumed my vigil by the front window. I could see some activity by the gate of the barracks and I assumed it was the follow up on its way. Then some movement to my right caught my attention. About 50 yards away, I could clearly see two men making their way down the side of a house in New Barnsley. Both had rifles and my view of them was such, that I even identified one of the weapons as an M1 carbine.

Inwardly I was screaming with frustration as I watched them both take aim, then open fire. The gun flashes seemed to illuminate them and I thought surely the lads must see them. Somebody thought they did; but they were either the worst shots in the British Army, or were just firing blind as once again, the flats next door copped it. Again and again this pair fired at the barracks and from somewhere further down I heard two longish bursts of automatic fire. I didn't see any of this as by then I had a mouth full of living room carpet and hot tea was soaking into my trousers; well I hoped it was tea!

It was all quiet again apart from a lot of shouting coming from the barracks. I then heard the unmistakable sound of PIG engines screaming their way up the hill. I stood up to have a look and was nearly blinded by the flash and bang of another explosion which shook the whole house, immediately followed by five rapid shots from an SLR. It was all activity after that. One of the PIGs stopped virtually outside the front window, accompanied by the familiar banging of the doors, shouted orders and pounding of feet. A loud voice told me in a 'polite' way to get away from the window so I joined the ladies in the kitchen and put a brew on, fully expecting company. We could hear the pounding of boots from the flats either side of us, but strangely, the expected 'size nine' through the door didn't happen. In a way, I was disappointed as I hoped for a chance to point out the fire position those two bastards had used.

I took stock of the damage to the house; there were four bullet holes above and to the right of the living room window; three holes in the wall adjoining the kitchen and three exit holes giving the flat its own built-in ventilation. The fourth round had entered the wall near the ceiling and left a scorch mark right across the living room ceiling before disappearing from sight. I blocked off all the holes as best I could with toilet paper and told my sister-in-law to wait till I left and then report the damage. Any problems and I would be a pretty good witness. She was actually moved into a much better flat out of direct sight of the barracks.

The PIG stayed outside for most of the night, so we all wrapped up with blankets and spent the night in the back kitchen listening to the sporadic shooting all over the area. My thoughts were with the lads in Vere Foster and I was fervently praying that none of them had been hurt, despite their lousy marksmanship. By daylight, all was quiet and I started to make plans for getting out of 'Dodge City'. Because of what had gone on the previous night, my wife decided to come with me. We had to put things on hold for a bit as throughout the day there were several shots and a couple of bombs directed at the barracks. Finally at about 4.30pm we made our move. The plan was that the wife and her mother would go to the house in Divismore Park where the wife's clothes were, while me and the sister-in-law would make our way to the Springfield Road and meet up with her near the Henry Taggart barracks.

As I went round to the front and onto the road, I had a look at the outside wall of the flats. They looked as if they'd been given a going over with a minigun. The one next door was well peppered with the windows all smashed and big chunks dug out of the walls. We were pretty fortunate to have been hit only four times.

After freezing my nuts off in the Springfield Road for about half an hour and drawing some suspicious looks from the front sangar of the Taggart [Henry Taggart Memorial Hall on the 'Murph which was commandeered as an Army base], the wife and her mother turned up with two cases. A quick tearful goodbye and we were off. There were no buses running because of hijackings so it was a long old trek down the road with the wife sobbing all the way and me cursing the weight of the cases I had to carry. I had decided to go to Mulhouse barracks off the Falls Road as it was familiar territory and the plan was that we would play up the incident where she was threatened and that I had come over to rescue her. It had to be good as I was in the shit being both AWOL and in a place banned for soldiers.

As it happened, all went well. When we got to Mulhouse, the company commander of the unit, the Glosters, was very sympathetic and apart from calling me a stupid bastard, which I was used to by now, was very helpful. An RMP vehicle turned up and we were bundled off to Albert Street mill. There we were given travel warrants to Woolwich in London, paid a £50 advance and escorted down to the ferry terminal. Fifteen hours later, I was repeating the story to the adjutant at Woolwich. He arranged accommodation for my wife in the WRAC block, but instead of ending up in the cells as I expected for being absent, he told me that I was chucked off the course but had to go to Larkhill to collect my kit. I was later grilled by some character from the Intelligence Corps who wanted to know all the ins and outs of a cat's arse about my 'adventure'.

Looking back now, I still can't believe how lucky and stupid I was. Many other soldiers were shot or kidnapped and murdered doing what I did. I also realise how selfish I had been because I had put everybody else in danger as well. I think that most soldiers who are 21 like I was possess a form of self belief and bravado that makes them think 'it can't happen to me!' Sadly, in many cases, that bravado proved fatal. Unfortunately, despite what we had been through, my marriage, like the majority of those with girls from the province, didn't last. Repeated Operation *Banner* tours and homesickness put paid to it.

You will appreciate my desire for anonymity, when I tell you that my ex-wife and kids kept my name and still live on the 'Murph.

UNDER FIRE ON BLOODY SUNDAY

Tommy Clarke, RCT

I had been married for seven months and we had just been posted from BAOR to my new unit 60 Sqn RCT based in Ripon, North Yorkshire. We were busy preparing for a tour in Northern Ireland, so we had to hit the ground running, doing things that civvies do at leisure, like finding your way around new surroundings, setting up home, finding shops, hospitals, doctors, filling in forms making new friends, oh, and finding out your new wife is pregnant! The unit sailed from Heysham on the car ferry, arrived in Belfast on 7 November 1971, where we were bussed from the docks to Palace Barracks the home base of 1 Para at the time and not a great distance. Some of us naively believed that the huge plumes of black smoke in some places were leftovers from Bonfire Night; how innocent some of us were.

It wasn't long before we were all split into sections and briefed on our detachments. Unlike infantry units we in the RCT not only had to learn our own SOPs [standard operating procedures] but had to be familiar with every other units that we had to work with; at times this did cause minor friction burns, but were mainly settled amicably.

Myself and six other drivers were sent on to attachment with 54 Field Support Squadron RE based at Castledillon, a large disused lunatic asylum just outside Armagh. It was what's called in the immortal words of most squaddies 'a shitehole.' The mud at the Somme was a sand pit compared to this place; I suppose the use by engineers and their heavy kit didn't help in this respect. Much of the work we did with them was moving huge amounts of kit to a place called Magillian Point near Limavady; this was a 24/7 job and went on for about five weeks. We were bollixed by the end of it and even missed Christmas that year.

My section then returned to Palace Barracks in mid-January and after two days off to clean, repair and service vehicles and personal kit, we were sent as small detachments supporting other units in and around Belfast. It was around about the middle of January that 'rumour control' intimated that there was something big afoot and we began to work more with the Paras; even to the extent of wearing their god-awful coloured berets, which didn't impress us at all.

29 January saw us transferring 1 Para from Palace Barracks in Belfast to various locations in and around Londonderry. Everyone knew there was going to be a large illegal march/demonstration and everyone knew that this was going to be a cover or excuse for the IRA to kick off. After we had disgorged our loads we along with other units not actively involved in policing the demo/marches, were all parked in a large grassed park area. We all sat around talking about how big an event this was when someone shouted 'Stand to and take cover.' Apparently someone had taken a shot at us and had hit one of the reserve PIGs.

I quickly followed one of my muckers into one of these, as it was safer than the back of a soft-skinned Bedford and as I slammed the back doors, two clangs sounded and I knew that we were under fire. This was probably coming from one of the blocks of flats [Rossville] which surrounded the park so there was no chance of us returning fire on the buggers trying to bump us off for fear of hitting civvies.

We did start to worry when we heard the buildup of noise and then the sound of 'Dick guns' and then live firing coming from the area where the march was taking place. Radio traffic was horrific but we could make out that the Paras had come under fire and were returning it; we too were under fire but couldn't see to return our fire, nor did we. By about 2200 hours we began to pull out from the park to pre-arranged pick-up points; luckily, the IRA sharp shooter was not all that sharp and no-one was hit, just a few vehicles.

It wasn't until we started to return our sections back to locations and doing mobile patrols around the area that I realised the extent of what had taken place. Everyone was interviewed by RUC/SIB officers and it was all over the media. As someone who was there at the time and knew how the IRA operated, I believe that it was they who staged this event in order to discredit the Army and it managed to achieve its aims.

BOMBS AND BRAVADO

Jock 2413, Royal Artillery

On arrival at Flax Street mill, we were told that a young kid had been run over and killed by a Ferret Scout car down in the New Lodge and the whole area had erupted. Our tasking had changed and my troop had to relieve a platoon of Queens' who were guarding the Ardoyne bus station. We all piled into the back of a Bedford which soon deposited us at the bus station. The Queens' lads hopped aboard and headed for the New Lodge. The troop sergeant soon sorted out guard positions and a stag list and we settled down to what we thought would be a boring task. By now it was after 1800 hours and it was quite dark. We heard the sound of gunfire in the distance and were told that four Protestant teenagers had been shot by gunmen from the New Lodge area. I was sitting with a couple of others in what passed for a rest area when one of the lads started shouting something and pointing at the rear wall. As we got up to have a look, there was this bright flash and a huge bang which stunned everyone.

We all ran to our stand-to positions. My ears were buzzing with the effects of the blast. Suddenly gunfire erupted from the direction beyond the front entrance of the station. It's strange, but if you are not the target, you have a tendency to count the number of shots being fired but this time I lost count though I remember it was more than ten. I didn't actually see it, but the story went that the lad who was at the front entrance came running into the garage proper followed by bullet strikes shouting: 'Sarge, Sarge, they're shooting at us.' It's funny now, but at the time poor 'B' was a quivering jelly. The shooting had stopped and nobody had seen where it had come from. The troop sergeant went up to the entrance and in a feat of bravado, stepped out into the road and shouted: 'Come on you bastards; we're ready for you.' Nothing happened and we were stood down to normal stags. The bomb had been thrown from the street outside the rear of the garage but instead of landing inside where it probably would have hurt some of us, by a fluke, it landed on top of the wall with its burning fuse glowing in the dark. This was what the lad who shouted out had seen.

As January 1972 came to an end, five British soldiers had lost their lives in the fight against terrorism. On that last day of the month, a senior member of PIRA stated all that all members of PIRA had been given 'permission' to shoot as many soldiers as they possibly could in retaliation for 'Bloody Sunday.'

On the following Sunday an anti-internment march – organised by NICRA – took place near Londonderry. Most of the world held its collective breath as it could so easily have resulted in revenge attacks. It passed without major incident.

During that awful month, seventeen civilians, four RUC and RUCR officers and four members of the IRA had been killed. Adding these to the deaths of the five British soldiers meant that the bloody month of January had claimed 30 lives.

It was not to be the worst month that year.

CHAPTER TWO

FEBRUARY

Mark Bolan was belting out 'Telegram Sam' – he was to be killed in a car crash in 1977 – and Chicory Tip's 'Son of my Father' would replace it in the British music charts by the end of the month. In Dublin, mobs of Republicans attacked, ransacked and burnt down the British Embassy.

Harold Wilson, the Prime Minister who had initially sent British troops into the Province in 1969 and by 1972, leader of the Opposition Labour Party, said that a United Ireland was the only solution to the conflict in Northern Ireland. William Craig, then Home Affairs Minister, suggested that the west bank area of Derry should be ceded to the Republic.

On 1 February, a mere two days after the tragedy of the Bogside, the events, the analysis, the recriminations and the hand-wringing in the world's media was still going on. However, the events of the previous Sunday were washed from the minds of Ian Bramley's family. On that day, Corporal Ian Bramley (25) a married man and father of two from the Cheltenham area was in the process of opening security gates at Hastings Street RUC station in west Belfast. As he went about this task, one of two rounds fired from gunmen who had taken a man hostage in Durham Street, hit him in the chest. He fell, mortally wounded, and was immediately rushed to the RVH, but died within minutes of being admitted He was the second Gloster to die in just 27 days.

An IRA gunman – masked as always – poses for a 'publicity shot', no doubt in part to impress the NORAID people in the US.

Impact marks of an RPG attack on an Army base in Vere Foster school on the Ballymurphy Estate.

On the same day two other soldiers were wounded in the Andersonstown area. In the Republican Short Strand, a Catholic woman was shot in the chest and badly wounded following more disturbances there.

On 2 February the funerals of eleven of the dead of Bloody Sunday took place in the Creggan area of Londonderry. Tens of thousands attended including clergy and politicians from North and South. Tensions ran incredibly high and were probably as high on that day as at any other time during the Troubles with the possible exception of the death of hunger striker Bobby Sands in 1981. Tensions ran no less high on the 'Murph that day.

The Ballymurphy estate in west Belfast – which is not the author's favourite place – suffered more than its fair share of tragedies, none more so than the accidental shooting of an innocent civilian on the 2nd. Thomas McElroy (29) was caught in the crossfire between the Army and IRA gunmen attacking the base at the Henry Taggart Memorial Hall; he left a young child.

Throughout the rest of Ireland, prayer services were held to coincide with the time of the funerals. In Dublin over 90 per cent of workers stopped work in respect of those who had died, and approximately 30,000-plus people turned out to march to the British Embassy. They carried thirteen coffins and black flags, and later attacked the Embassy with stones, bottles and petrol bombs, and the building was extensively damaged.

On the next day, in what bore all the hallmarks of a Loyalist attack, a Catholic bar in Stewartstown, Co Tyrone was bombed. The device destroyed the bar, injured five, and killed Louis O'Neill (49) a father of six. Several days later, two IRA men in the process of planting a bomb on a barge on Lough Neagh were killed when the device exploded prematurely. Phelim Grant and Charles McCann died instantly.

Lost Lives (p151) reports that, on the same day as the IRA 'own goal' at Lough Neagh, a former soldier David Seaman (32) was 'probably' killed by the Official IRA. Seaman, described as a 'Walter Mitty' character had led a bizarre existence during the Troubles; he was abducted and found murdered in the area of Castleblaney on the Irish border. Earlier, he had appeared at an IRA press conference where he had claimed to be a British spy.

Another former soldier, Bernard Rice (49) was killed on the 8th, but this time it was a sense-less sectarian murder by the Red Hand Commando. He was walking towards the Ardoyne when he was shot from a passing car on Crumlin Road. Miles away in Rio de Janeiro a Royal Navy sailor was murdered, and although his name does not appear on the Roll of Honour, his death is noteworthy in that there is a tenuous connection with the Troubles. David Cuthbert (20) was shot and killed in a taxi in the Brazilian capital and pamphlets were left describing the murder as 'an act of solidarity for the Irish Republican Army … against British Imperialism'. The family of Cook David Cuthbert, from Powys in Wales, was presented with the Elizabeth Cross in recognition of his service and death, at a ceremony in May 2010.

The next day, another IRA 'own goal' fatally wounded two bomb makers. Patrick Casey (26) and Eamonn Gamble (27) were planting a device near Keady on the border when it exploded prematurely. The two badly injured terrorists were smuggled across the border to hospital in Co Monaghan; Casey died shortly afterwards and Gamble on 8 March. Once again the Gardai were seen to be turning a blind eye and further fuelling Loyalist suspicion and hatred. On the same day, Joseph Cunningham (26) was wounded in a gun battle with the RUC at Glengormley to the north of Belfast as he prepared to ambush an off duty UDR soldier. He died of his wounds the following day.

On the 10th, an IRA landmine was detonated in the Newtownhamilton area when an Army mobile patrol was attacked as it drove along the border. Newtownhamilton – or NTH as it was known to a generation of soldiers – is in South Armagh, and although it would still be several years before the then Secretary of State for Northern Ireland Merlyn Rees coined the cliché 'bandit country' the area was fast becoming a very dangerous place for the security forces.

On that Thursday a team of bombers concealed across the border detonated a device as a Land Rover containing Devon and Dorsets' Sergeant Ian Harris (26) from the Channel Islands and Private David Champ (23) from Warwickshire drove near Freeduff. Such was the force of the explosion that the vehicle was totally disintegrated, killing both soldiers instantly. *Lost Lives* (p153) states that it was over a day before the second body, or body parts were discovered. Sergeant Harris and Private Champ both had young children.

On the following Sunday 13 February, the Official IRA, ever seeking a soft target and having intelligence from their army of dickers, abducted Private Thomas McCann, an Irishman by birth, whilst he was off duty. Private McCann (19) was a victim of the Officials who were trying to bloodily emulate the Provisionals as each murderous faction sought to gain 'revenge' for Bloody Sunday and assert themselves as 'guardians' of the Nationalist community.

He had, unwisely, crossed the Irish border to visit his elderly mother and was en-route to Dublin. It is a source of speculation as to where exactly he was abducted, but his bound and hooded body with a gunshot wound to the head was found at Newtownbutler just inside the Ulster border. He was a member of the Royal Army Ordinance Corps and was the third member of the 'blanket stackers' to be killed by the IRA.

NORTH HOWARD STREET MILL PONG PATROL

Mike Heavens, 'B' Company 1 Glosters

It's now so long ago that it is almost as if it didn't happen. It was part of another life; different and cold and very intense and now relived as a series of images and fragments. The images are firstly of the huge old and defunct Victorian cotton mill that was home for those months. It was called North Howard Street Mill, in the no-nonsense, cold logic of military thinking, because it was situated in North Howard Street. It was a part of the Clonard area of Belfast and the street was a through link to the Falls Road and Albert Street to its south and the Shankhill to the north and had been a rat run for several sectarian killings in the past.

Eventually, the military had blocked the road and built the base there because it dominated the peace line. The base was surrounded by a high concrete wall and the only entrance was through two giant heavy metal gates that covered the road way in and with a smaller pedestrian gate alongside. Both ways passed close to and were controlled by the giant road sangar which looked down at the Falls Road. Its seven floors had a winding stone staircase at one end and a wider, normal stone staircase at the other. The very top floor was living accommodation and on the roof was another giant sangar which overlooked the peace line. Loosely following Cupar Street, and over the Falls and the Divis flats complex and around and up to the Shankhill area. The sangar was surrounded by a steel mesh anti- rocket screen with armoured steel portholes and kitted out with radio, a squawk box (an internal comms system) and a land line phone. Naturally, it had a GPMG [General Purpose Machine Gun] and various surveillance devices and finally a system the squaddies called 'Clarabelle.' This was an echo location device designed to find the firing point of the prat who had just shot at you; because of all the surrounding buildings, the normal 'crack and thump' training given to squaddies for locating incoming fire was impractical and unusable. It had a face similar to a compass and as the high velocity round impacted close by (but hopefully not too close!) the face spun around and an arrow indicated the direction of the shot so you could tell the Ops room. It didn't stop the smelly 'adrenalin' filling your underwear and then trickling down your leg, though!

It was from this dark forbidding home that foot patrols left on what were delightfully referred to as 'ground domination' patrols. Search teams visited various nominated homes with the early morning 'knock, knock!' We also had to search derelict buildings and waste ground looking for weapons caches and the like.

The Clonard Monastery dominated the area and was only some 500 metres away from the mill. Its head at that time, was a very sympathetic padre (sympathetic that is, to the 'cause'); on one occasion this godly priest leapt upon and bit, quite savagely on the throat, one of our lads. Poor 'Maggot' Mosley – a member of the search team tasked with looking at graves for signs of entry as it was known that the 'Boyos' were storing weapons in some graves – was the victim. The man of God had to be forcibly removed from the aforementioned squealing squaddie, whilst the vitriolic language from the priest had to be heard to be believed. He went on, it is believed, to hold high office in the Roman Catholic Church in Northern Ireland.

We had the pleasantly named 'sewer patrols' known for obvious reasons as 'pong patrols' which were required because the monastery also covered a large area of sewers which 'fed' this area of Belfast and it was a frequent task of the North Howard Street mob to 'clear them'. The CQMS was issued with a stock of 'boots, Wellington rubber', which the 'pong patrol' put on during this

Was it a joke? Decide for yourself if the sign was genuine.

highly sought-after job! Clambering down steep rung ladders into the bowels of Belfast's sewer system was a job not for the faint hearted or weak stomached amongst us. It took several showers until you were allowed once more into the choggie shop, or even into the dining hall and everyone knew who had been on the latest venture 'down under' that day.

SERGEANT JOHN GREEN

Mike, Royal Artillery

Our tour was only four days in when information came in that a bomb had been set at one of the border towers. One of our batteries was working the border at the time and a patrol was sent to investigate and found the biggest device seen up to that time; 48lbs of gelignite. ATO was ages away so one of our sergeants, John Green took it upon himself to have a go. He disconnected the alarm clock timer and as he threw it away, the alarm went off. Clean underwear all round, but he got a bollocking off ATO and a pat on the back from the Major; nowadays, he would probably be decorated.

Another time, we were in Balaclava Street, Belfast when we tried to retrieve a hijacked tanker. Petrol bombs were falling like rain and some 'Rupert' was running about shouting 'Don't shoot them!' Then John Green's voice boomed out: 'Shoot the next bastard who throws one!' It all stopped as if by magic; what a man. He was sadly killed in a helicopter crash in Canada in the late 70s.

Three days after McCann's murder, two soldiers were to lose their lives. Private Michael Prime (18), a young married man from Derbyshire was travelling in a convoy with the Royal Regiment of Fusiliers on 16 February. At Moira roundabout near Lisburn, around 2000 hours, the IRA attacked with automatic weapons and explosives from the top of a motorway bridge. Private Prime was from Matlock and his funeral took place there.

On that very same day Private Thomas Callaghan was murdered by the IRA. The UDR Private, unusually for a member of that regiment, was a Catholic who lived in Limavady and was a bus driver. Some months earlier, another Catholic member of the UDR had been murdered by Republican terrorists and it was clear that they sought to intimidate or murder any of 'their' community into severing all links with the security forces. The 47-year-old man was driving his bus when he was forced to halt by armed and masked gunmen whilst in the Creggan area of Londonderry and driven off in a car. Several hours later, his body was found near Foyle Road in

Despite the IRA's much vaunted 'no go areas' covert British Army patrols still entered. An officer has been badly wounded in the leg. This was, it is thought, taken in Londonderry.

the Creggan area; he was found bound, hooded and with the customary IRA shot in the back of the head. The 'heroes' of the IRA had made yet another widow and clearly advanced the cause of Republicanism in the eyes of no-one but their own sycophantic and bloodthirsty supporters.

After the murder, bus services in the area were suspended and members of the public protested at the cold-blooded killing. Petitions were handed into both the Army and RUC claiming that UDR soldiers living in the Creggan and Bogside should be provided with 24-hour protection.

LENADOON NEAR MISS

Lance Corporal Ken Anderson, Royal Corps of Transport

I did my one and only tour of Sunny Belfast between March and July of 1972; just missed the Bloody Sunday (my birthday) and the joyride of 'Motorman' and its aftermath. Before we got out to Ulster, we spent a week learning how to drive Saracens, but when we got there we didn't even see any; we got PIGs and Land Rovers.

I was in the escort section which had two Land Rovers which were 'armoured' with Makralon. It looked like plain fibre glass to us, but we were assured it was next to bullet proof! It was actually anti-fragmentation, but had been upgraded by the rumour dept. They're the lot that tell you your armour is proof against all known weaponry, and then go on to tell you that your weapon can penetrate all known armour! We found out that a well aimed brick would shatter the stuff, and the local youngsters were renowned for their aiming of bricks! Along with the 'armour' there was a wire mesh screen and an angle iron spar that stuck up in front to cut cheese wire traps, which we never encountered incidentally. The tailgate was suspended on its chains where the two gunners with rifles stood as protection.

We had two Corporals from REME in charge but, fine as they may have been at radar installations and other electrical marvels, they were totally unprepared for commanding a section of mixed Belfast 'pirates' which is how we saw ourselves. We were 2 REME, 2 'troggs' [RCT] and 4 'drop shorts' [Royal Artillery] ready to go.

Our arrival saw us in Palace Barracks Hollywood, where we heard bombs going off down in the city. We were nervous but somewhat relieved when we left there to go to Sunnyside Street TA Centre for a few weeks. The TA lads supplied the guards on the lookout towers and the gates, so we were spared that tedium. Our days consisted of replenishment runs to the other batteries in Lenadoon and Andersonstown Bus Garage, taking them fresh food rations and fuel etc.

One day we were doing our normal delivery of fuel and rations to two of the batteries, and I was driving the rear Land Rover in convoy with the two four-tonner lorries and another [Land] Rover. Suddenly, several shots were fired at us, passing between my vehicle and the lorry in front. The gunners standing in the hip ring of my vehicle ducked inside for cover, but seconds later we arrived at Lenadoon, where we unloaded our provisions and got ready to set off again.

I was a bit pissed off with the Gunners for not being more 'workmanlike' and I decided that I would stand in the hip ring of the lead vehicle for the next leg. I took up my position, and off we set. I had cocked my weapon, my thumb was on the safety catch and my index finger was taking up slight pressure on the trigger. All it needed was a small twitch of my hand and a bullet would be speeding on its way towards making another martyr for 'auld' Ireland.

Warning on a British Army base; the last thing the soldiers would see before commencing a foot or mobile patrol.

As we left the camp gates we were on edge, knowing the gunman might still be waiting for our return. I was facing forward and out of the corner of my eye I saw a man heading in our direction, swinging a weapon up into the aim and pointing straight at us! I immediately swung my body round to line up the shot; the safety came off and I took up a smidgeon more pressure on the trigger. My heart stopped; it was a gentleman wearing a pin-stripe suit complete with bowler hat, and he was swinging an umbrella, and I so very nearly shot him. I didn't stop shaking for the rest of the day.

BELFAST MOMENTS

Trevor Johnson, Glosters

We were sent out to Northern Ireland sometime in late 1971 and I was the youngest NCO in 15 Platoon. I remember not being scared when we were told over in Germany that we were going to Belfast as we just had a job to do. What bothered me was when we were given a straight-from-Sandhurst Second Lieutenant and I knew that he would end up getting us killed. Anyway, after we kicked up a fuss, we were given a Lieutenant from REME who clearly had a bit of sense and, more importantly, experience of patrolling in Northern Ireland; hopefully he was going to keep us alive.

Maybe we all had that 'what if' fatalistic attitude but just before we left Germany, all the younger lads drew out their money and spent it on having a good time just in case we got killed. Several of us also had our blood groups tattooed on our arms, you know, just in case our dog tags

Republican area, thought to have been taken on the Ballymurphy Estate, Belfast.

got lost! As soon as we arrived, we were transported out to Albert Street Mill in west Belfast and immediately set upon doing foot patrols around the area.

I well remember the night that Tony Aspinwall was shot – he was a member of 'D' Company of which I was also a member. We were in the Falls Road area and we were moving along Raglan Street, close to Alma Street when we came under fire. Bullets were just pinging down the street and I think that Tony managed to fire quite a few rounds back at the gunmen even though he'd been hit. We knew that we had to find some cover and even tried the doorways along Raglan Street. One of the lads – 'Lofty' – tried to kick in a door but it wouldn't give so he went in through a window instead and then discovered that it had a bloody big steel bar across the door. We did have a good laugh about that later on but it was tinged with sadness because Tony was hit and badly injured; he died the next day.

That same night, we all received Christmas presents from home; I remember that it was mostly toothpaste and soap and stuff like that which just made me laugh! Just before Christmas Day, we were moved from Albert Street Mill to Mulhouse, close to the Rodneys' area, where we remained for the rest of our tour. I remember it being either Christmas Day or Christmas Eve and I was standing in the front sangar and a little old lady approached me; she would have been roughly my Gran's age. She just said to me: 'Merry Christmas, son; I hope yez get shot!'

When Bloody Sunday happened, we were resting up at RUC, Mulhouse but we were ordered straight out on the ground as trouble was brewing. Now, before we did a foot patrol, we would always sort out the route first, and I would generally lead, but for some reason, on this one particular occasion, I decided to change it. Anyway, thanks to the changing of the route, we avoided a bomb which exploded right at the time we would have passed by it. But then we were told on the radio that there were some kids in the wreckage and we had to go straight there. We started to search through the rubble – and it was a mess I can tell you – and we were abused and called 'English bastards' even though we were searching for their kids!

There was this one night which I will never forget when one of the patrols was out and 'Scouse' Brown – a 'full screw' – was walking up the street and this woman put her head out of the door to see what was going on and this wee fella' fired a gun from the street corner and hit this poor woman right in the side of the head. 'Scouse' tried to help her, but when he put his hand on her head he could see that there was a bloody big hole, and although he tried to save her and ended up covered in her blood, I think that she died. [The woman is thought to have been Elizabeth English (67) who was shot and killed in Barrack Street, close to the Divis.]

We were in Hastings Street one day, inside a PIG, and one of the lads was messing about and had an ND. He had a round in the breach and was pissing about with the safety catch on his SLR when it fired and the round shot against the roof and ricocheted around the PIG. Every single person in the vehicle was cut by the bits of metal flying around and he was lucky that he didn't kill anybody. Another time, we were out patrolling in these vehicles and I was in the lead and 'Lofty' was in the rear one. Suddenly, a car came up behind the rear one and started shining his main beams at it and were sure that we were being 'dicked' and being set up for a hit. Lofty jumped out and went up to the car and told the driver to put his lights out but he refused.

Whereupon 'Lofty' just smashed the headlights with the butt of his SLR and turned back to the PIG, but some lights were still showing, so he went back and finished off the job! The driver complained to the RUC but he was sent off with his tail between his legs. There were other exciting times like when we had an IRA informer with us and he was pointing out who to lift and things like that; we ended up dropping him off at Palace Barracks for interrogation.

Towards the end of the tour, 'Scouse' was shot at and we raided a local house afterwards and I found a rifle and two handguns and in a corner of the yard, after I smelt something odd, some explosives in a bag and I got ATO involved. He had wanted to blow it up, but we were left there to keep watch in case a terrorist who we thought lived nearby, came back for it. Unfortunately our radio failed and we were pulled out. There were other incidents ...

The IRA brought a great deal of influence to bear on the institutions of the Republic. The RUC had occasion to stop a hearse as it crossed the border from Dundalk en-route for the Ardoyne in Belfast. Medical certificates, allegedly signed by medical staff at a hospital in Co Louth, stated that the individual had died from a 'non-infectious disease.' It was shown that David McAuley (14) of the IRA youth wing had in fact died of a gunshot wound. Speculation followed speculation and theories ranged from an accidental shooting in an IRA training camp to being wounded in a shoot-out with the Army. Whatever the cause, another young life, drawn by the 'romantic' image

Outside Army base in West Belfast where an attempt had been made to ram the security gates.

Bullet holes in a
Land Rover seat.

of the terrorists, had been snuffed out. The border country was a very dangerous place for those farmers whose properties straddled the dividing line from the Republic and their 'friends in the North' especially those UDR or RUC Reservists (RUCR) who chose to live and work there.

There are many members of the SF who allege that both the *Garda Siochana* (Irish Police) and the *Óglaigh na h-Eireann* (Irish Army, and not to be confused by the IRA's use of the term) looked the other way where the IRA was concerned. Many of the police – including their political masters in *Fianna Fail*, the Irish Republican Party and often in government – were Republican by politics and by nature. The very fact that the Irish government – *Rialtas na hÉireann* – had, embodied within the framework of its constitution, the stated aim of taking the North back into the country of Ireland, gave tacit support to the IRA. That they saw the terrorist acts committed by both wings of the IRA as 'political' was enough for any border incursion by them to be ignored. However, at the same time they came down hard on border crossings by the British. IRA men would cross back to the Republic immediately after a murder or a bombing with impunity, and dozens of OTRs – IRA members on the run – would set up home within a few miles of the border.

The areas around Castleblayney, Dundalk, Cavan and a myriad other border towns inside the Republic would often have large numbers of OTRs, waiting for their 'on the run' money from the IRA Army Council or setting up new attacks inside Northern Ireland. One of the 'godfathers' of the IRA, Joe Cahill, was reputed to be the paymaster and took this money to the men on the run on a weekly basis.

The Republic gave the IRA an astonishing degree of leeway. An excellent but tragic example of this was the killing of Corporal Ian Armstrong (32) of the 14/20th Hussars who was shot on 29 August 1971 near Crossmaglen. His two vehicle armoured patrol had accidentally crossed into the Irish Republic into the Sheelagh, Co Louth area and was attacked by a mob of Irish citizens. The village is less than a mile from the border and comparative safety. One vehicle was set alight and soldiers had to scramble clear and were immediately attacked by a mob. Whilst this was on-going, the police and Irish Army did nothing and it transpired that gunmen from within the Republic were summoned and opened fire on the troops. They confirmed later that they had been more scared of the mob – who they felt would tear them to pieces – than the armed men.

It was during repairs to their remaining vehicle that an IRA gunman shot and killed Ian Armstrong and badly wounded Trooper Ronald Ager; both the Garda and the Irish Army denied that they had refused to intervene. Strictly speaking, as the event in question took place in 1971, the following personal account is outside the scope of this book. However, as it illustrates perfectly the inertia and often complicity of the Garda and Irish Army, I have chosen to include it.

THE DEATH OF CORPORAL IAN ARMSTRONG

Soldier P, Royal Tank Regiment

On the afternoon in question, I was commanding a three vehicle re-supply convoy of soft skinned Land Rovers, detailed to Crossmaglen. At the time we were based at Markethill, but had a troop of four Ferrets, (rotating), based at XMG. You must understand that at the time, the location of XMG was nothing much more than an armoured RUC police station, and bore no resemblance to what it became later as a large forward patrol base. Our job was to deliver petrol and rations, and apart from an LMG and personal weapons, we had no heavy machine gun.

We were met two miles out from XMG by a half section of Ferrets from the base, at a pre-arranged location, to be escorted in. That half section was commanded by a Second Lieutenant Ross, and the other Ferret by Ian. After a brief chat, we were escorted into the base, the Ferrets continuing on towards the border at Cullaville with the intention of checking the border crossing. The other half section, commanded by Sergeant Tottman (MID), was on another road, and the intention was to meet up on the northern side of Cullaville.

However, (for reasons never explained), Ian Armstrong became detached from his Troop Leader, and crossed the border at Cullaville. He proceeded through the village for over a mile, before being alerted to his true position on spotting a green telephone box. Ian then returned the way he had come, but the locals had seen him enter the village, and immediately blocked the road between two houses with a furniture van and a load of scrap metal. When Ian drew up to this barricade, the locals refused to move it, and a standoff began. Ian radioed for assistance and all units in the area made a dash towards the location.

Now at XMG, I became aware of the situation from the Ops room, and gained permission to take three men armed with SLRs in a Rover, with instructions to de-bus on our side of the border, and set up a fire position to cover the scene. However, in the interim time, Ian had ordered Ron Agar to drive over the scrap metal, whilst he himself threatened the locals with his turret Browning. Meanwhile, a Sioux helo from Bessbrook was in the air along with the Regimental Commander, who took command of the ensuing operation. Ian and Ron got back over the border, but they had punctured a tyre, (a run-flat), reporting the same on the net. On REME advice, the Colonel ordered Ian and Ron not to proceed, but to change the wheel for the spare, which they started to do. This was bloody stupid, as each Ferret run-flat had 100 miles flat running time on them, and XMG was only six miles away.

In the meantime, the local battalion of the IRA had ascended a hill to the left and behind of the village, and opened fire on Ian and Ron. A high velocity round [.303], hit the road near to Ian, ricocheted up under his flak jacket, and through his heart, killing him at once. A second round hit Ron, smashing his shoulder. He then crawled into a nearby ditch for cover.

Sgt Tottman's half section was approaching, and they now came under intense fire from the Provo unit. Halting, they returned fire with their Brownings. My Rover was now approaching the scene, and we de-bussed. Ordering the men with me to take cover, I made my way to Tottman's Ferret, and spoke to him from the rear of the vehicle, as it was under sustained fire. I told him that I intended to proceed around the bend, and make my way along the left hand ditch towards Ian's Ferret, which lay about 200 yards down the straight. Taking one man and the LMG, [Light Machine Gun] we got around the bend, but could not enter the ditch (or if we had done, we couldn't proceed), because of large amounts of brambles growing there. I could see the whole scene in front of me, with Ian's body next to his vehicle. The two of us crawled up the left hand side of the tarmac, but then it seems that we came into the view of the Provo unit on the hill, and they fired at us, ripping up the roadway into clods of tarmac; scary stuff. I returned fire with the LMG, and we carried on, crawling, firing and then crawling again.

We came to a point some 50 yards from Ian's body, but could proceed no further. I had noticed this chap who kept running behind the distant furniture lorry, which was still in place from the earlier barricade. He was carrying ammo tins and bandoliers up behind the hill, and so when he reappeared some five minutes later, I put half a mag into his legs as they appeared under the lorry. He went down and didn't move again.

I could hear a Saracen behind us, and saw that it was reversing past us towards Ian's Ferret. Of course, all the Provo fire was directed towards it, and away from us. The back opened, and two corporals jumped out (Elsdon and McVay), grabbed Ian's body and Ron from the ditch. God knows how they weren't hit; I think that such was the weight of fire now being directed towards the hill that it put the gunmen off. As this was happening, I saw two Irish Army Land Rovers pull up in the village, along with a Garda car. They all got out, and just stood around, watching the action! They made no effort to intervene, (they could have got the gunmen hands down), and seemed to be treating the whole thing like a tennis match.

My mate and I then pulled back down the road after the Saracen, the fire having by now slackened. I next saw Ian's Ferret about a week later, burnt out. It had been recovered from its location about four days after the incident, and of course the good people of South Armagh had looted it before firing it. As far as I am aware, no other Ferret was involved in the incident, but now I must admit that I'm not all that sure, after reading your report. Certainly I only saw one burnt Ferret, which I was told at the time was Ian's, but there lies the question. Did both Ferrets cross the border? I think not, but hell, it's been 40 years; I might be wrong.

All I can add is that Tottman got a Mentioned in Dispatches, Elsdon and McVay each got GOC Commendations for bravery and I used 240 rounds. The IRA admitted to losing two men, both from the Dundalk Active Service Unit.

On the 21st the IRA lost four of its members in another premature detonation. An IRA bomb team was taking a device to its target when they were recognised by an RUC patrol and they turned their hijacked car back towards the Republican Short Strand in Belfast. The bomb exploded inside the car on the Ballygowan Road, scattering pieces of metal and human flesh over a wide area.

Three of the terrorists were killed instantly and the other died of his terrible wounds in hospital the same day. The dead were Gerard Steele (27); Gerard Bell (20) whose brother was later killed by the UVF; Joseph Magee (30) and Robert Dorrian (29).

After the events of Bloody Sunday the British Government had braced itself for a revenge attack by the IRA. The first took place in the garrison town of Aldershot, spiritual home of the esteemed Parachute Regiment. The Regiment – with battle honours including Normandy, Arnhem, the Rhine Crossing and Suez – was based at Maida Barracks in the small Hampshire town. For their attack, the Official IRA chose the Officers' Mess at 16 Parachute Brigade HQ, determined to hit as many high profile targets as they could.

On the morning of Tuesday 22 February a car – demonstrating the naivety and laxity of Army security – pulled up outside the mess. Moments later, a device, thought to contain 200lbs of explosive, detonated and devastated the building. Seven people died and many more were injured. High ranking 'Ruperts' were the IRA's target; instead they took the lives of an Army Padre and six civilian members of staff. Killed that day were Captain Gerry Weston, MBE (38); Jill Mansfield (34) a mother of one; Margaret Grant (32) mother of four young children and married to a Paratrooper; Thelma Bosley (44); Cherie Munton (20); Joan Lunn (39) mother of three; and John Haslar (58). All five of the dead women were cleaners and John Haslar was a gardener.

The IRA claimed that they had killed at least a dozen officers in the 'revenge' attack; they claimed 'Our intelligence reports indicate that at least 12 officers were killed.' Even when it became obvious that they had killed only innocent civilians, a spokesman told journalists that this was propaganda and an attempt by 'reactionary and hypocritical politicians' to attack them and condemn Republican actions. Later, however, their 'department of pious and hollow apologies' was wheeled out to claim that they 'regretted' the deaths of innocent civilians; yet more overtime for that over worked 'department.'

The commanding officer of the 2 Para paid tribute to Captain Gerry Weston, who died in the explosion.

> Padre Weston was an absolutely tremendous Roman Catholic priest. He did a huge amount to try and bridge the gap between the Catholic community and the Catholic Church and our soldiers. And he was continually going around into Catholic estates to try and achieve this, very often by himself and obviously completely unarmed and dressed as a priest.

UNDER FIRE: ARDOYNE BUS STATION

Jock 2413, Royal Artillery

The night in question, we were back inside the base when there was a loud bang from the other side of the rear wall which shook up the buses but strangely, not us. A few shots were also fired but came nowhere near us. It looked like the bomb aimer still couldn't get it right and there was a goodly collection of squaddie type insults thrown in his direction commenting on his aim, his ancestry and the reason he had no strength in his right arm.

It was getting on for about 0300 hours and I was posted at the corner of the rear and side wall. I was a bit exposed at the side wall as it was brick to a height of two feet topped with six-foot railings but when the Belfast confetti got a bit close, I just ducked behind a bus which was parked next to me. There was an alleyway opposite me and I saw this character run up to the entrance and lob something in our direction. It was quite large and must have been heavy as he bowled it like a cricket ball. It bounced on the road which I thought strange and came to rest on the pavement just out of my sight. As he started to run back down the alley, I jumped onto the rear platform of the bus to get a better sight of him and had just put a round up the spout when suddenly there was the cracking of close passing bullets. I could hear the whip crack of high velocity and the 'pang' of low velocity shots all coming from the left.

Because of the railings, I couldn't see far enough down the street so I thought to use the stairs of the bus to get some elevation and had just started to move when there was an almighty flash. I can't remember any bang, just this force which nearly deposited me in the luggage compartment. I was pretty stunned and I remember hearing my name being called but it seemed from far away. One of the lads came to check on me as I was getting to my feet. Apart from ringing ears and a sore shoulder, I was ok.

A quick fag and a couple of squares of chocolate obtained from a 'bomb damaged' vending machine found in the bus drivers' rest room and I was fit enough to accompany the boss on a look around for the firing points. We saw nothing in the dark but there turned out to be three gunmen involved using rifle and handguns.

The official total of shots fired was twelve but we knew there was more than that as a lot of the shots were overlapping each other. Luckily for me, and Graham, who was stood at the wall where the front of the bus was, the low brick wall took a lot of the blast from the bomb. I got a good-natured ribbing from the lads for 'hiding' on a bus instead of shooting the bomber; stag on was the cry.

ON THE BORDER

Jim, Argyll and Sutherland Highlanders

It was my first tour and I was heading for the border; you have to remember that for 1972, Crossmaglen, Forkhill and Newtownhamilton were platoon locations. That meant eight-man section patrols. The IRA on the border were the most experienced and together group in the whole of Ireland and we were put up against them, young and inexperienced. We were armed with SLRs and carried around 40 rounds of ammunition. The South Armagh Brigade of the IRA had Armalite rifles (no doubt diverted from the war in Vietnam) as well as heavy machine guns, homemade bombs and eventually RPG7s [Rocket propelled grenades].

As a platoon we were split into three sections: guard, standby and patrol. Guard duty was manning the front and back sangar, one guy on two-hour stags, and standby was just that, you were on standby in case of, well, anything that the IRA could throw at us. Basically it was a rest time with maybe a town patrol. The helipad was the playing field behind the police station, and whenever a helicopter was coming in the standby section had to run out the back and man the four corners of the playing field. Around this field was a concrete wall and wire fence and the two farthest away corners were the least favourite to have to man, having to run 500–600 metres into the unknown, so that each corner was covered, allowing the helicopter to land, drop off whatever and leave.

There was also road clearing, looking for bombs halfway up to Newtownhamilton. A section from there would clear the road down and we'd meet somewhere in the middle. We'd clear other sections of road on a regular basis, giving us some tarmac we could use to drive on for a couple of hours.

We were doing eight-man patrols, basically showing a presence around the area. The Moybane and Drummuckavall area were generally the most active, running close to the border. These patrols were a few hours long and it was a hot summer that year; funny, I don't remember rain or wind. For the most part we avoided the roads, preferring the fields, scrub land mostly and it was often hard going so we'd take breaks on higher ground, observing the terrain. Of course patrolling tended to bring us closer to the border and the chances of a contact were that bit higher and they did come. One minute you're walking across a field, next would come the crack of the rounds passing by you and you found yourself in a fire fight with only an approximate area to fire back at. These folk tended to pop up, fire a burst and then crawl away over the border.

As we got settled in we would tend to go out on night patrols, leaving the base around 11pm and returning for breakfast around 7am. We'd use some roads but take to the fields and lie up to watch for IRA units. Sometimes a day patrol might find us on a hill overlooking farmhouses of interest. I remember one night patrol that one of the sections went out on. They were going to

Snatch squad in action used as an IRA propaganda poster.

observe a farmhouse in the Drummuckavall area. Sitting in the base at about midnight we heard the first shot, followed by burst of automatic fire. The patrol had come under heavy fire while we sat in that police station listening. That was another of those memories that suddenly come back. No matter where you went in that area, back at base those contacts would be heard.

Three days later, Gerard Doherty (16) an IRA member accidentally killed himself when a faulty pistol went off in his hand. His body was abandoned in a derelict house on Londonderry's Creggan Estate.

'MUSHROOM' COMPANY

Trevor Johnson, Glosters

Our CSM was called Pete Goss and he was great in Belfast, on the ground and he would back us to the hilt. At the time of the 71/72 tour, I was the company sniper and I was usually on the roof at Mulhouse. I had taken out a slate so I could watch, unobserved, the barrier at the top of Mulhouse Street and I remember CSM Goss telling me that if I saw any civvie leave anything there, I was to immediately shoot them. We were allowed to do that under the 'yellow card' and I always knew that he would back me to the hilt.

The Company OC was Major Long and he seemed to volunteer us for absolutely everything and anything going; any dirty job at all! In fact we were kept in the dark and fed with shit so much, that we were known as the 'mushroom' company!

I remember that we had a lad called Flower, a mate of mine, and we were searching this filthy old house on the Falls and this old dear told him that all he would find in her house were fleas. She was dead right and he ended up with his legs all covered in itchy flea bites for days! On that entire tour, we only actually had one night's sleep in a bed. It did us no harm mind, and we were all mates doing the job that we were paid for.

The Official IRA tried their hands at assassination on the 25th when they attacked the Northern Ireland Minister of State for Home Affairs, John Taylor. Although he was shot and wounded several times, he escaped death. On the next day, the UDR lost Thomas Moffett (48). 24280400 Private Moffett lost his life in circumstances unknown. The best efforts of both the author and NIVA have been insufficient to record how or why this soldier died. What is absolutely certain, however, is the cause of death of his UDR comrade Sergeant Harry Dickson (46) who was murdered at his home three days later by the IRA.

The 2nd Battalion soldier, the father of three children, was shot and killed in his hallway around 22:00 hours as he answered his front door. The brutal and cowardly killing was witnessed by his young daughter who was also shot and wounded as masked gunmen poured a hail of shots into his head, killing him instantly. The murder further demonstrated the IRA's avowed aim of attacking soft targets and to hell with whoever got in their way. This Leap Year February ended with the loss of 30 lives; 8 soldiers, 12 civilians and 10 members of both the Provisional and Official wings of the IRA.

The slogan above the smiling faces identifies the area as Loyalist. It was marginally safer here for British soldiers than the Republican areas.

CHAPTER THREE

MARCH

March and the promise of an early spring arrived; eleven soldiers from five regiments would die. There was Republican graffiti on virtually every gable end; 'Brits out!' was a popular one as was 'We stand by the IRA' and 'Don't ball lick the Brits! Fight 'em.' Many had the Irish tricolour (illegal in the north) or a balaclava-wearing gunman brandishing a revolver.

William Whitelaw was appointed as the first Secretary of State for Northern Ireland, as Prime Minister Heath belatedly recognised that the Troubles would not be a short term phenomenon. It finally dawned upon the Heath government that troops would be on the streets of Ulster for a considerable period of time to come and it began taking steps to both formalise and 'legalise' their presence and actions. Prior to this legislative change, the soldiers had fewer powers of arrest than the police and had no real dispensation for their activities. The Army could be shot at, bombed and hit by rioters' missiles and yet were restrained in their response.

While the British were passing laws, the IRA was becoming more adept. Desmond Hamill, author of *Pig In The Middle* – a fine account of the Army in Ulster 1969–85 – describes how the IRA was becoming more skilled and observant of Army tactics. He writes of an incident in the spring of 1972 when soldiers were engaging terrorists on the border. One man chose what he considered an ideal firing position, unaware that it had been used previously by men from other units. The Provisionals had observed this and pre-planted several explosive devices on the exact spot where he lay down; the man's foot was not found for some considerable time.

The IRA continued their attacks on the UDR. Tommy Fletcher (43) was a farmer and forestry worker who lived with his wife on a farm at Frevagh on the shores of Lough Melvin close to the Irish border; he was also a Private in 'A' Company of the UDR's 4th Battalion. Shortly after daybreak on the morning of 1 March, and in full view of his horrified wife, several masked gunmen arrived at the farm and pulled him from his car as he was about to leave for work. They made assurances to the woman promising that he was only going to be held temporarily, but after marching him several hundred yards into the Irish Republic, they stopped near Kiltyclogher and shot him. He was reportedly hit some fourteen times and died more or less instantly; his body was dumped in the safety of the Republic where they knew that neither Army nor RUC would or could pursue them.

Following this murder four other families with connections to the UDR were moved from the area to safer locations and taken on as permanent voluntary call out (VCOs) by the battalion; their livestock was sold and the land leased or sold at knock-down prices. They did not receive any help or compensation from government sources to help them relocate and settle into their new homes.

The IRA struck again over the next several days as they stepped up their war of terror, justifying the deaths as revenge for Bloody Sunday. The epithet 'Bloody' would be used again later that year when they tried to devastate the city centre of Belfast, but that day was still some months away and the 'penny packet' killings would continue.

There existed within the ranks of the Provisionals a sense that the shootings and bombings were a kind of game and although there were psychopaths aplenty, there was also an element of ordinary men doing it for fun. In some of the IRA biographies by apologist writers there are descriptions of men 'hogging' rifles and jostling to shoot at a British patrol. The words 'disputed circumstances' and 'controversial' are always added to reports of the death of a terrorist in such publications, and it is this hypocrisy which sickens one. Incidents of IRA assassinations and shootings of unarmed soldiers and civilians are equally 'controversial' and 'cowardly', terms used by one IRA spokesman in reference to a shooting by the British Army. I await the use of these terms by apologists for the IRA in connection with the killing of a soldier.

'BLUE ON BLUE' PREVENTED

Mike Heavens, 'B' Company 1 Glosters

There are memories of number 219 Springfield Road which was a large house that had been commandeered and fortified because it looked out over the Mackie's Factory which had a mixed workforce of Catholics and Protestants and was therefore a possible flash point. The Protestant workers of Mackie's had to walk to and from work via Lanark Way and this was close to the 'wrong' side of the peace line; clearly asking for trouble. On a week rotation, a platoon would occupy and patrol from number 219. It had been bombed once before with a large device placed against an outside wall during some renovations. The resulting blast demolished the new wall and killed a soldier working behind it. Being surrounded by 'Indian country', windows had been bricked and sandbagged up, until the only views were through the myriad of cameras that festooned the place from the top bedroom. This looked into the Clonard area and had two giant mirrors that the sentry looked into, because a normal viewpoint would have lost him his head.

Blast bombs were frequent presents from the locals, being lobbed over the rear wall, and the perpetrator would then scurry down the connecting alleyways before the sentry could react. On one occasion we had gone out on foot patrol and around midnight whilst returning, a shadowy figure was observed crouching in the hedges some 50 metres away on the opposite side of the Springfield Road. It was always difficult to see anything clearly at night as it was before Starlite scopes or any night vision devices and all the street lights were regularly shot out to give us cover from snipers. We decided to completely ignore the yellow card rules of engagement, so the lead man fired three rapid shots at the figure and to our surprise and not too little discomfort, three different firing points blasted back at us and a massive fire fight developed. After a couple of minutes and just as we were beginning to run low on ammo, a very Scottish voice shouted from the shrubbery across the road, 'Stop! Watch and shoot!' the standard fire control order of the British Army, and our platoon Sergeant shouted out: 'Is that you Jock?' To which a very irate Scottish accent boomed out: 'You fucking English bastards have frightened the fucking life outa me!' At this 'meeting of minds' the patrol from the KOSB coming out of the 'Murph went their way and we went ours. However, explaining to the OC why so much ammo was expended and there were not thousands dead was a bit of a nightmare! It was almost a 'blue on blue' and there is nothing friendly about friendly fire.

The company that was based in North Howard Street also had to supply sentries for the three giant sangars on stilts that looked out over the peace line wall of wriggly tin. They ran down Cupar Street and were very lonely and very much out on a limb; it was not a task anyone liked. Freddy Standlick, one of the platoon members, had a very lucky escape when fired at during one sentry tour; the rounds struck about an inch above his head. Fortunately, as Freddy is a short arse of 5 feet 4 inches in his socks, apart from stains in his shorts no damage was done. Willy Tong was not so lucky. During a heavy rain storm (they are very frequent in the Emerald Isle; that's what makes it so green) the foundations had been washed away under two of the four legs and the structure collapsed into the road. Tons of sandbags and heavy timber buried poor Willy and the rescue team took many minutes to dig him out of the debris. His injuries were slight; just lots of cuts and bruises but he had a very severe fear of enclosed spaces for a while!

The day after Tommy Fletcher's death, an RUC officer, Thomas Morrow (28) died of his injuries following an IRA shooting near Newry on 29 February. On the following day, they attacked a mobile patrol in Manor Street, Belfast and killed a dismounted soldier. Private Stephen Keating (18) was observing a local pub and stood on the corner of Annalee and Manor Streets when he was hit by automatic gunfire. The Manchester boy died at the scene and his distraught mother was moved to write a moving and poignant open letter to the gunman concerned. The Provisionals were cynical and cold-blooded about their killings and even the grief of a widow, orphan or distraught parent was unlikely to move them.

The day after (the 4th) was a Saturday and Belfast city centre was packed with weekend shoppers. By late afternoon the centre was still very busy and in the Abercorn Restaurant, close to Belfast's Cornmarket, many shoppers were enjoying a tea and a cake. The popular cafe was situated on Castle Lane, close to Donegall Place. Two young girls were seen to stand up and walk out and leave their bag behind. Minutes earlier the RUC had received a bomb warning which was traced to a Republican area, warning of a bomb in another part of the city centre. At approximately 16:30 a large device exploded and instantly killed Ann Owens (22) and her friend Janet Breen (21) and injured over 120 more. Amongst the horrifically wounded were a bride-to-be and her bridesmaid; both women lost both their legs in the blast.

BLACK BUSH AND BELFAST

Starlight, Royal Army Medical Corps

I have thought long and hard about 1972 and it is almost impossible for me to isolate any one incident; it was truly a horrible year for those of us on Operation *Banner*. At the start of the year I was in the Short Strand bus station, where I was a Company Medic with the Queen's Own Highlanders, but also supported the RUC SPG [Special Patrol Group] out of Mountpottinger Police station. So much happened, incident and contact followed incident and contact with bewildering speed, so trying to isolate events becomes painful. Memories of bodies lying where shot, burning flesh, traumatic amputations as a result of car and pub bombings. The sounds of sirens, falling masonry, broken glass all seem to form a kaleidoscope of intrusive thoughts from those years long gone.

I vividly remember that just after Bloody Sunday we were hammered by everything they could throw at us for about a week. Specific incidents which I attended with the SPG include the bombing of Lavery's Pub on the Lisburn Road as well as the massive bomb in a beer lorry in Callender Street. This caused dozens of casualties amongst young girls who were enjoying the first warm spring day of the year. The bulk of the injuries were deep lacerations from glass and shrapnel, the screams of the injured, the awful facial injuries in ones so pretty and the smell of burning are still vivid to this day. I also attended the awful bomb in the Abercorn Restaurant with SPG under the leadership of 'Tommy the Peeler' (Inspector Tommy 'M' RUC); it was another milestone, a well documented atrocity. Shortly after the Abercorn bomb I was injured myself ending up in the RVH for six weeks. In the intensive care ward beside me was a man who lost both his legs in that atrocity.

In all of these incidents, we had the horrific task of rescuing and giving immediate aid to the wounded, many suffering multiple injuries and amputations. It was hard to keep going at times, and I will be truthful, smuggled Black Bush [whisky] and the black humour of Blue SPG and us Jocks kept us going. No counselling, TRIM or other restorative methods in those days; just get on with it. We did get a day's R&R in Killyleagh and we stayed in a TA centre from memory and got very drunk.

Desmond Hamill, writing in *Pig In The Middle* (pp100/1) describes an explosion:

A bomb blast in a confined space is devastating. First the shock wave spreads out, faster than the speed of sound. Some heavy objects deflect the waves, but other solid material is changed instantly into gas, creating an enormous increase in volume and pressure. People in the way can have their limbs torn off, and in the millisecond which follows, the energy waves go into their mouths and upwards, taking off the tops of their skulls and other parts of the body so that sometimes all is left is the spine, held together by the vertebrae. The shock wave, travelling at 13,000 miles per hour pulverises the floor immediately below the explosion. It slows down quickly, but more damage is done by the blast wave which follows at half the speed. This has the pressure of pent-up gas behind it and it can also tear off limbs, perforate eardrums and smash up furniture, the pieces of which in turn become deadly weapons. For a few seconds a fireball goes with it, singeing hair and removing eyebrows and eyelashes.

THE ABERCORN RESTAURANT

Soldier 'W', Att Parachute Regiment

There are many things in life that I will never forget. For example, I will never forget the birth of my first kiddie, my wedding day, my passing out parade and lots of other things that as I pass 60, I can look back on and smile. But there is also one very black cloud which will blight my life and will stay with me until I go to the final reunion with the lads who have gone before me; I will never forget the Abercorn Restaurant. I will never forget the black heart of the Provisional IRA and I will never forget what they did.

Soldiers from the Parachute Regiment and a comrade, thought to be UDR, carry away dreadfully torn bodies after the IRA attack on the Abercorn Restaurant on 4 March, 1972. (Belfast Telegraph)

It was a Saturday in early March – it was the 4th, I'll never forget that – and we were in the city centre of Belfast. The first point that I got wind of what was happening was when I heard some officers and NCOs shouting at the lads and telling them to get people moving away from the shops and cafes at the bottom end of Castle Lane. The place was packed and it was mainly women and kids and there weren't too many men around, just women with shopping bags and them department store carrier bags. It's funny, but I remember that there was a bit of panic and I suppose all those lads in uniform trying to get people to move might have made them panic a wee bit. I also remember that there was one fat woman with a head scarf on and she had loads of bags and I could see that the strings or the handles on the bags were digging into her fingers and there was red marks and white marks on them as she tried to rush past, no doubt wanting to hang on to her shopping and all.

The next thing I knew was a strange silence, only it probably wasn't, if you understand what I mean and things just seemed to slow down to a crawl. Then I saw a huge yellow flash and then a huge boom and I was knocked off my feet and as I fell I saw people just being bowled over and falling down. I remember sitting on my arse and feeling as though all the air was being sucked out of my lungs and I couldn't fathom out what was happening to me and I wanted to laugh and then I was gasping for air. All of a sudden there was a cloud of smoke or dust and I thought that we were all on fire and something flew over my head and I later found out that it was a leg with a sock, but no shoe or any other clothes; just a leg and a sock. I found the leg later where it had hit a wall or a shop doorway across from the restaurant. Looking back, it might have been a burned ankle and not a sock.

I couldn't hear a sound but I could see some of the lads and they seemed to be shouting and the women looked shocked and dusty and their mouths were opening and they seemed to be screaming but it was as silent as the grave and I thought that I was going to cry as I just didn't know what was happening.

In basic training I had heard thunder flashes go off and had watched EOD officers exploding old ammo and the like but it didn't prepare me for this. Very quickly all the dust – masonry dust I think – had started to settle although there was a fair bit of cloud around us and I saw a couple of shoes; one black and one brown and both were really dusty, just sitting there and then I noticed that there was sticky, red blood under the dust and it seemed as though it wasn't real. At that moment, seeing all those screaming women – even though I couldn't hear them – and seeing all the panic and the shock and abandoned groceries and new clothes and boxes of presents, I still hadn't realised that it was a bomb!

Then there is a growing realisation as you know what has happened! Suddenly, in addition to dust-covered soldiers, there were dust-covered RUC men and then there were firemen and ladders and still women running around. There was this young girl – a Saturday shop assistant because she only looked fifteen – and her hair was all over the place and she was filthy and I'm thinking her mum and dad have let her come down to the city centre for her Saturday job and she could have been killed!

The lads were taking some sheets and blankets into the still smoking Abercorn and covering the bodies and bits of bodies and I was dragged in to help and that's when I saw all the blood and the injured people and limbs; God, nothing but limbs and I was praying that I wouldn't have to work out which went where. I felt so useless and I tried to remember that I was a soldier and I got a woman who was black-

Tom McFarlane, a shocked Abercorn survivor. (Belfast Telegraph)

ened from top to bottom, head to foot, and I gently lifted her out of the ruins and took her outside to an ambulance man. I could hear her a little bit, despite the ringing and she was asking where her shoe was and she had high heels on, or rather she had one and when she walked, she went up and down until I got her clear. As I left her, she said something like 'Don't be forgetting me bag, wee man!' I just looked at her and ran away and tried to look busy, but I was useless that day. That's all I want to say about the Abercorn, but I would have liked to have had that twat Adams there and he could have seen the misery and the maiming that he caused that day!

I would have loved to have had all those IRA bastards there that day and they could have explained to the women with no legs and the girl with most of her face gone just why they had planted that bomb that day. Bastards, bastards, bastards!

Under the headline of 'For God's sake, why?' the *Daily Express* of Monday 6 March reported the grim aftermath of the weekend's explosion at the Abercorn Restaurant. Their staff reporter wrote as follows:

> John Robb is a surgeon in Belfast. As a medical man, he has seen many tragic sights, but after this weekend's work he is sickened 'more than words can say'. So upset by the horror of the Abercorn Bar bombing 'that I must speak out. It is not often a surgeon gets involved in anything outside his work. But I must try and get home to some people what they are doing.' Mr Robb – he is 40 – was at home with his wife and three children when he heard the news.

The surgeon went on to describe working among the broken bodies of innocent people at the city's Royal Victoria Hospital. He spoke of the casualty department being full of 'terrified, hysterical people' and of seeing a small boy with a piece of metal in his skull; 'it was such an appalling scene'. He stated that a total of ten people had lost limbs in the attack.

> For God's sake, what sort of people can be responsible for such a terrible thing? … When it is all over do they believe they can put the bodies of our society together any more than we surgeons can put back together the human bodies when they have been destroyed irrevocably? … For days afterwards all you smell is burnt hair and flesh. You bathe, you do anything to get rid of it but you can't. You get used to ghastly smells in hospitals, but you never get used to this one.

The Taoiseach (Prime Minister) of the Republic, Jack Lynch was reported as saying: 'We are filled with horror at the ever rising toll of deaths and feel deeply for the victims, their families and friends.' Final condemnation of the Provisionals' murderous and irresponsible act came from the Roman Catholic Primate of Ireland, Cardinal William Conway; 'This was a horrible deed and nothing can justify it.'

THE GHETTOS

Terry Friend, Royal Artillery

Everywhere we went it was the same old Victorian terraced houses. Endless rows of identical streets with attached back alleys, a most depressing environment. The whole place looked like a city in decline, filthy, run down and demoralising. How on earth, I wondered, did people live in such a state! The Protestant ghettos were bad enough, but the Roman Catholic enclaves were fifty times worse. Even when the sun came out the place still looked bleak. It really was like stepping back in time to the harsher days of the forties and fifties! Personally speaking, I was highly offended by the constant and ever present pervading atmosphere of animosity and hatred that each community had for its opposite number. The first time I saw the red, white and blue painted kerb stones and Union Jack bunting in a Protestant enclave called the 'Village', I was astounded! It seemed to me to be medieval, barbaric almost! Long haired and sullen faced youths hung around the street corners in small gangs and glared at us as we drove past. The hostility was so palatable; you could almost taste it in the very air itself!

The Roman Catholic ghettos were even worse with their Republic of Ireland flags flapping in the breeze on the lamp posts. It did offend me that these people dared to hoist a foreign flag on UK soil. Would anyone have had the affront to raise the Swastika over London in the forties? And I bet half of these bastards were gratefully holding their hands out to receive the benefit payments, courtesy of the British taxpayer!

I remember how seedy, run down and rotten the place seemed to be, you could literally almost taste the damp and decay. They do say that poverty has its own particular smell; I smelt it throughout that tour.

Many soldiers have spoken of the routine searches which they had to carry out in order to stifle the movement of arms and of the animosity which it attracted.

SEARCHES

Lance Corporal, Royal Green Jackets

Now and then – more now than then – we had to carry out searches of the locals and sometimes we got a player and bagged some important finds. But more often than not, we just succeeded in pissing off the locals and as they eventually walked off, you just knew that you had handed a big propaganda boost to the Provos. We would hit a pub where we had had some grief and get all the drinkers outside and sometimes in the inevitable melee, a few drinks were spilled, if you get my drift?

We would herd them outside, sometimes with the odd SLR butt to 'encourage' them and line them up along the pub wall and start searching; doing name and address checks and sifting out the ones on our 'lift list.' If you were on it, you'd be picked up straight away and taken away by the 'peelers' to the local nick or to the interrogation centre at Castlereagh. As I say, we got some prime players but most of the time we just pissed off the locals.

We'd often do the same things in the hardline Prod areas and we got the same shit from them. One minute they'd be your pal and the next, they were spitting at you and gobbing off like the nationalists. Sometimes you didn't know who the fuck was your enemy and who wasn't!
On 8 March it was back to easy prey for the IRA and this time the target was a 'lance jack' from the UDR's 3rd Battalion, Joe Jardine (43) who worked as a vet. He was shot in the afternoon working at a government agriculture centre at Middletown, Co Armagh on the Irish border, killed after a long burst of machine gun fire. Over two dozen shots were fired and the part-time soldier was riddled with bullets, dying at the scene. He was the father of two children.

The UDR then lost Private George Curran (46) four days later in circumstances unknown. The author notes that he is named on the National Arboretum's roll of honour. The very same day, Bernadette Hyndman (24) and mother of a young child was shot and killed by the Official IRA when she was caught in crossfire as an Army patrol was attacked; she would not be the only one killed by IRA carelessness during that month.

The Royal Army Ordinance Corps (RAOC) is known, some say affectionately, as the 'blanket stackers' but, given the highly dangerous job which their Explosives Ordinance Disposal (EOD) men carried out, they were truly 'front line' in Ulster and abroad in every definition of the word. In *Bullets, Bombs and Cups of Tea* the death of Staff Sergeant Tony Butcher is poignantly and lovingly dealt with by his brother Gerry and his daughter Tracy Abraham. It would not only be disrespectful but also superfluous to try and match their words and I will not begin to try. It is enough to say that, on 15 March, two EOD specialists were killed in Grosvenor Road, Belfast when a suspect car exploded. Sergeant Anthony Stephen Butcher (24) and Staff Sergeant Christopher Robin Cracknell (29) had been called to a suspect vehicle in Willow Street, just off Grosvenor Road. After a controlled explosion, they were returning to the car when a device exploded; both were killed instantly. Staff Sergeant Cracknell was from the Leamington Spa area and was the father of a young son.

On the very same day a young RUC constable who had been wounded following an IRA ambush in Coalisland the day before, died of his wounds. William Logan (23) was in a joint RUC-Army patrol when they came under heavy machine gun fire from IRA gunmen hiding at the roadside.

On 16 March, in an attack which bore all the hallmarks of the UVF and/or the UFF, a small but deadly device was left in the ladies' toilets in Market Street, Lurgan. Tragically Mrs Carmel Knox (20), mother of an eighteen-month-old baby chose to use the toilets located underground near the centre of the town. When the device exploded she received horrific injuries and was probably killed instantly, while her distraught husband waited close by.

Soldiers from the Royal Tank Regiment had been patrolling through the town when a massive explosion 100 yards in front of their vehicle brought them to a halt. The soldiers saw people scattering through swirling clouds of thick black smoke, and quickly cordoned off the area and mounted guards to provide cover against snipers in case it was a set up. They saw and heard a man screaming at policemen and pointing at the toilet, shouting that his wife was inside. One of the soldiers raced towards the man who was becoming hysterical. The RUC man was adamant that the toilet was empty, but an NCO grabbed the policeman's torch and took two of his men down the massive hole in the ground, climbing over the rubble and through floods of water. They scrambled around until they were warned that there was a suspect car in the street above them.

At that point, one of the searchers found a woman's shoe and they continued to dig frantically with their bare heads. When they found her, they stated that she looked like a large rag doll smashed to pieces. All that was left of her clothing was a piece of rag around her neck; her body had suffered massive tissue loss and one of the soldiers covered her with his jacket and carried her out to an ambulance. The woman was clearly dead; later one of the rescuers heard a local woman shout disparaging sectarian remarks to the tune of 'She was only a Catholic'.

Two days later, the Paras lost Private Anthony Kelly (27), killed in a road traffic accident at Holywood, Co Down; no further details of his accident can be ascertained at the time of publication. The excellent website maintained by the Palace Barracks Memorial Gardens does

'Dear Mum; this is how we live.' The glossy recruiting brochure images of British soldiers were totally unlike the grim living conditions of the 'temporary' security bases.

list most of the soldiers killed in Northern Ireland RTAs. The list is incredibly long and whilst many were UDR soldiers – generally killed in accidents caused by fatigue – it also includes many men from other regiments. It is a site worth perusing even if only to demonstrate the sheer scale of the carnage on Northern Ireland's roads. For a more detailed explanation of RTA-related deaths in the UDR, please see *Bloody Belfast* by the same author. It would appear that the long hours, working two jobs and the relentless pressure of policing known and suspected players and then having to live virtually next door to them were prime factors in the accidents. One former UDR soldier said: 'You might have just stopped one of them at a VCP, "P" checked him and then maybe seen your mates give him a bit of hassle, then later on, you're in the same pub as them! After that, you had to sleep with one eye open.'

WAS IT A WAR?

Corporal Keith Page, King's Regiment

Generally, when you fight a war you can see your enemy; the enemy we were fighting in Northern Ireland wore civilian clothes and hid behind their own people. I agree with the statement that we had one hand tied behind our back as we had the yellow cards to quote and we also had a government which was scared of its own shadow or to give us the power to do our job.

I personally remember having to shout halt on three occasions then warn someone that I was cocking my weapon; what a load of bull. The guy who had just tried to kill me was around the corner and out of sight and probably laughing his head off at me; we were a joke to them. I remember chasing a known player across Strabane fields after a contact, and he just walked across the border and the Garda didn't even flinch. When we shouted at them to stop him they just looked at us.

On one occasion, I was drenched from head to toe in petrol by a five-year-old (yes, five!) whom I nearly shot, and I still have nightmares and cold flushes even now. Today I suffer from PTSD and have had two nervous breakdowns; have nearly killed myself twice with tablets and slit my wrists and lived on the street after losing everything I owned and held dear to me. I have good days but mostly bad days due to the fact that I never got any counselling other than a crate of beer on arrival back at camp in the UK and told to get drunk if I still felt bad. Just recently I have received some counselling for my troubles and am on twelve anti-depressants a day just to get me out and about and to stop me going over the edge. That is what Northern Ireland did for me!

THE OFFICER WHO WANTED TO BE A HERO/ANDYTOWN CIVVIES

Lance Corporal Ken Anderson, Royal Corps of Transport

The driver of the other Land Rover in our section was my mate Roddy; a Jock from Bonnybridge near Falkirk. I like to think that I latched on to him to keep him from trouble, as he was not too bright in the IQ dept, but it had a plus side in that beside him, it made me look almost intelligent.

One time we were inside the RAOC stores compound near the docks, picking up rations, when this officer – a Colonel – came striding over to us. 'Don't you salute officers?' he demanded of Roddy. 'Och no sir,' said my mate, 'We was told nivver tae salute an officer oot here, in case yon snipers should tek a bead on ye, sir,' he replied, nodding in the direction of the city. This was, of course, some miles away over the water! But that Colonel didn't care for us one bit, and he had a good look round our ration vehicle and condemned it outright for breaking whatever passed for Health & Safety in those days. 'Get the inside painted white before you dare bring it into my compound again!' Needless to say we obeyed, and next day we were unloading sides of bacon with gloss white paint all over 'em!

One of our first outings as escort section was taking a guy we called the 'mad Major' on a trip round various church halls and Women's Institutes, picking up donations 'for the troops' in the way of fancy cakes etc. We in turn gave them to the local hospitals. It sounded like a nice cushy little number, but the downside was that this Major seemed intent on getting us all killed or covered in glory. Whenever we had him aboard we just prayed that no gunfire could be heard within ten miles, for if he heard it, he would order full speed ahead to the sound of the guns!

He got us lost on one occasion, right in the middle of a nasty looking part of 'Toy Town' which I'm guessing was the Falls or Andytown. What I do know was that there were definitely no Union Jacks in evidence; just signs of recent rioting. The lead vehicle suddenly lurched to one side and swerved around an obstacle in the road, and I immediately followed suit because the object was what we now call a 'stinger' thrown across our path. A few shots rang out and we sped off like scalded cats until we met a couple of Ferrets who escorted us out of trouble. The Major seemed pleased with all the excitement; the prat! It wasn't only the vehicles that were soft-skinned mate, I told him (under my breath of course).

Cups of tea were always accepted when in 'safe' areas, but we were warned not to accept in Catholic areas owing to the likelihood of powdered glass or other substances added to get back at us. However, on one occasion the locals around Andersonstown bus depot gave us tea which we did accept. It was after a large bomb had exploded on a bus stopped outside by the gate guard whose job it was to search all buses returning to depot.

When the bomb exploded it blew out all the windows in the street nearby, and it was our blokes who were up all night boarding up their windows and clearing the mess. This upset the Protestants, who stopped supplying beverages for a couple of days in protest.

There was a very young local lad of about six or seven years old, who was 'adopted' by the lads in 'Andytown' depot. He was an absolute picture of urban poverty, but he seemed to be friendly with some of the guys in Rocket Troop. One of the lads had shrunk his heavy duty jumper, so they dressed him up in that and got some other decent clothes for him including boots and let him have the run of the camp. But his mother complained loudly, calling them all sorts of nasty names and even going so far as to make a show of clipping the poor lad's ear for associating with soldiers. In private, behind her closed front door, she thanked the lads for their kindness and explained that her husband was 'behind the wire' and she was terrified that he would get to hear and have her and the child punished from inside his cell. After that, the child was dressed in his army gear only when inside our camp, and changed into his rags on leaving.

I TOO WAS THERE

Mike Heavens, 'B' Company 1 Glosters

I have many memories of that '72 tour especially of the unlucky ones; ten or so shot and wounded in January and February and of the three that were shot dead. As is the way in small county regiments, all of these had brothers serving in other rifle companies and that makes it worse to bear. There was Ned Buck, hopping around and swearing profusely after a high velocity round had passed close to other members in the patrol then struck him in the foot removing some of his toes. It was difficult to shoot or run when you're laughing your head off with fright and hilarity at the same time and all in the same thought process!

The Mill's outer wall had the badges of all the different units who served there painted around the vehicle park area. This area was festooned with sheets which criss-crossed the park on lines of string like bird scarers in an allotment, so that the snipers using the Divis flats couldn't get a good shot into the area. The walls of the relaxing areas, the dining room and bar had high standard graffiti on them, some of it slightly pornographic; it was an attempt to give the areas less of a feeling of a hardcore prison complex.

1972 turned out to be one of the hardest years of those Troubles for the PBI [Poor Bloody Infantry]. To those who did it and survived, it was great to have been a part of that group and to have known such a group of men like them; to those who didn't survive, whilst my memory of the many events may dim, it will not of them. It was a time of our history that they contributed so much to and that I will always be proud to say that I too was there.

On 20 March, the IRA killed seven people when they detonated a car bomb in Donegall Street, Belfast, close to the city centre. At 11:58 after a series of misleading calls, a car containing 200lbs of high explosive detonated, devastating the area; the *Belfast Telegraph* described the area as a 'battlefield'. It was indeed a battlefield, because it was the place where the IRA was waging its so called 'economic' war against the Ulster infrastructure; it was a war of unadulterated terror.

Two RUC officers, one off duty UDR soldier and three civilians were killed and a fourth terribly injured, dying sixteen days later in hospital. The dead were RUC Constables Ernest McAllister (38) and Bernard O'Neill (26), both fathers of two children each; off duty UDR soldier Samuel Trainor (40), Ernest Dougan (40) and James Macklin (27). The latter three were all refuse collectors doing their jobs when the IRA struck. Also killed that day was Sydney Bell (65) who was driving a delivery van past the car as it exploded. Henry Millar, at 79 one of the

Opposite, top: Monday 20th March 1972, Donegall Street, central Belfast and the aftermath of a car bomb which left six dead, including two RUC officers and an off-duty part-time UDR soldier, with a seventh victim dying from his injuries two weeks later. *Opposite, below:* Another badly injured casualty from that atrocity. (Belfast Telegraph)

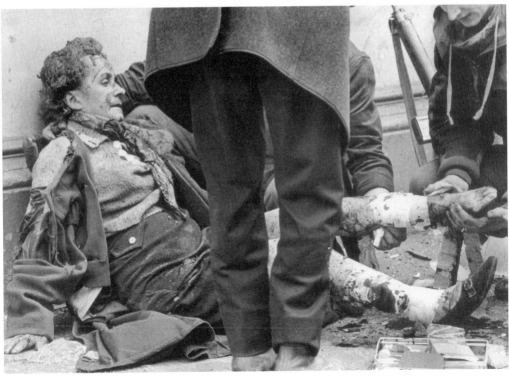

oldest victim of the Troubles, died on 5 April as a result of the wounds that he received in the explosion. Victims of the attack – many of them women shoppers – were strewn about in the blood and rubble. A policeman openly wept as surgeons performed life-saving amputations on the pavements.

Not content with this carnage, the Provisionals then exploded a series of bombs in Londonderry, killing none but badly injuring 26, and later damaged over twenty shops and businesses in Enniskillen.

Clearly, the deaths were not enough to satisfy the IRA and later that same day, an IRA sniper, hiding near the council swimming baths in William Street, Londonderry shot Rifleman John Taylor (19) from 2RGJ. He was rushed to nearby Altnagelvin hospital but was dead on arrival; he was the eighth 'Jacket' to die since the start of the Troubles.

On 26 March, RCT soldier Driver Stephen Beedie (21), a Derbyshire boy was killed in a road traffic accident whilst on duty; another casualty of fatigue? It is a point of constant irritation to this author and many other Northern Ireland veterans that, whilst the MoD chooses to include non-battle casualties in the toll for Afghanistan, the same does not appear to apply for the Northern Ireland conflict. Two days later, this time in Limavady, Co Londonderry, an IRA car bomb exploded outside the RUC station, killing Joseph Forsythe (65) and Robert Mitchell (26); both were innocent bystanders.

LOYALIST VCP

Lance Corporal Ken Anderson, Royal Corps of Transport

We were driving towards Kinnegar [Palace Barracks] taking weapons to them, when we came upon a Protestant barrier across our path. This was one of several barriers set up by them in protest at the British Army allowing the 'no go' areas of the Catholics to exist unchallenged. I was driving lead vehicle, so I stopped 100 yards short of the barrier. The two REME corporals had no idea of how to proceed, so I decided to take the initiative and stepped out of the vehicle and started to walk towards the balaclava-clad Loyalists as they stood guard behind the barrier.

Then I remembered that I had left my rifle in the vehicle and, not wishing to be caught unarmed should war break out, I turned back to retrieve it, slung it nonchalantly over my shoulder and resumed walking towards the vicious looking band of thugs ahead. I got within talking distance and told them of my plight: 'I have a couple of scared shitless corporals back there who need to get to Kinnegar, lads. Is there a way round you that I can take so as not to give the poor buggers a heart attack?' 'Ah, ta be shure; ye just need ta take a roight turn at this road here, then ye turns left at da next junction; roight again at da next, and ye'll be back on ya way, me boyo.' So ended the confrontation with the 'men with guns'. A few days later our tour had ended; 'Motorman' followed soon after.

On the 27th, the Ulster Vanguard organised a two-day industrial strike against the imposition of direct rule. The strike resulted in the stoppage of public transport, cuts in power supplies and many firms closed. William Craig, then leader of Ulster Vanguard, spoke at a meeting of right-wing MPs at Westminster. He said that he could mobilise 80,000 men to oppose the British government; 'We are prepared to come out and shoot and kill. I am prepared to come out and shoot and kill and those behind me will have my full support.' It had its roots in the Vanguard or Ulster Vanguard wing of the Ulster Unionist Party (UUP) who were opposed to the policies of the party's leader and last Prime Minister of Northern Ireland, Brian Faulkner.

The Ulster Vanguard movement was originally a political pressure group within the UUP. It was formed on 9 February 1972 and was led by William Craig (former Minister of Home Affairs at Stormont) with its deputy leaders the Rev. Martin Smyth and the former Stormont MP for Carrickfergus, Captain Austin Ardill. At its first meeting in Lisburn, on 13 February 1972, Craig made the first of a number of bellicose pronouncements, declaring 'God help those who get in our way for we mean business.'

Prime Minister Edward Heath announced that the Stormont Parliament was to be prorogued, and Direct Rule from Westminster would be imposed on Northern Ireland from 30 March 1972. The announcement was greeted with outrage from Brian Faulkner and Unionist politicians. The main reason for the suspension of Stormont was the refusal of Unionist government to accept the loss of law and order powers to Westminster. He was also putting more and more pressure on HQNI with a view to getting tougher on both the gunmen and their 'allies', the ever present rioters. It was about this time that orders from 'on high' were filtering down to the troops on the ground that certain constraints were about to be removed. This has never been admitted officially and can be added to the myriad speculation about the Troubles in the early 1970s.

The legislation responsible for direct rule was the Northern Ireland (Temporary Provisions) Act. Under the legislation, a new Northern Ireland Office was established at Stormont which was supervised by a new Secretary of State for Northern Ireland, William Whitelaw. Ulster Vanguard organised a two-day industrial strike against the imposition of direct rule. The strike resulted in the stoppage of public transport, cuts in power supplies and many firms closed.

The month ended with the loss of two further lives. On 29 March, Martha Crawford (39) was shot and killed by the IRA who they were attacking soldiers in the Andersonstown area. A gun battle between the terrorists and an Army patrol in the Ramoan Gardens section of 'Andytown' had actually been stopped to allow the evacuation of children. As the gunmen withdrew from the scene in a crowded shopping area, Mrs Crawford was shot and fatally wounded, leaving ten children motherless. Further terrible luck was to hit the Crawford family in August 1975. One of the children Patrick (15) was killed by IRA crossfire as they attacked soldiers in the Falls Road area. A further family member who was a member of the Official IRA was also killed, this time by Protestant terrorists, in January 1974.

On 29 March, the IRA had left a car in Wellington Street, Belfast, with the intention of damaging the City Hall. EOD Major Bernard Calladene (39) from the York area and a father of three children arrived at the scene and, as he neared the vehicle, it exploded, wounding him dreadfully; he died very shortly afterwards in hospital. Major Calladene had defused another car bomb in the city centre only hours earlier.

March ended and 40 more lives had been lost; eleven soldiers – the worst month to date for the Army, 4 policemen, 13 civilians, 11 IRA and one Protestant terrorist. The Republicans did not have a monopoly when it came to killing civilians; Protestant terror gangs killed two of the innocents in March.

CHAPTER FOUR

APRIL

April is a month of rain showers; this April was no different. 'Amazing Grace' was at the top of the music charts but, given the military band that was playing (Royal Scots Dragoon Guards) one wonders how many Nationalists from the Turf Lodge or the Ardoyne would have allowed it to be heard in their homes. The US resumed its carpet bombing of Hanoi as the ground war stepped up and Apollo 16 landed on the moon.

It was during this month, that the hastily convened tribunal under Lord Justice Widgery reported on the events of Bloody Sunday. Lord Widgery's report concluded that the soldiers had been fired upon before they started shooting; that the soldiers acted as they did because they believed their orders justified such behaviour; and that there was no proof that any of those

A soldier from the Royal Regiment of Wales walks uneasily past Loyalist paramilitaries in Clonduff Drive, south east Belfast. (Belfast Telegraph)

killed were shot while handling weapons or bombs, but there was strong suspicion that some had been doing so during the afternoon.

Widgery was faced with testimony from the soldiers that they had been shot at, while the marchers insisted that no-one from the march was armed. Widgery's report took the Army's side; his fiercest criticism was that the firing 'bordered on the reckless.' The Widgery Tribunal was denounced by many, including future Labour Prime Minister Tony Blair, as a 'whitewash.'

In the early part of the month, the UDR lost Private Donald Kane (30) under circumstances unknown. Whether he was on duty or not is a moot point, as he is recorded on the National Arboretum's roll of honour at Alrewas. It was a commonly held view that the part-time soldiers of the UDR were far more susceptible to fatigue – which often resulted in traffic accidents – than their full-time counterparts. Duties were long and arduous and even when off duty, UDR personnel had to sleep with one eye open under the constant threat of assassination in their homes and places of work. They never seemed to have enough men or patrols and it was not uncommon for them to go 40–50 hours without rest. If Donald Kane died in an accident due to exhaustion, then he is, in my eyes, as much of a battle casualty as a soldier shot by a sniper.

In that month a confrontation between a Loyalist mob and scared Catholics in the Short Strand area of Belfast took place, described by Kevin Myers in *Watching The Door*. It demonstrated not just the hatred of the mob but the attempts at impartiality by the Army. The Short Strand (*an Trá Ghearr*) is a Catholic area in the east of Belfast, situated on the eastern side of the Lagan which neatly bisects the city. It is hemmed in on virtually all four sides by the Unionists, and is part of Ballymacarret.

Myers describes how a baying mob of Protestants, in protest at the ending of Northern Ireland rule, were chanting obscenities at the Catholics whilst a small Army patrol attempted to keep them from attacking houses. The 'thin red line' was ever thus! Against cries of 'Fuck the Virgin Mary' (*Watching The Door* pp70/71), was a group of RUC officers with a line of British soldiers guarding the Catholic homes. In charge was a young subaltern who demanded that the RUC stop the mob or at least move them on. When the most senior officer there refused, the soldier informed him that he and his men would do the job for them. The RUC man told the soldier that as he, the policeman, had jurisdiction, no such action would take place. In sheer frustration, the subaltern shouted at him: 'This is a fucking scandal! I did not join this fucking army to see bigoted mobs rule our streets. This is a disgrace and you are a fucking disgrace, and by God if things were just a bit different I would shoot you for what you're doing here today!'

Shortly afterwards, demonstrating the amateur nature of the IRA's bomb-making department, three more would-be terrorists were killed in an explosion while handling gelignite. Samuel Hughes (17), Charles McCrystal (18) and John McErlean (17) were killed when the bomb exploded prematurely in a garage in the Bawnmore area of north Belfast.

The father of one of the three boys was a former TA and UDR man and had brought up his son – John McErlean – on a quiet, uninvolved Catholic estate; he was forced to identify the remains of the three teenagers. The young naive boys, no doubt swayed by the events of the previous January at Free Derry Corner, were 'claimed' by the IRA as members of 'E' Company, 3rd Battalion of the Belfast Brigade. Bawnmore had hitherto been ignored by the Loyalist terror gangs but further tragedy was to befall the Catholic oasis in the Protestant desert over the coming years. Relatives from two of the dead boys' families would be killed later in Troubles-related violence.

On the 7th, following an incident in the Ballymurphy estate, a local bus driver and his conductor stopped their bus outside the Army base at the Henry Taggart Memorial Hall in order to speak to soldiers. Lance Corporal Peter Sime (22) of the King's Own Scottish Borderers Regiment was shot by an IRA gunman and died at the scene. The young Borderer lived in Edinburgh and was the father of a baby son.

In the early evening of the following Monday, a foot patrol of the Royal Artillery were in the process of investigating a suspicious package placed inside a hut of a bowling green at Brooke Park, Londonderry. As they were doing so, a stone-throwing mob of children approached and, in the immediate vicinity of the package, began attacking the troops. Despite the danger to their own lives, two soldiers, fearful of injuries to the children, forced them to disperse. As they did so, the package exploded and Bombardier Eric Blackburn (24) from Kent was killed instantly and his comrade, Lance Bombardier Brian Thomasson (21) of Bolton died very soon afterwards. That the IRA could plant a device in the immediate vicinity of children was either callousness in the extreme or incredibly well calculated. No children died that day at the hands of the terrorists and that was due entirely to the selfless bravery of the Gunners. Time and time again professional soldiers proved that they were men of honour.

Lost Lives (p175) quotes the poignant words of Eric Blackburn's widow: 'I heard on the television about the soldiers being killed and I just knew that one of them was Eric. I just burst into tears. Later the Army confirmed what I had already guessed; that Eric had been killed.'

Above: 'Made safe.' Assorted-vintage SLRs in a Mk 1 (amateur chippy-armourer constructed) rack, with the first plastic bits beginning to replace the original wooden stocks, grips and fore-ends. A superb rifle, for both left and right-handed use. *Opposite, top:* Private Ernie Taylor (Light Infantry) seen relaxing with comrades. KPs had to be the most boring duties on the planet, so a draughts or chess board, ciggies and a couple of tins passed an hour or two when not on stag. *Opposite, below:* Ernie Taylor in a Belfast street, with what looks like another PIRA Redevelopment Corporation job in the background.

CAR BOMB IN NEWRY

David Mitchell, Gordon Highlanders

I was sent to Northern Ireland for the first time during 1972, which was, I understand, the worst year of the Troubles. I was based at Lurgan and was attached to 321 EOD, the bomb disposal chaps. My role as an infantryman was as escort and close protection for the full four months of the tour.

Things were uneventful at first – insomuch as Northern Ireland during that time ever could be – and then, one night we were called out to do the job we were paid for and were informed that something was happening in Newry. We set off and were told, en-route, that a car bomb had been placed outside the town hall. Well, we arrived in the centre of Newry in the early hours of the morning and there was an eerie silence on the streets and a very odd feel about the whole place.

We were walking slowly towards the suspect car and had reached a spot about 50 yards away from it. We halted around the corner of a building and then all we could do was to watch the ATO [Ammunition Technical Officer] go into what they called the 'ponder mode' and he took a good look at the car. All of a sudden there was an almighty explosion which illuminated the whole street and we could feel the sheer heat of the shock waves. Then, all of a sudden, one of the car's wheels came flying through the air, followed by red-hot shrapnel, which peppered the wall right next to us.

I probably didn't think of this at the time, but if the ATO or myself had stepped out from behind the corner, we would have been, as the Ulster folk say 'tatey bread' and I wouldn't be telling you this now. Perhaps my 'Maker' decided that my time was not up.

BLAME REME

Soldier, Royal Tank Regiment

I attended the morning briefing as to the patrol tasks of that day, and we were to escort a convoy of 'military materials' from an air base to Castlereagh docks via west Belfast. We were told to anticipate an imminent RPG 7 attack, as apparently the IRA 'knew' that we were coming and immediately I felt sick. I couldn't face any breakfast that morning, Colonel's parade or not. I looked in the washroom mirror and I thought that I could see part of my head missing; was this an omen? Two soldiers had been killed in that same week; was my number up? I was think-ing about the padre knocking on my parent's house front door saying: 'Your son was killed this morning in Northern Ireland. Mind you, at least we got the convoy through!' All sorts of thoughts were buzzing through my head.

We loaded our weapons and mounted the Land Rovers, and as 2IC of the 'brick' and driver, I was trying to keep my composure. I had to be seen as strong especially in front of the younger lads. One of my colleagues, a young trooper, was visibly shaking though not from cold weather. I patted his arm, 'Aye up lad. We'll be laughing about this tonight in the bar. Just keep ya chin up and eyes peeled for them rockets.' Sometime later we arrived safely at the air base and picked up the consignment of 'materials' and then headed off for the docks passing a few rock ape [RAF

Regiment] VCPs on the way. As we moved through west Belfast, I felt that I could see and hear for miles. I was 100 per cent alert and could feel the hate in the air. Suddenly the Land Rover engine misfired. 'Hurry, hurry,' the lads on 'top cover' were shouting. The engine was making an awful row and we could only maintain about 20mph. Our radio wasn't working properly and we were rear vehicle and could not signal the front 'landy' to slow down. We were basically a sitting target. Everybody in our vehicle was swearing at each other, and it was cutting out and kangaroo-hopping. People on the streets were all laughing at the sight of us four arguing as to who was to blame for the state of the engine. It must have looked like a scene out of the Keystone Kops!

The REME eventually got the blame, and after about ten minutes of sheer terror we eventually arrived at the docks unscathed and back to our base intact. Later when I'd breathed hundreds of sighs of relief and got some time to think about the day, I thought that either we had been very lucky or the terrorists were so amused at our predicament that they didn't bother contacting us or that perhaps they had no idea that we would be there escorting such a hazardous cargo. In any case I drew the conclusion that my number wasn't up; at least not that day, anyway.

The IRA, for reasons never explained, decided to bomb the centre of tiny Ballymoney, Co Antrim. They detonated a 100lb device in a van which killed Elizabeth McCauley (65).

Irish-American money continued to pour in to fund terrorist acts; about this time an organisation under the banner of Irish Northern Aid Committee (NORAID) began funding the IRA in Northern Ireland. Ostensibly a fund-raising body to help the Catholics over the water in Ulster and provide aid and comfort to families dispossessed by the Troubles, it was nothing more than a front for the Provisional IRA. It was one of the major sources of weapons and explosives and bankrolled Republican terror. Brendan Hughes when interviewed by Ed Maloney (*Voices from the Grave* p270/1) talks of meeting NORAID officials holding 'briefcases full of cash' and of holding such an anti-British hatred that they were advocating shooting postmen!

With a huge Irish-American vote to cultivate, many US politicians either turned a blind eye to NORAID's activities or openly became apologists for them. The US Supreme Court behaved over the course of the Troubles in much the same way. US support for terrorism, overt or otherwise, finally came to an end on 11 September 2001 when they were attacked by Al Qaeda. On that day, amidst the death and destruction, there was a sudden awakening as to what 'terror' really meant.

Thus the country which had given succour to Irish terrorism, refusing to extradite known and convicted IRA terrorists, suffered itself. This was the country which had provided safe haven for murderers, gun-runners and bomb-makers; it had welcomed Gerry Adams, now President of Sinn Féin and member of the power sharing executive, believed by many to be Belfast Brigade Commander for the IRA on Bloody Friday; this was the country which entertained Martin McGuinness, allegedly IRA commander in Londonderry and widely believed responsible directly or indirectly for SF deaths. This was the country whose President was photographed shaking hands with the men of violence inside the White House. All this was apparently encouraged by one of the IRA's biggest apologists and 'celebrity' supporters: Senator Edward Kennedy.

As one observer remarked, after the events of 11 September: 'Imagine the outcry amongst the Yanks if we had invited Osama Bin Laden to Britain and then feted him at 10 Downing Street?'

AN AMERICAN SNIPER IN LONDONDERRY

Soldier, REME

I was based in Londonderry in 1972 and was attached to various units. Because I was warned not to tell this story, I will reveal only my cap badge but not to whom I was attached. It was late evening, and a brick from the Welsh were on patrol going away from Fort George, and another brick from an unnamed regiment was returning to the fort on a path that would cross at right angles to the Welsh. Because of the ever present danger of a tragic 'blue on blue' occurring, even though they were well behind them, they were aware of each other. However, at this stage, they didn't have visual contact in what was an area of small terraces.

At this point, a shot rang out and one of the Welsh lads went down. Immediately, the other brick saw an armed figure on a roof top and dropped him with a few superbly aimed shots. The lads on the ground radioed the contact in and backup was called for; this included the RUC of course. The gunman, somewhat unusually, had no back up; no one came to get him or the weapon before we got there. We were aware that they had dickers and other helpers ready to pull the dead or wounded man away and dispose of his weapon, often broken down into its constituent pieces and deposited in a dozen or more safe houses.

[An IRA shooting would generally only take place in a nationalist area where they could rely – either through natural support or forced acquiescence – on a small army of helpers or places of shelter. Often an IRA gunman would lie on a blanket and if hit, his body along with spent shell cases would be dragged away by the helper. They would only generally target SF members in their areas of support so that help would be near at hand. For this reason, they were therefore unlikely to try an attack on the Loyalist Shankill or Woodvale or Sandy Row in Belfast, knowing that their means of escape were extremely limited.]

Later on, we heard from an officer that the downed squaddie was not seriously hurt, and although wounded, would survive. The RUC later gave us some info, stating that they had tested the rifle and this showed it to have been used several times in sniper attacks but always on Saturday nights; they believed this to be the infamous 'Saturday night sniper.' He was thought to have been a US soldier stationed in England, with a strong Irish-American background. It is understood that he had been taking his service weapon, catching the Friday night ferry from Liverpool to Belfast, hiding by day and sniping by night. It was further believed that he caught the Sunday night ferry back to Liverpool in time to be back for duty Monday morning.

There was never anything official revealed – how could they – and the whole matter was hushed up and we were told by the brass not to tell anyone of this. Someone, somewhere in both the US and British governments knew all about this; will the truth ever be revealed? Somehow I doubt it.

ANOTHER LONDONDERRY YANK

Jock 2413, Royal Artillery

My regiment deployed to Londonderry in 1973, and part of our TAOR [Tactical Area of Responsibility] was the Brandywell area which was the also the responsibility of a company from DWR [Duke of Wellington's Regiment] who came under our command and were based at Bridge Camp. My troop were designated as regimental reserve so we had to familiarise ourselves with every area. Day three saw myself and one other as part of a DWR foot patrol under the guidance of a corporal. This guy was pretty switched on and gave us the guided tour of all the nasty places in the area. As we were moving along the Lecky Road, we spotted a group of young adults who looked totally out of place compared with the usual collection of scruffy 'Herberts' who populated the area. Stopping them for a 'P' check, we discovered they were Americans. Not only that but they were American sailors and produced ID cards to that effect. After an exchange of what you might call less than pleasantries, they were allowed to go on their way.

Back at base, after debrief, I was having a brew with this corporal and I commented about the presence of Yank sailors and as to why they were so anti towards us. He proceeded to relate a story to me that had been passed on to him by one of his predecessors.

One night in late 1972, a foot patrol in the Bogside was making its way down Elmwood Road near Garten Square when they were illuminated by a very bright light being shone from a service road on the other side of Westland Street. The patrol came under fire and some of the return shots were directed at the source of the light. During the follow up a vehicle was found, fitted with a large spotlight, and lying next to it was a body of an adult male. Whilst waiting for the ambulance, the patrol commander searched the body and found a wallet identifying the male as an American sailor. Realising the hot potato he had uncovered, he passed this over to the RMP who were in attendance and they advised him to keep quiet about his find. The ambulance whisked away the body and the whole incident was dealt with in a very low key manner even putting about the story that the man had already been killed before the contact. Obviously word had got out and it was my turn to be told. I must admit at the time, I didn't give the story much credence.

Two years later, I was back doing a different kind of job. I recalled the tale of the spotlight and, having access to all sorts of INT goodies, I tried to find some mention of this incident. I found the contact report and the intsum [intelligence summary] but there was no written word about a dead American sailor. I was on the point of writing the whole thing off as bullshit when somebody from the Int Corps who was in the office at the time asked if he could be of help, so I told him what I was looking for. He just gave me a funny look and said that I would find no mention of it anywhere. He also added that it wasn't too clever an idea to go asking anyone else about it either. I took the hint, but that comment of his convinced me that the story was true after all and somewhere out there is an ex-patrol commander who has a hell of a story to tell. I don't know how delicate that incident was or is nearly 40 years on. I'm fairly sure it was not the only incident that happened over there involving American citizens.

I am indebted for these two accounts from known and trusted sources. Indeed, I have had the same story from extremely reliable sources in both the Royal Corps of Transport and the Royal Artillery and I remain convinced of the veracity of this report. Of course I cannot prove it and readers must draw their own conclusions; what is interesting is the fact that the 'Saturday night sniper' never appeared again. To admit the fact would have caused great embarrassment to the governments of both the UK and the US and for this one reason, I do not believe that the truth will ever see the light of day.

In a concerted attack in almost every major centre in Northern Ireland, the IRA placed and detonated 23 bombs; fortunately, there were no deaths. They planted bombs in towns and cities across Northern Ireland, and there were also fourteen shootouts between the IRA and security forces. There has been much speculation that this series of attacks was possibly a dress rehearsal for Bloody Friday.

On 15 April, in what Republican apologists describe as 'disputed circumstances' a leading name in the Official IRA was killed by soldiers in Belfast's Markets area. Joe McCann (25) is widely thought to have shot and killed Corporal Bob Bankier (RGJ) in Cromac Square (see *Bloody Belfast* pp 69–71) on 25 May the previous year. Although he had been briefly held in custody, he had absconded to the Irish Republic and returned to Belfast probably in April 1972. In Kevin Myer's *Watching The Door* the author says he was later told by McCann that he didn't shoot Bankier and only claimed to have done so in order to boost his standing and reputation as an IRA gunman. He did murder Private Robert Benner (25) of the Queen's Regiment who was gunned down whilst unarmed and visiting his fiancée in Dundalk on 28 November the previous year. He was also allegedly responsible for shooting another unarmed soldier who was returning from a visit to his mother in Dublin. Private Thomas McCann (no relation), RAOC was murdered on 13 February 1972.

What follows is speculation, but I have put together the following from both a Republican source and a senior Royal Green Jacket NCO. At the time of Joe McCann's shooting, the Provisionals were engaged in preliminary conversations with the Heath government and various ceasefire options were being discussed. The Provisionals knew that McCann was back in the area and, knowing of his reputation, were keen to have him removed in order not to complicate the discussions with the British government. It is a source of controversial speculation that they 'shopped' him to the authorities.

McCann's MO was to approach VCPs or foot patrols and, knowing that he would be recognised, immediately run off and lure the unsuspecting troops into a carefully pre-laid ambush. British Intelligence was aware of his presence in Belfast and troops were naturally briefed to 'lift' him, or 'scoop' as the Provisionals termed it. Unfortunately for McCann, the first time he tried it on with the soldiers, he chose the wrong regiment. He was being followed by a pair of RUC SB (Special Branch) officers and they identified him to a Parachute Regiment patrol as being worth a 'lift' in the event that he was armed. He was spotted and the Paras just weren't 'prepared to play' and as he ran, he was shot and killed in Joy Street, close to the spot where he had allegedly murdered Bob Bankier ten months earlier.

Later the same day, a UFF murder squad driving a stolen car drew up close to two Catholics on the Crumlin Road and beckoned one of them over. When Sean McConville (17) approached as they requested directions, he was shot three times and died at the scene. Later a gang, possibly from the same Loyalist organisation, shot and wounded two other Catholics in the same area of Belfast; both men survived.

The following day – 16 April – three soldiers, all from different regiments, were killed. Private Martin Robinson (21) from Sutton-on-Sea, Lincolnshire was manning an OP in Foyle Road, Londonderry when gunmen firing from the walls of the City Cemetery shot and killed him. It is thought that the gunmen, from the Official IRA, had been briefed to exact some revenge for the earlier killing of McCann when they attacked the Worcester & Sherwood Foresters. Later that day, a short distance away, the Officials shot and killed Corporal Gerald Bristow (26) a father of one from Newport in Wales. The soldier from the Royal Welsh Fusiliers was part of a patrol in the Lecky Road area.

A few hours later IRA 'gunmen', some as young as twelve and thirteen, in the Divis Street area fired what many observers thought was a 'lucky' shot through the observation slot of a

PIG parked in Durham Street, Belfast. The round hit Second Lieutenant Nicholas Hull (22), a Bedfordshire boy, in the chest and he died within hours. The shooting was witnessed by a reporter who stated later that there were several children, some with rifles almost as big as themselves, who poured a hail of fire at the PIG, one shot of which entered the visor and killed the young officer. At the time, the Army was convinced that the IRA had some sort of 'super sniper' who could penetrate the vehicle's viewing slot, seemingly at will. It will have come as a great relief to discover that the truth was somewhat more prosaic; it will have been no relief whatsoever to the mother of Lieutenant Hull.

In *Watching The Door* (pp 76–8) Kevin Myers describes how he was in the stairwell whilst what he described as 'demented children' poured a purely haphazard hail of fire at Lieutenant Hull's PIG. Led by what he describes as an 'infant-Rommel' (who he later learned had been the juvenile Gerard 'Dr Death' Steenson) the children continued firing until that one chance round hit the young officer. One of the most poignant aspects of his death was that he had only just arrived an hour or so before at Belfast docks on his first day of his first tour, and was killed without even getting to know or be known by many of his men.

Steenson, dubbed 'Dr Death' by the RUC for the sheer number of murders in which he was involved, later joined and then left the INLA (Irish National Liberation Army) and was himself killed in the internecine struggles between the Republican paramilitaries in the 1980s. He was shot along with a friend Tony McCarthy by INLA gunmen including Dessie O'Hare on 14 March 1987. The feud was between INLA and IPLO (Irish People's Liberation Organisation) although there is a school of thought – largely unsubstantiated – that Steenson was shot by undercover soldiers in a covert OP. This is not entirely unfeasible as the Army had much to gain not only in the paramilitaries killing each other, but being observed killing each other! In addition to being involved in the shooting of Lieutenant Hull when he was just fourteen, two years later he shot and killed leading Official IRA member Billy McMillen on 28 April 1975. This was during a feud which saw the formation of the INLA; truly a mad dog was dead. The INLA was itself a violent offshoot from disillusioned members of the Official IRA.

NICK HULL

Sergeant Mick 'Benny' Hill, Royal Anglians

I knew Nick Hull quite well as he had served in Germany before going to Belfast. He must have been delayed on a course to have arrived there after his platoon. Belfast certainly wasn't his first posting. Until reading your account I was unaware of exactly how he had died, as we were just informed that he had been shot whilst the front seat passenger in a PIG. Later on the day he died, I was on an OP, and had cause to open fire. Much later I came down from the OP, and was met by one of the senior officers of the battalion. He wanted me to confirm that I had opened fire; I replied that I had and he asked if I had hit my target. I indicated my L42 and told him that I didn't often miss. He didn't say anything, but the hand squeezing my shoulder was far more eloquent than words could ever be.

I have never told anyone that before, like so many of our colleagues I suppose I just filed it in that part of the brain under the heading: 'Do Not Open.' Over the many intervening years, I have just tried to forget about it.

Soldiers from a Royal Anglian foot patrol make 'hard targets' as they patrol in North Belfast.

The Army was involved in the tragic death of a civilian shortly after Nicholas Hull was killed, when Patrick Magee (20) was shot dead at St Comgall's School close to the Falls Road. Troops opened fire on what they thought were gunmen and Magee was fatally wounded. The day after, in what was seen as a propaganda coup for the IRA, the Army killed another innocent civilian when they shot what they thought was a gunman. Patrick Donaghy (86) was observed in the window of his eighth storey flat in the sixteen-storey Divis Tower in Belfast. Soldiers opened fire and the man was hit and died shortly afterwards although his body was not found for some time. The author in no way justifies either of these two deaths and will not be as hypocritical as the IRA. However, in those life and death situations where a moment's hesitation could – and did – cost lives, split second decisions had to be made. Far more soldiers were killed by delaying those decisions than the number of civilians regrettably killed by soldiers. But again, the decision to use urban streets as a battle ground was entirely of the IRA's own making. As a fall back, they could of course, always wheel out an IRA representative with an articulate, well rehearsed but totally meaningless apology.

HOW THEY LIVED

Soldier, Royal Anglians

I was brought up in a council house in the Ipswich area in the 50s and 60s and I thought that I knew what poverty was, but even though there were a lot of us, mum always kept the place clean and tidy and even when dad was out of work, we kept food on the table. You would not find him, legless, down at the pub if he wasn't bringing in a wage; he would always put us first. Now, I was based near the Falls Road and we patrolled around the lower end of it as well as around the Divis. It was all Nationalist and there was trouble every single day and it was not a nice place to be.

Almost without exception, when we raided a house – either looking for players or doing an arms search – it was one of those filthy two-up two-downs with outside lavvies and only a tin bath for washing. Judging by the stench in those houses – usually stale piss or even staler cabbage – they never did much cleaning. You would usually find an old woman of about 60 or 70 who was the gran and her daughter who didn't look much younger and upwards of six or seven kids. If you did a dawn raid and surprised them in their bedrooms, you could find five or six in a bed, top and tailed and the bedding was filthy and stank of piss and soiled nappies.

Every house had a big framed picture of either Jesus or the Virgin Mary or both and there were always religious sculptures around. Such a pity that the fucking priests didn't teach them a bit more about birth control or personal hygiene! There was one fat old bitch who lived on the Clonards and she stank like a fish market; she had a wee runt of a husband who was in and out of the nick and he was skinny and emaciated and always seemed to have her pregnant. I used to gag at the thought of those two at it! Every foot patrol which passed her house got the same greeting from this hag: 'Yez wee English c★nts!' Charming language it was; usually in front of her filthy brats.

I'm told that the Prods kept them under the thumb with no equality of housing, poor education facilities and no equality of employment. My platoon commander told me that at one time employers could state in their adverts 'No Catholics need apply!' I do feel, looking back, that the

Prods made the Catholics the way they were, poor housing and all, but there's no excuse for the way that they turned them into pig sties.

After Lieutenant Hull was shot near the Divis, the locals cheered and took the piss every time we patrolled around there. He was only a young lad and none of us had time to get to know him, more's the pity. We all wanted to get in there and bash some skulls but our NCOs reminded us that we were twice the people those bastards were and we had to show professionalism and restraint.

The previous contributor speaks of the discrimination which was rife and, amongst the ruling Protestant classes, perfectly normal. It certainly was the case that the two-thirds of the population who 'ruled' Ulster had a measure of institutionalised prejudice with which to hold sway. Many Protestant employers would not take on Catholics and even with the distribution of housing stock, one's religion determined where one might be allocated a place to live. Little known organisations such as UPA (Ulster Protestant Action) made it their job to ensure that Catholics were excluded from employment. Their avowed goal was to make places such as Harland & Wolff, Shorts Engineering and Mackies as Catholic-free as possible. When vacancies arose they tried to ensure that no Catholics applied or if they did, influence matters so that they didn't get beyond the application stage. Catholic applicants might lie on their forms about their religion, but often their surname gave them away; if that didn't, their place of residence or former schools certainly would. That said, there were many fair-minded Protestants and Catholics who simply wished to live in harmony with the other side. It was Ulster's tragedy that the men of evil in both communities dragged Ulster into the depths of the maelstrom for such a long period of its history.

On Wednesday 19 April, the body of UDR soldier Corporal Jim Elliott (36) was found in an isolated spot on the Irish border close to Newtownhamilton. He had been abducted by the IRA two days earlier whilst delivering soft drinks from his lorry. He had just crossed into the north on the main Dublin Road when he was stopped, abducted and taken forcibly back into the Republic. He had been treated with sickening brutality and torture by his captors, and was shot eleven times. With the utmost depravity, his killers had booby-trapped his body with devices weighing over 500lbs which, once the body was disturbed, would have exploded with devastating consequences. It was felt that the very obvious booby-traps were not so much designed to kill SF but to cause revulsion amongst Elliott's Protestant community.

While Loyalist youths smashed windows in Catholic business premises and houses in his home town, the RUC's suppression of the gruesome torture details and insistence on a 'closed' coffin probably saved nationalist lives in Rathfriland during the time of his wake and funeral. He left a pregnant widow and the aforementioned Protestant backlash and damage to Catholic homes in the vicinity were precisely the divisive reaction desired by the IRA.

Just minutes before the day ended, two men were abducted from the Andersonstown and Suffolk areas. The two men were brothers and were suspected of being informers. One of them, Martin Owens (22) was shot dead and his body was dumped in the Suffolk area; his brother was released after questioning. The abductions and killing bore all the hallmarks of an IRA 'kangaroo court' where, often on the flimsiest of evidence, men could be tried and dealt a summary execution by their fellow Republicans. It is alleged that the older brother deliberately lied and confessed to a crime which he had not committed in order to save his equally innocent brother.

The following day, in what the Belfast Coroner described as a 'meaningless sectarian murder by … so-called heroes', the UFF shot and killed a taxi driver. They had called into a taxi office in Clifton Street, Belfast close by Crumlin Road and requested a taxi to the Ardoyne. Gerald

Locals ready themselves for a confrontation with soldiers on Etna Drive, Ardoyne.

Donnelly (22) took the men and drove off up the Crumlin Road. However, they shot the man several times and then ran off leaving him dying in Harrybrook Street, some 300–400 yards away from Clifton Street. The author has met Loyalists, both as a young soldier and in later life and they have always claimed that we were on the 'same side'. I will condemn these paramilitaries and murder gangs with the same force as I condemn their Republican counterparts.

Further tragedy struck when a schoolboy was accidentally killed by soldiers firing baton rounds at rioters in the area of the Divis flats on 20 April. Francis Rowntree (11) was struck on the head and died in hospital two days later. A young boy was dead at the hands of the Army but indirectly at the hands of the IRA who turned his play area into a battlefield.

On 24 April, Private Dennis 'Taffy' Porter (22) of the RAMC from the Cardiff area was killed by an ND in the men's quarters at the Musgrave Park Hospital. Despite being aware of the circumstances of his death, the MOD will permit me only to state that he died from what is euphemistically termed 'violent or unnatural causes.' In *Bloody Belfast* by the same author, there is a section which deals exclusively with deaths by 'violent or unnatural' causes and whilst there were some – in truth too many – suicides, there were a large number of deaths attributable to NDs. In most cases, the ND was caused directly from what the Army terms somewhat euphemistically 'horse play' and was most definitely avoidable.

THIS IS WHAT YOU GET!

Alan Lengden 14/20 King's Hussars

We were down at Forkhill RUC station not far from Newry and looking for a place where we could park our wagons and have some kip; we settled for a place around the back. The station was situated on the main road opposite the communal hall and we were informed by the RUC that a known player was suspected of hiding in there. Apparently, Catholics – innocent civilians as well as those on the run – often camped in there overnight before heading south to the Republic.

Anyway, me and Scotty, another lad called John Wood, our commander and an RUC man went over to the hall where we found it locked and silent. I was thinking 'Thank God for that' but the policeman went to find the caretaker and get a key. The caretaker came and told us that all the people had already gone in the early hours but the RUC officer insisted that the door be opened. In we went and the place was like an empty gym but the policeman then asked if there was a cellar and the caretaker said that there was but it was empty. Scotty looked at me and said 'It'll need to be checked' and with that, my stomach full of butterflies, down we went.

I asked if anyone knew what the bloke we were looking for looked like, but nobody knew! In I went and I called out the name of the player (long since gone from my memory) but there was no response. The place was empty save for loads of mattresses and blankets. We gave a sigh of relief and went up and reported back; end of incident.

Sometime later, we received a postcard and I have never forgotten what was written on it. 'We are coming to get youse Hussars and cut your bollicks off.' A week after that, a policeman was shot dead in the sangar at the front of the station. Opposite was a dip in the ground which led to a river and then a forest; it was ideal sniper ambush country and was the firing point for the shot which killed the officer.

An RUC officer, totally exhausted after a day of rioting and shooting and mob confrontations, rests against the nearest wall.

Later on, another one of our patrols was stoned by local youths and Corporal Mick Greenwood told his driver to stop, jumped down and chased them into a field, caught one, threw him to the ground and sat on his chest! He pressed his cap badge into the yob's forehead saying 'This is what you get when you stone the King's Hussars!' Then he just carried on with the patrol.

The King's Own Scottish Borderers, still mourning the death of Lance Corporal Peter Sime, lost another man on 26 April. Lance Corporal Joseph 'Barrie' Gold (19) died of his injuries, having been shot in the neck whilst manning a VCP in the Falls Road area. The young soldier from Edinburgh was the father of two young children.

BLOWING HIS COVER

Paul Stride, Parachute Regiment

Early on in the tour, I was on a six-man foot patrol on the New Lodge Road; as usual any stranger in our area we would stop and search. It was morning rush hour, and the workers were making their way to Gallagher's cigarette factory at the bottom of the New Lodge Road. We took the usual verbal abuse, but occasionally some little old lady would say 'God bless you son; you may not think so but we are so glad that you are here.' These poor people were living in such fear of those IRA thugs, who collected protection money from even the poor and were told it was for the cause.

Ginge, who was opposite me patrolling on the other side of the road, stopped this scruffy looking stranger, and spreadeagled him against the wall of a terraced house. He began searching him, whilst Gary covered him with his 'widowmaker' pointing at the stranger's head. I was covering the rear of the patrol, on a corner, when suddenly Ginge jumped back, the stranger fell to the deck and Ginge shouted: 'He's got a fucking pistol! I'm going to kill the c★nt!' and let his safety catch off. In them days we always carried a round up the spout, because you had to be quick off the draw on drive-past shootings.

'Stop,' Walley shouted over to Ginge, 'you haven't read him the yellow card,' so he went over and took the pistol from the stranger's trouser belt. The man insisted we take him back with us as we had compromised him, saying he was an undercover soldier. Not believing this, we confirmed on the net. Back at Girdwood nobody had been told that specialist units were even in Belfast, but now we knew that there were a few here on recce. He was made to get into his uniform and do stags on the sangars until he could be returned to his unit. He stayed with us for about a week sussing out the form.

On the same day as Lance Corporal Gold died of his wounds, Driver Laurence Jubb (22) from Doncaster in South Yorkshire was driving an Army recovery vehicle in Armagh City when it was attacked. The vehicle went out of control, jack knifing and then crashing on Killylea Road, crushing Driver Jubb and trapping other soldiers. He left a young widow who gave birth to twin daughters within days of his tragic death.

THE DEATH OF DRIVER LAURENCE JUBB

Geoff Moore, Royal Engineers

At some stage I worked in the Regimental workshops and I was aware of Laurie driving AEC 10 tonners and other plant; however he was not a regular acquaintance of mine. As to the circumstances of his death we were given to understand back in 1972 that he was driving a Scammell Constructor with its trailer when he was stoned by youths, as was their wont at the time. Whether he lost control or tried to avoid those in the road was a moot point, because the vehicle turned over and he was severely injured, not sufficiently to discourage the youths from continuing to stone him. I believe some of the public went to his aid but he soon succumbed to his injuries.

As the month of April breathed its last, yet another civilian was shot and killed by the IRA in a further 'crossfire' incident. Rosaleen Gavin (8) was walking along the Oldpark Road in north Belfast when IRA gunmen opened fire on an Army position at Finiston School. She was hit in the chest and died instantly and another man was also wounded. The IRA somewhat sanctimoniously claimed afterwards that the young child had been killed by Protestant extremists.

April and the accompanying rain showers had ended and May and the promise of warmer weather was just around the corner. During the month, 23 people lost their lives. In all, 10 soldiers, 9 civilians and 4 members of the IRA were killed as a consequence of the Troubles. It is worth noting that one of the civilians was killed by Protestant terrorists.

A third of 1972 was over and 110 people had already lost their lives. Claudy and Bloody Friday were just around the corner.

Photo taken during a foot patrol near Belfast city centre; a soldier keeps a watchful eye on the street ahead.

CHAPTER FIVE

MAY

Marc Bolan and T-Rex were top of the British music charts with 'Metal Guru'. President Richard Nixon ordered the mining of Haiphong harbour in North Vietnam, Governor George Wallace of Alabama was shot and Ceylon changed its name to Sri Lanka.

May Day fell on a Monday but for those who worked at Courtaulds in Carrickfergus before the introduction of public holidays it was an ordinary day. Ordinary that this, until the IRA – after a series of misleading telephoned warnings – detonated eight bombs, one of which killed David Currie (26) a married man from Lambeg and a father of two young children.

On the 4th, a Protestant terror gang – probably UFF – murdered a 20-year-old Catholic seaman, Victor Andrews, as he returned home to Belfast on leave; his body was found just off the Antrim Road with multiple stab wounds.

The UDA, a Loyalist paramilitary group formed in September 1971, undertook an armed campaign for almost 24 years. Most UDA attacks were carried out using the name Ulster Freedom Fighters (UFF). The UDA's declared goal was to defend Unionist areas from attack and to counter Republican paramilitaries. However, most of its more than 250 known victims were civilians. The majority were Catholics, killed in what the group called 'retaliation' for attacks on Protestants. Amongst their operations were the Milltown cemetery massacre, led by the mad dog, Michael Stone, the Castlerock killings and the Greysteel 'trick or treat' massacre. The UDA declared a ceasefire in 1994, although sporadic attacks continued until it officially ended its armed campaign in November 2007.

The Ulster Defence Association had its origins in the Shankill Defence Association (SDA). The SDA was led by a rabid anti-Catholic thug called John McKeague and he was allegedly involved in explosions and violent unprovoked attacks against Catholics. He is also known to have led many of the attacks on the Catholic Unity Flats. It was formed as an umbrella organisation for vigilantes called defence associations; these had the responsibility for defending Protestant, Unionist and Loyalist areas. Its first leader was Charles Harding Smith, and its most prominent early spokesperson was Tommy Herron.

The UDA's original motto was 'law before violence' and it was a legal organisation until it was banned, far too late in the author's opinion, on 10 August 1992. At its peak it had about 40,000 members. During this period of legality, the UDA committed a large number of attacks using the name Ulster Freedom Fighters, including the assassination of SDLP politician Paddy Wilson in 1973. The UDA was involved in the successful Ulster Workers Council Strike in 1974, which brought down the Sunningdale Agreement, one of the first attempts at power sharing in Ulster. It was an agreement which many Loyalists thought conceded far too much to the Nationalists.

A British soldier, his arm slashed by debris from a car bomb, is treated by his mates. Thought to have been taken on the Crumlin Road, Belfast, 29th May 1972. (Belfast Telegraph)

The UDA enforced this general strike through widespread intimidation across Northern Ireland. The agreement, which most of the hard-core Loyalists rejected – was also resisted fiercely by the Provisionals and there was an alleged plot to assassinate the Unionist leader Brian Faulkner. The IRA were rumoured to be planning the murder but back-pedalled when they realised the backlash which the Catholics would face from the Protestants would far outweigh any benefits.

The UFF's campaign of violence began in 1972 when in May the UDA's leader Tommy Herron decided that responsibility for acts of violence committed by the UDA would be claimed by the UFF. Its official position was that if the IRA called off its campaign of violence, then it would do the same. However it threatened, in the event of a British withdrawal, to out-terror the IRA.

It may strike the reader, especially one not involved directly in the Troubles, how almost impervious to prosecution and legal retribution the Loyalist paramilitaries were at this stage. Indeed, the Heath government did not begin treating them in the same way as the Provisionals until well into the following year of 1973, when Loyalists began to be interned. When troops and RUC started their dawn swoops in August 1971 and began rounding up known and 'suspected' terrorists, often with poor intelligence lists which were hopelessly out of date, the absence of Loyalists was noticeable. Internment which was seen by Heath as a panacea to the growing and seemingly out of control bloodshed turned out to be the clarion call that the 'recruiting officers' of the Provisional IRA had been seeking.

Internment had alienated the moderate SDLP of Gerry Fitt and he was just the man that the British government and Army had needed to keep the door open with the increasingly alienated Catholic community. The Protestants on the other hand took heart from the fact that, however woefully out of date the intelligence lists were, scores of their enemies had been removed at a stroke. The Catholics saw internment as anti-Catholic rather than anti-terror and this further drove a wedge between themselves and the SF.

'He went thataway!' Rare help from a civvie as Green Jackets patrol near Belfast city centre.

By the second month of 1973, when Heath finally began to take heed of the increasingly grave threat that organisations such as UDA/UFF and the UVF posed and began to act against them, it was probably too late. Nationalists saw themselves as victims and the Loyalists saw themselves as almost equal partners with their 'brothers' in the Army and felt 'respectable' and as having an equivalent status as the soldiers.

Although outside the scope of this book which deals with the events of 1972, the UVF, regardless of whether they saw themselves as 'allies' of the British, were involved in some terrible and sickening sectarian atrocities. None more so than the attack on Casey's Bottling Plant in Millfield, Belfast. Millfield is close to the far eastern end of the Shankill Road where it becomes Peter's Hill and North Street near to the city centre. An armed UVF gang shot dead four Catholic workers – two of them sisters – in appalling circumstances in which eye witnesses stated that the killers made some of the victims lie down on the floor. Three of the murdered Catholics were shot personally by Lenny Murphy, leader of the notorious 'Shankill Butchers' of whom we shall hear more later.

A Jackets foot patrol ponders its next move.

The King's Own Border Regiment lost one of their men on 10 May, when Private George Ridding (29) collapsed on duty and died shortly afterwards. Representations to his regiment's museum in Carlisle have failed to elicit any further information. The King's Regiment is drawn in the main from the Merseyside area and are known by squaddies as the 'hub cap nickers' and I am proud to state that I have many personal friends from that regiment. May 1972 was a tough time for this tightly-knit bunch of lads and they would lose three men in west Belfast.

The first soldier to be killed that May, as a consequence of a terrorist act was Private John Ballard (18) who was shot by the IRA in Sultan Street, Falls area as he covered some colleagues on 11 May. The Royal Anglian Regiment squaddie came from Grimsby.

LEARN AS YOU GO

John Bradley, 23 Engineer Regiment

We were very young but obeyed orders without question, not understanding, for the most part, our reasons for what we thought we were accomplishing. We passed the time playing cards and reading our yellow cards. What a joke. 'Sergeant, do we have to give three warnings if we are being shot at?' or 'Sir, what if they are too far away to hear me warn them before I shoot?' These were the kind of ramblings on over those silly yellow cards. Later one of our squad corporals would find out that he should have adhered more closely to that card and its rules; but that's another story.

Equipment and maps issued and briefings over, we were off to fight the good fight. It was an exciting time and we were all glad to be doing our part. We ran into some lads who were on the rear party of the regiment we were taking over from. They said: 'You will be needing these,' and gave us a bunch of 7.62 rounds. I thought 'why would I want these things?' How naive of me. I later learned that extra rounds would come in handy. They also showed us how to enhance a rubber bullet and told us that in a tight situation this modified 'dildo' would be useful. Simply slip the bullet out of its cartridge and saw off the back inch. A penny was about the same size. Insert enough pennies to replace what had been cut off and replace the bullet into the cartridge. How ingenious, although we were thinking 'What damage could this do?'

Off we drove, four to a Rover, driver, NCO and two idiots standing on the tailgate. I remember like it was yesterday because I felt like a moving target in a shooting gallery. Over the next eight days we learned that this was the chosen method to familiarise us with the local landscape. We got to know the street names and where our lads had sangars and guard posts, which streets were supposedly friendly and which were hostile. Being engineers we picked things up very quickly. I liked being around my old and steady Sergeant Exton. He was the only one I trusted. He had seen action in the Suez and wore a red beret. He had my complete respect. That was until I came across our WO1. 'Mick the nick' we called him and being a Paddy himself he was having fun locking up curfew dodgers.

I got stuck humping the old and heavy walking packs [radios] issued back in those early days. One night on a foot patrol I remember we had been out for just over an hour and not much going on until we came to a very dingy, half-darkened street. I had forgotten to check in with a 'sit rep' and, as I realised, my guts jumped into my mouth. We crept along silently, listening to a few noises coming from the derelict housing ahead. Suddenly '23 foxtrot; sit rep over.' My radio squawked and I almost pissed myself. 'Taff' and Sammy squealed at me 'Turn that thing down.' I did and we walked on a bit further. That's when I turned to Taff and suggested we check in and report the noises we heard. 'Bollocks, we've got nothing yet,' he barked as we crawled further down the street. Taff led the way and off we went to the end of the street. As we reached our mark he turned to me and said 'OK Ginge,' (my nickname in those days) 'give HQ a sitrep.' I did so but when their reply came in, I was stunned as several times it was repeated back, loudly to me, from a nearby house! It blared from the house window behind us, clear as day. Taff took a couple of steps backward and peered through the window. He saw that the broadcast was coming through crystal clear from the resident's television. The bloody telly was rebroadcasting all of our transmissions. And it wasn't just that one house. Every house with a television could intercept our communications. When we returned to HQ later that night all hell broke loose over that one. 'Mick the nick' was none too happy. We were ordered to keep radio traffic to an absolute minimum while on the street and two weeks later the patrol NCOs got issued police walkie talkies complete with ear pieces. It was a 'learn as you go' tour.

On the 10th, the IRA planted a series of devices inside the huge Co-operative department store which included incendiary devices and caused severe damage; no lives were lost as they stepped up their economic war. The store, a major symbol of the financial and commercial heart of Belfast was almost destroyed; the gutted ruins were a monument to the bankruptcy of the IRA's scorched earth policy.

On 13 May, the same day that Protestant terror gangs launched a series of bomb and gun attacks on Catholic bars and clubs which led to the deaths of four people, the Kingos came under fire whilst attending the scene of such an attack. Corporal Alan Buckley (22), a Geordie, was sitting in the turret of an armoured vehicle outside Kelly's Bar in the upper part of Springfield Road, Belfast. He was shot and killed and another comrade was wounded.

NECESSARY VANDALISM

Corporal Paddy Lenaghan, King's Regiment

I remember sitting in the TV room there at Springfield Road RUC station – the 'barracks' as the locals called it – apparently, next to Crossmaglen, the most besieged police station in Ulster. There was about three or four people watching the TV, knowing that shortly afterwards we were going out on patrol and vehicle escorts. An RP [Regimental Police] Corporal got up and annoyingly switched TV channels and one of the Kingos who had been watching the programme to take his mind off things, stood up and switched it back. The RP switched again and the Kingo did the same, but as the RP Corporal walked over to switch again – no remote controls in those days – the Kingo cocked his SLR pointedly in the direction of the RP. No words had been exchanged in all of his and at the cocking of the rifle, the RP sat down and again no words were exchanged. I was there; I saw it happen.

It was shortly after Alan Buckley had been killed – our first fatality – and our Adjutant, Major White didn't want anyone ringing home and blabbing out the news before his NOK [Next of Kin] had been informed. We didn't know at the time and the Major came straight out of the Ops room and I was the first person that he saw. He just said to me: 'Corporal Lenaghan; put the telephone out of use!' I didn't think twice and just ripped the phone straight out of the wall, wires and all and just handed it to him; him with a look of shock on his face.

A short time later, there was a chorus of moans from people who had promised to call home to their families and there were all sorts of violence being offered up to the 'vandal'. Me; I just kept as quiet as a mouse.

A night or two later, and I was stagging on up on the roof of the police station; it might have been a Saturday night; not sure. Watching the young ladies of the night, walking west down Springfield Road or east towards Grosvenor Road and the city centre or up and down the Falls Road. They were singing and taking the piss as they had heard of the death of one of our Kingo mates up on the 'Turf. They were singing 'Pistol Packin' Momma' as they passed the front sangar. They also sang things like 'If you shot a British soldier, clap your hands. If you a shot a British soldier, clap your hands. If you shot a British soldier, shot a British soldier, shot a British soldier, clap your hands.' It angered us but it stopped you getting bored on stag!

In a scene reminiscent of the street fighting in Normandy in 1944, a prone soldier covers his comrades with the belt-fed GPMG (General Purpose Machine Gun) known as a 'Jimpy'.

The 13th was a day of insanity which ended with five people dead. First was Tommy McIlroy (50) the father of three children, then Robert McMullan (32) was found dead in the Springmartin area. He had no terrorist connections and speculation still exists as to whether he was shot by the Army accidentally, or by a Loyalist terror gang. Loyalists then murdered Gerard McCusker (24), a Catholic, close to the Shankill Road. A member of the Fianna (nominally the youth wing of the IRA) Michael Magee (15) was then shot and killed, accidentally according to a Republican organisation, in New Barnsley close to the Ballymurphy estate. A few hours later, an Army patrol returned fire after coming under attack in Chamberlain Street, Londonderry and killed IRA member John Starrs (19) and wounded another IRA man.

The killing continued as Loyalist terror gangs killed two more innocent Catholics as the 'Protestant backlash' gained momentum. On the 14th they killed schoolgirl Martha Campbell (13) as she walked home. UVF gunmen firing down from a multi-storey flat hit her in the neck and she died in the arms of a local man who bravely dashed into the road to rescue her. Within hours the UFF abducted a salesman, Bernard Moane (46) a father of six from the Shankill Road where he was working. He was taken to a place called Knockagh where, bizarrely, they drank with him before shooting him in the head. The poor man must have thought that his life was in no danger.

On the same day, the IRA shot and killed Sapper Ronald Hurst (25) of the Royal Engineers as he worked outside of the fortified RUC station at Crossmaglen in the heart of 'bandit country.' Perhaps inadvisably, he was outside in the open and was not wearing either steel helmet or flak jacket; he was hit twice and died shortly afterwards. I was given access to a photograph of the dead soldier and the sight of the man, lying there with such a shocked expression on his face, is one which will haunt my dreams.

FOREVER YOUNG

Corporal Roy Davies RRW

On one occasion, Corporal Prosser and I went at speed in a rover to Flax Street, and I really put my foot down, as we faced a hail of stones and a few bullets on route. Sounds of bullets and their ricochets bounced all around us. Just as we arrived back, we saw a terrible sight. We rushed through the gate of the mill; the sentries had seen us coming and opened and closed the gates quickly with us safely inside, but the firing continued and was being answered from the sangars at the mill. Then I saw Private Hillman being carried down from the gate sangar, and he was bleeding from a bullet wound in his face. Though he was 'out to the world' he was trying to make speech which did not seem to make sense; it sounded like he was speaking Russian in a loud voice.

Someone told me that he had been shouting at some young children to get out of the line of fire when a sniper got him from the empty house opposite. He died a few days later; recently I went to see his grave in the Welsh valleys. It is strange how we all felt so grown up in those Belfast days. John's grave showed his age as just 29. I was comparable age at the time; I'm 63 now; how time flies. Our battalion lost six on that tour.

On 18 May, while manning the top sangar at Flax Street mill in Belfast's Ardoyne, Lance Corporal John Hillman (29) was shot; he died three days later, leaving a pregnant widow and two young children in Monmouthshire. On the 19th and 20th two fifteen-year-old schoolboys, one Protestant and the other Catholic, were shot and killed.

In the first incident, Protestant schoolboy Harold Morris (15) was talking with friends in Boundary Street, close to the Shankill Road in Belfast. A gunman, almost certainly a member of PIRA, opened fire from the general direction of the Falls Road and hit the teenager in the head. He died shortly afterwards. A foot patrol arrived on the scene and an eyewitness pointed out where the gunman was as the soldiers then came under fire. Despite the man's help, the troops were unable to return fire.

On the following day, there was a shooting in Londonderry by troops of another teenager, this time Catholic, which caused much ill-feeling. Manus Deery (15) was walking along Lecky Road, having visited a fish and chips shop to buy supper for his family who lived in Limewood Street in the Bogside. A soldier manning an OP on the city walls fired a single shot which hit a brick wall and both the young man and a friend were hit by bullet fragments. Deery died shortly afterwards and a later coroner's inquiry cleared the soldier who stated that he had fired at a gunman.

JOHN HILLMAN'S DEATH

Major Allan Harrhy, Royal Regiment of Wales

I was a Sergeant in the April or May of 1972 and was sent to Signal platoon at the Flax Street Mill. Even today, my memories of the place are mixed; I thought that it was an amazing place, rather like what I expect the 'Alamo' to have been like.

I remember poor John Hillman who was in my company; a nice lad, a lovely little fella, a very helpful, very friendly young soldier. He was allocated the roof sangar. This position was very exposed and 1972 was a very nasty year and the Ardoyne was an exceptionally dangerous place and people manning sangars had to be very careful.

I can't be sure, but he may have stuck his head out of the observation slit just to get a better view of something. He was hit in the head by a shot fired by an IRA sniper but not killed outright. I heard two, maybe three shots from where I was, down in the mill below where John was; it wasn't unusual to hear incoming rounds. Then there was a shout that someone had been shot and you go cold inside wondering which of your comrades has been hit. We had a good medical team which would 'crash out' a casualty to the RVH in double quick time.

As I said, poor John had been hit in the face, but he didn't die outright and in the evening we were informed that he was in a bad way but was hanging in there; he hung on for three days and then we were told that he had sadly died from his awful wound.

The Ardoyne lies to the immediate north of the Crumlin Road and is a fiercely Republican area. Kevin Myers wrote of the Old Ardoyne 'barely two hundred yards by two hundred yards … it was composed of a huddled jumble of houses made for proletarian elves who once toiled in Flax Street Mill, which was now an army base.' (*Watching The Door* p.29)

On 17 May, as if to further illustrate that they were as sectarian as the Loyalist murder gangs, several IRA gunmen opened fire on workers leaving the Mackie engineering works in Springfield Road, Belfast. Although the factory was situated in a Catholic area it had an almost entirely Protestant workforce. There were no fatalities amongst the workers.

A lone rioter wearing a motorcycle helmet for protection confronts two Saracens on Springfield Road, Belfast.

LEARNING THE GAME

John Bradley, 23 Engineer Regiment

We poor engineers had to complete two tasks; building bloody sangars and street patrols. Mind you, it made the time go by a lot better. We were split into different groups for different tasks. Search teams made up surveillance teams and engineer teams. Occasionally we'd bump into some covert guys, and stupidly, we'd say hello. Someone should have told me. I recognised a sergeant once; long side burns in civilian clothes. I went over to say hello and got bollocked.

One of my more exciting assignments was a two-week stint I did with my fellow engineers, a real job doing bomb disposal. Now this was interesting stuff. Me and my mate Kenny were assigned to guard these two from the bomb disposal unit. Cars were the biggest target for these lads. If a vehicle had a package in it and was parked on a street where it didn't belong, we were called. One job involving an old Morris comes to mind. I remember it because it got the 'shotgun treatment'. That was when a car, once given a quick walk around, was blasted with a shotgun from 75 yards away. They would blast a couple of well aimed shots at the boot and bonnet (glad it wasn't my car) and two more random shots. If it still didn't blow, then the engineers were called to haul it away with an armored Allis Chalmers loader. I'm glad I wasn't in that moving target.

Just like in a few big cities today, some stupid people created their own entertainment by leaving boxes and packages with protruding wires in the middle of the street or down a dark alley. They'd get their kicks watching us dismantle the phoney bombs. I think early on, before the serious trouble began, a few idiots got their jollies watching us play soldier. We were always on alert for an ambush, set up a dummy to shoot a dummy we said.

On 20 May, Lance Corporal Henry Gillespie (32) was patrolling with his UDR comrades a few miles outside Dungannon, Co Tyrone. As his mobile patrol neared the hamlet of Killyliss, IRA gunmen opened fire and he was fatally wounded, dying shortly afterwards.

GUTLESS BASTARDS

Paul Stride, Parachute Regiment

On a mobile patrol one lovely sunny evening, I was sitting on the tail gate of the rear open Land Rover, as usual covering with my warm 'widowmaker' cocked and ready with the safety on. We noticed that the multi story flats area of the New Lodge were unusually quiet as we approached a cul de sac. CRACK CRACK CRACK CRACK CRACK as shots were fired at us. The lead Land Rover hit the curb and went up on two wheels presenting its underside in the direction the shots were coming from. As we were being shot at by AK47s, Paddy Doolin, the MT driver of the lead Land Rover, had swung his wagon round on two wheels and sped out of the ambush area. As we followed suit, our wagon went up on two wheels, and me and Al put a couple of covering shots through a low wall, where the shots came from, to keep the enemies' heads down and give us a chance to escape the ambush.

We escaped with just a couple of bullet holes in the vehicles, but we were seething, and wanting to get after the gutless bastards who shot at us. As usual we gave the contact report on the radio, and tried to contact the backup patrol. They had also come under fire from a different position, and had returned fire believing to have got a hit, but there was also bad news, as Mick our patrol commander had been hit three times in the chest, and his driver wounded in the arm and leg. We had to get them casevaced, so the follow up had to be delayed because as usual we never had enough bods for a standby section.

Mick was sent back to Blighty to the Cambridge military hospital in Aldershot, and came back to us six weeks later. He didn't have to, but such was his loyalty to his buddies, he knew we were always under-manned; besides he wanted to get the bastard who shot him, as did we all.

On 21 May one of the most controversial killings of the Troubles occurred in Londonderry. Ranger William Best (19) of the Royal Irish Rangers was abducted and murdered by the Official IRA after one of their customary 'kangaroo courts'. Ranger Best was based with his battalion in Germany and wished to return to his home in the Creggan Estate. His worried parents had contacted the commander of the IRA in the Creggan – now a politician – and permission was given for him to return safely home.

Having been abducted he was beaten and then murdered. The following day, an Officials spokesman stated 'Once we had him, there was nothing we could do but execute him.' His body was found dumped on waste ground by a passing nurse who tried to help him. Over

400 women attacked the offices of Official Sinn Féin Derry following the shooting of William Best. There is unproven and unsubstantiated speculation in some quarters that the current Deputy First Minister of Northern Ireland, Martin McGuinness, believed then to be IRA commander in the Creggan, was involved in Ranger Best's death.

Only weeks earlier, the Official IRA had captured an off-duty soldier who was visiting his heavily pregnant wife in the Bogside. To the utter disgust of the more militant Provisionals, the 'stickies' released the soldier on 'compassionate' grounds; that would probably be the last act of compassion shown by any of the Republicans.

It is thought that the derisory term 'stickies' was coined by locals because of the Officials' habit of wearing or 'sticking' an Easter lily on their lapels during the annual celebrations of the Easter Rising. The Army initially called them 'IRA Goulding' after their leader Cathal Goulding and the breakaway Provisionals as 'IRA Brady' after their nominal leader Ruairí Ó Brádaigh. After the Officials' ceasefire in 1972, many of their disaffected members joined the fledgling IRSP (Irish Republican Socialist Party) and its military wing, the INLA (Irish National Liberation Army). The INLA was a terrorist organisation even more vicious than the Provisionals. Its most notable 'scalp' was the murder of Airey Neave MP on the car park ramp of the House of Commons in 1979.

Airey Middleton Sheffield Neave DSO, OBE, MC who had risen to fame during the Second World War as one of the few Allied PoWs to escape from Colditz, was Shadow Secretary of State for Northern Ireland in Thatcher's Shadow Cabinet. He was killed by an INLA car bomb just weeks before the 1979 General Election that the Conservatives were widely tipped to win – which they did – when he was expected to become Secretary of State for Northern Ireland in the first Thatcher cabinet.

Airey Neave was killed on 30 March 1979, when a car bomb fitted with a mercury tilt switch exploded under his car just before 15.00 as he drove down the ramp of the House of Commons car park. Both his legs were blown off and he died in hospital an hour after being freed from the wreckage. The INLA – already banned in the UK under the Prevention of Terrorism Act – claimed responsibility for the killing.

In November 2008, the author in an emotional return to Northern Ireland stood by William Best's grave in the city cemetery. His black marble tombstone reads 'Erected by Officers and Men of 'B' Company, Royal Irish Rangers in memory of a loyal comrade.'

On 22 May the IRA shot yet another member of 'their community' as they apparently 'mistook' William Hughes (56) as he sat in a car in the tiny village of Moortown, Coagh; to the best of the author's knowledge, they never actually explained who or what they 'mistook' him for! The following day, another of the wounded from the UVF/UFF attack on Kelly's Bar died; he was John Moran (19) a student who was working to supplement his grant.

Later that same day, the Kingos lost one of their black soldiers, Eustace Hanley (20) when the IRA shot him as he guarded comrades in the Springhill Avenue close to the Ballymurphy estate. Peter Oakley, a former CVO for the regiment, speculated that the IRA may have been targeting black and Asian soldiers in order to try and discourage recruiting into the Army from the ethnic communities of Britain.

MAKING FACES

Corporal Paddy Lenaghan, King's Regiment

I remember that we had some bigwig, some visiting VIP, and I was chosen to ride as 'shotgun' and we were en-route for one of the Company locations. We were driving through one of the dangerous sectarian interfaces, when there was the distinctive sound of an HV [High Velocity] round passing close over our heads. At this, incredibly, the driver slowed the vehicle right down making us an even easier target and I was speechless for about a quarter of a second. I then screamed at him 'What the fuck are you doing?' and he just replied 'Trying to find where the round came from!' I was again speechless, but this time for only about a tenth of a second and screamed back 'You fucking gormless, fucking idiot! Fucking drive out of here; put your fucking foot down!' As posterity has recorded, we did get out of there, but perhaps I was only delaying the inevitable and the IRA got Jimmy and badly damaged me just a few days later [see below].

Before that happened, there was another incident, this time, I am pleased to report, it was a funny one. I was stood on a VCP with another Kingo, a black lad like Jimmy Doglay and Eustace Hanley who were both later killed. Leon Smart was the lad's name, smashing lad he was; anyway, as I say, we were manning this VCP and a little old lady approaches with a cup of tea. She gets chatting to Leon and asks him 'You a Protestant or a Catholic?'

Now, you have to remember that Leon is black and just a few yards away, we have a hostile crowd of the local yobs and they're screaming 'Get the nigger! Get the nigger!' Leon looks at the old lady and said gently 'Lady, don't you think that I have enough problems?'

Another time, we were together in the front sangar, watching the front of the station when this local woman walked by. Now, Leon was, as I said, black and although he was a real 'gentle giant', he was a big tall lad and a member of the battalion boxing team. The lady with a kid in a pushchair walked by, cold-shouldering us as the locals did and the kid turns around in his pushchair and stares at Leon. Well Leon just does this huge, ugly face thing and scares the kid to death. Well, the kid is in hysterics and the angry mother is looking around trying to find who caused it! You then have to imagine two Kingos, desperately trying to keep a straight face and look totally innocent! I imagine that poor kid still has emotional problems even today!

On 26 May an IRA car bomb on Oxford Street in Belfast city centre exploded and killed Margaret Young (60) as she left work; no warning was given. Ranger Best's regiment lost another soldier that day when Ranger Thomas McGann (20) was killed in a RTA. Over the next two days, the UVF and the UFF shot and killed two innocent Catholics; James Teer (21) and Gerard Duddy (20) were simply in the wrong place at the wrong time as the Loyalists – or 'Orangees' as the Catholics knew them – tried to emulate their Republican counterparts. There are observers who might say that the Loyalists did not merely emulate their murderous rivals; in many ways they surpassed them.

A tragedy was about to befall upon the Catholic community, the very people both wings of the IRA professed to be the guardians of. During what the Belfast folk call the 'wee hours' an IRA bomb making team was busily assembling a device at a house in Anderson Street in the Catholic Short Strand enclave of east Belfast. The device, made of nitrobenzene exploded and killed all four members of the IRA team instantly. Tragically, four other innocent Catholics were also killed; John Nugent (31), Geraldine McMahon (17), Harry Crawford (39) and Mary Clarke (27). By some miracle, none of the latter's three sleeping children were killed.

SHORT STRAND BOMB

John Bradley, 23 Engineer Regiment

We had one more bomb in store for us. There was a small side street that ran between the Short Strand bus depot and a row of houses. We had watch towers at either end. I think it was about 03.30hrs and we had just come off patrol and returned to HMS *Maidstone* from the fan works roof when we heard the most deafening noise from about three miles away.

'That was a big one,' Sammy screamed. Little did we know that it was a couple of hundred yards away from where we had just come from! We had just got into bed when Danny boy came into the room and told us we were going out again. Pissed off, tired and hungry, we got back in the Land Rover and followed orders to go back to the bus depot. It was about 05.20hrs and the sun was just coming up. As we got closer we could see the plume of smoke rising from right next door. Bloody hell; what a mess! There were ambulances and fire engines everywhere. It looked like the whole street had gone. The last six houses had just collapsed in on themselves and there was broken windows and glass everywhere. 'What a mess,' we kept saying, 'what a mess.' Paramedics tended to a couple of our lads who were so close they were deafened and blinded by the blast.

'Why would the IRA bomb themselves?' I thought. They must have been building bombs right under our noses in that row of houses and something went wrong. It was the only logical explanation. It turned out to be true. Search teams, more lads from HQ, were brought in to help clean up the mess. The usual bags, gloves and masks were issued and we were given an area as our own to search. We were looking for bodies of course, but we had no idea what was really in store for us. There wasn't an intact body left in that rubble; little arms and feet and bits of intestines all gooey and slimy and bloody. I don't know who it was, but one of the boys always seemed to find humour in a bad situation. Seagulls had been swooping down on a double decker bus on the other side of the wall in the station. On the roof of the bus was obviously a piece of flesh that looked like someone's arse. It took the gulls about a half hour to finish it off. That was one body part that never made it into a bag. Good Navy food or not, I still didn't eat for three days.

On the 29th, the Official Irish Republican Army announced that it was calling a ceasefire, reserving the right of self-defence against attacks by the British Army and sectarian groups. Although the 'stickies' were involved in a number of incidents following the ceasefire, it was to mark the end of the military wing of Official Sinn Féin. However, the Provisional IRA dismissed the truce as having 'little effect' on the situation. The Northern Ireland Secretary, William Whitelaw, welcomed the move and a spokesperson said it was 'a step in the right direction'. A statement issued at the time by the Officials read 'The overwhelming desire of the majority of the people … is for an end to military actions of both sides.' It went on to say that a suspension of activities would be a chance to prevent all-out civil war in Ulster.

A spokesman for the Official IRA insisted it would continue a campaign of civil disobedience and the political struggle until its demands were met: release of all internees, an amnesty for 'political prisoners', withdrawal of the Army from Northern Ireland and the abolition of the Special Powers Act.

JIMMY

Corporal Paddy Lenaghan, King's Regiment

We all have memories; some are vivid and unforgettable. But, with the passage of time and problems of ageing and the frequent re-telling to those who will listen, sometimes I have to ask myself: did it happen? I often lapse into the realms of: did this happen like this; am I merely repeating what someone else told me?

My memories in any case end suddenly and violently on the afternoon of Tuesday, 30 May in 1972; that's when my mate Marcus 'Jimmy' Doglay was killed and I was blown up and airlifted back to England after an IRA bomb blew up the rest room of Springfield Road police station.

On 30 May 1972 the IRA killed 'Jimmy' Doglay at Springfield Road RUC Station. 23868738 Kingsman Marcel James Doglay (28) known to all of his mates as 'Jimmy' was born in the Seychelles, half a world away from the blackened stone terraced houses of west Belfast. He left a wife and four small children, a lasting legacy to this 'gentle giant'. He is buried in St Patrick's Churchyard.

The RUC station, described by Paddy Lenaghan as one of the most beleaguered and besieged places in Ulster, was located strategically on Springfield Road. The area, at first mixed, later became overwhelmingly Catholic and Nationalist and as such a prime base for the Provisionals. The 'barracks' were only yards from Grosvenor Road and Dunville Park and the Falls Road and a short stroll to the Divis and Leeson Street, close also to North Howard Street Mill. Soldiers based there could be rushed very quickly to all the local Republican hot spots in a very short space of time.

At the very height of the Troubles, huge metal security gates were erected across the entrance to Violet Street. This effectively made the front of the station more defendable and the sides less vulnerable.

At the time of the attack that killed Kingsman Doglay, the station was being renovated for purposes of strengthening it and making it into more of a fortress. A number of civilian workers – some with obvious IRA sympathies, perhaps even a member or members – were working on the station at the time. The civvie workers had to pass an armed sentry to gain access and this was where the lapse in security occurred. The device was placed inside a fire extinguisher and was designed to detonate when the rest room was full of soldiers. As it happened, the room was not packed at the time because the TV was faulty. To the author's knowledge, no-one was ever charged with the attack.

PROVO CAUGHT WITH HIS PANTS DOWN

Paul Stride, Parachute Regiment

One night I was lucky enough to be on a mobile when we got the brief that one of the 'ladies of the night' was entertaining a known Provo in his car. We parked around the corner and dismounted the Land Rovers and left the PIG at the end of the street with its lights and engine switched off. It was parked at the top of a gradual slope, so that when the driver released the hand brake it would just roll down towards car. Pete crept up to the car and when he stuck his thumb up, the PIG rolled down behind the car and suddenly put his lights on full beam. The occupants were in a state of undress, the Provo with his trousers round his ankles. We put him against the wall and his vehicle was searched. However, all we found was some photos of himself with some other characters which we discreetly pocketed for our intelligence boys.

Left: Guardsmen occupy a position on a street corner near the Falls in Belfast. In the background is a Saladin armoured vehicle.

Below: 'This is more interesting than shopping, girls!' A group of women take a keen interest in a Cheshire Regiment foot patrol on Lisbon Street, east Belfast.

AGEING ON THE JOB

John Bradley, 23 Engineer Regiment

Without a doubt the toughest night for me was when we were called over to guard this new estate in the dead of night. It was the Turf lodge, somewhere in the upper Falls Road district. I was with about 50 lads that were sent to this area to wait for trouble in the absolute dark. We had learned that an illegal meeting was taking place and Bernadette Devlin herself was in the area. We had been called in case of booby traps and the like. We never found Devlin or any booby traps that night, but as Kenny and I agreed later, waiting for trouble for four hours in the pitch black was enough to make anyone soil their trousers. Waiting in the dark for something to happen put us all on edge. I think it's when I first began to fear the unknown. We aged on that job I tell you.

But May wasn't finished with, certainly not as far as the SF were concerned. Lance Corporal Michael Bruce RCT (27) was in a mobile patrol in Andersonstown when the IRA opened fire from a hijacked vehicle. He was hit and died shortly afterwards in the nearby Musgrave Park Hospital.

It is worth noting that the UDR lost a further four soldiers during that month; all but one died in circumstances unknown but all are recorded on the ROH at the National Arboretum. The men were Corporal Brian Heron (24); Corporal Sidney Hussey (45); Sergeant William Reid (28); and Sergeant Major Bernard Adamson (30).

LOVED BY BOTH SIDES

Keith Williams, Royal Regiment of Wales, Att: UDR

In 1969, I was a student at the All Arms Drill Wing. The course included formal instruction on funeral drill; little did I realise that I would be instructing so many bearer and firing parties just a few years later in such tragic circumstances. The shock, dismay and total anger I felt when Sergeant Major Bernard Adamson – a NRPS Instructor and close friend – was shot on training exercise at Letterbreen by a member of a demonstration squad from HQ 3 Bde who mistakenly loaded his weapon with live ammunition instead of blanks. Regrettably he died of his wounds a few days later.

He was an English Roman Catholic ex-RAC regular soldier who served in Ulster before the Troubles. He married an Enniskillen girl and enlisted in the UDR on their formation. He was universally popular with all ranks and straddled the religious divide. At his military funeral the RC church in Enniskillen was packed with both Protestant and Catholics alike. He died because the golden rule about mixing live and blank ammunition was on this occasion disregarded.

May was about to slip into the summer months, but the toll was heavy with no less than 47 people killed. The Army lost fifteen, its worst month of the Troubles so far; 26 civilians were killed, many at the hands of the Loyalist murder gangs and six members of the IRA were also killed, four by their own hand.

CHAPTER SIX

JUNE

June arrived and if there was any sort of lingering optimism in military or governmental circles, it would soon be dashed. For the overworked CVOs, the month which heralded the start of summer and the lengthening of the days culminating in the longest day on the 21st; it would be sad and extremely busy time. This month would result in twenty visits to the loved ones of dead soldiers and it would be the worst single month for the British Army since the end of Empire when 23 British soldiers were killed in Aden in June 1967.

Don Maclean's melancholic 'Vincent' was number one in Britain and even the pious Republicans could join in with the mournful dirge. In the US, the Watergate scandal was just

For this little girl en route to school in West Belfast, the sight of armed soldiers was merely part of her daily routine.

kicking off and Nixon had started the long, painful process towards either impeachment or resignation.

June began badly. On the 2nd, an IRA team hiding over in the Republic detonated a massive device which caught a Royal Artillery patrol at Derryvolan on the border near Rosslea. Two young lads were killed instantly, leaving two widows and four fatherless children over on the mainland. Gunner Brian Robertson (23) from Sunderland and Gunner Victor Husband (23) from Middlesbrough were both killed in the blast.

Derryvolan Bridge is on a minor cross-border road 2.25 miles north of Rosslea village. Crossing the Finn River which runs north-south and marks the international boundary in that area, Derryvolan is a scenic and peaceful location, with high ground on the Republic's side making it a perfect ambush site. The Gunners were probably observing the area from a copse to the west of the road. The hilltop to the east (in the Republic) would have been an ideal and safe spot for the PIRA's 'button man'. As a former UDR man said to the author, 'It was a typically cowardly attack; leaving another four wains without their fathers.'

A further sectarian killing by the Loyalists was followed by the killing of Private George Lee (22) on 6 June. He was a Leeds man and a member of the 'Duke of Boots' as the Duke of Wellington's Regiment are known. The soldier was on patrol on the Ballymurphy estate when he was hit in the neck by a high velocity round fired by an IRA sniper and killed instantly. An armed gang had taken over a house, holding the family hostage before the fatal shot. He is buried at Hipswell Military Cemetery on the Catterick garrison.

On 7 June yet another soldier from the Royal Artillery was killed, less than a mile away in Andersonstown, or 'Andytown' as the soldiers called the sprawling council estate of post-war housing which sits immediately to the west of the Turf Lodge. Sergeant Charles Coleman (29) was hit as several shots were fired at his mobile patrol which was travelling near Tullymore Gardens. He was rushed to the Musgrave Park Hospital (MPH) where he died shortly afterwards. As his comrades began follow up operations, they came under heavy brick and bottle attack from the 'natives' of the area and were forced to withdraw so as to lessen the risk to the lives of civilians.

Five days earlier, UDR Private Edward 'Ted' Megahey (45) had been badly wounded when his mobile patrol was attacked in Buncrana Road, Londonderry. He died in hospital on 7 June. The very same day, the regiment also lost 8th Battalion member Corporal Roy Staunton (27), shot whilst off duty. The part-time soldier worked at a factory on the edge of the Andersonstown estate which is fiercely Republican and not a safe place for a member of the security forces. As he drove out of the gates of the factory, a young member of the IRA stepped in front of his car and opened fire, killing him and wounding two colleagues whom he was giving a lift. He died at the scene. This was no opportunistic hit; it was well planned and demonstrated the ability of the IRA's intelligence units. Throughout the course of the Troubles the SF consistently underestimated just how professional the PIRA was to become.

'Andytown' was also the scene of a third killing in as many days, when Jean Smith (24) a local woman was shot by unknown assailants. She may have been killed by a Loyalist murder gang, she may have been shot accidentally by undercover soldiers or she may have been killed by the IRA; over 38 years on, no-one has admitted to her murder. There were two more sectarian killings by the UFF before the Army killed another member of Fianna during a fierce fire fight in the Berwick Road area of the Ardoyne in north Belfast. The dead member of the IRA's youth wing was Joseph Campbell (17), yet another young man seduced into the art of violence by the leaders of the Republicans.

On 11 June Loyalist Norman McGrath (18) was shot by soldiers from the Parachute Regiment as they returned fire after being attacked by gunmen in the 'interface area' between the two warring sectarian sections of north Belfast. Many soldiers had mixed feelings about incidents in the Loyalist areas as these were the people who professed to be 'on the side' of the Army. Indeed, the following year – as author and former Parachute Regiment officer Tony Clarke points out in *Contact* – a major fire fight between his unit and Shankill gunmen saw at least five shot.

On the same day, William Raistrick (18) from the Royal Artillery was shot at a sentry post in Brook Park in the Creggan. The young Halifax man was killed instantly and immediately a major gun battle broke out in the nearby Little Diamond area. Over 300 rounds were fired at the soldiers but thankfully there were no further fatalities.

'AS A MEMBER OF HER MAJESTY'S FORCES, I ARREST YOU!'

Mike, Royal Artillery

With those immortal words, you have guaranteed yourself membership to that group of soldiers called 'Courts Witnesses'. Before the advent of RMP [Royal Military Police] arrest and find teams, it was the soldiers themselves who had to take the various miscreants down to the local cop shop and give a statement of events leading up to the arrest. This incidentally, was ponderously written down in longhand by a patient constable. But if you thought that was it, you couldn't have been more wrong. Depending upon the seriousness of the offence, it could be

Illegal Vehicle Checkpoint (IVCP) A member of the Provisional IRA checks the identity of a civilian in a Republican area of Belfast.

days, weeks or even months before the case came to court. Offences such as riotous behaviour and the like were usually tried at the local magistrate's court whilst terrorist related offences were tried at Crown court.

From 1972, a system of judgement was brought into force called the Diplock Court. Due to the chances of jury intimidation by the various terror groups, it was decided to do away with the jury system and each case was decided by a single judge. Despite what opponents to this system thought, it was actually more difficult to obtain convictions using this system as judges tended to lean towards the accused unless the evidence and witnesses made the case watertight. It was therefore important that soldiers were schooled in the art of giving evidence so a special unit was set up for this purpose. Army witnesses were shown films and put through mock trials to prepare them for what was to come. They were told to stick to the facts as written down on their police statement. Basically: 'I am, I was where and when, I saw or found' etc and not to allow the defending lawyer a chance of tripping them up.

All very straightforward you'd think. The problem was that most soldiers' experience of the legal system usually involved a quick left, right, mark time in front of the 'old man' [Commanding Officer] for being drunk and fighting downtown. Nothing could prepare them for the intimidating experience of giving evidence in a court which was packed with friends and relatives of the accused.

My experiences of magistrate court was in Londonderry. The court itself was located in Bishops Street Within, almost opposite the Masonic Hall used as an Army base. Riotous behaviour offences were usually tried a few days after the arrest, so the chances were that the Army witnesses were still in the Province so they turned up in uniform. There was a small side room just to the left of the courtroom where we gathered waiting for our name to be called. I can tell you that it was a bit disconcerting the first time, hearing your rank and name being called out by the clerk and you have to walk in to the witness box next to the judge, knowing that every person in the gallery now knew who you were. All this 'Soldier A' or 'Soldier B' and giving evidence from behind a screen business did not apply to the normal soldier. You had to front it out facing the hatred of the gallery. The case itself usually only lasted a few minutes and the judge didn't hang about giving his verdict either. If the accused was found guilty, it was fines or probation or anything up to six months in the clink, depending on the seriousness of the offence. Then it was 'next case'. A lively weekend in the Bogside could see as many as twenty or thirty of the local yobs being dealt with in a conveyer belt-like manner.

However, if it was the Crown Court in Belfast, this was situated in the Crumlin Road. This was where most terrorist offences were tried. Although a much bigger set up than Londonderry, the arrangement for Army witnesses was similar. The case usually kicked off with the accused turning their backs on the judge and saying that they refused to recognise the court. It didn't do them any good as the case would go ahead anyway and all they had achieved was pissing off the judge. One difference was that the defence solicitors were more professional than the public appointed ones. A tactic that was used was to refuse a public defender and engage the services of an expensive lawyer. When he started on the case, they would say that there was no money to pay him so his fee came out of the public purse.

This contributor was involved in court appearances as a military witness right through until 1977. Although this is outside the scope of the subject year of 1972, a further contribution in this context appears later in the book.

On 11 June Alan Giles, a Cardiff boy from the Royal Regiment of Wales (RRW) was shot and terribly wounded in Alliance Avenue, Belfast following a firefight. He died in hospital the following day, a few hours after his parents arrived from Wales. I was told by a close personal source from the RRW that he clung onto life just long enough for his distraught parents to reach his side. For many soldiers' families, coming from the poorer areas of the mainland, air travel was still not, in 1972, a familiar experience. Often it was the first time grieving family members went on a plane, and the bewilderment exacerbated their fears and anxiety.

THE YELLOW CARD

Roy Davies, Royal Regiment of Wales

When we first got there, people were being pushed out of their houses and there were old people in wheelchairs. There was children and a lot of shooting behind them. Then in later tours, we was able to get to grips with the ones causing the trouble.

The yellow card; oh yes. If this person had a gun, you still had to shout 'Halt or I'll fire!' Well I never done that, see. I used to fire and then shout 'Halt or I'll fire!' I thought: what's the difference? Cos' if I shout "Halt or I'll fire!" he's gonna have me before I have him!'

Terry Friend, Royal Artillery

You can imagine; you're in a situation and some bugger's gonna chuck a petrol bomb at you. You have to shout: 'Put it down; I'm gonna shoot!' Well, if you had to shout it three times, by the time you've finished, he's thrown it and gone; absolute nonsense! [With thanks to Emma and Mike Ford, Point of View Productions for use of comments from their excellent History Channel documentary *Soldiers' Stories*, 2009]

On 13 June the IRA had invited William Whitelaw, Secretary of State for Northern Ireland, to meet them in what they termed 'Free Derry'. The British government rejected the offer and reaffirmed in a statement their policy not to allow part of the United Kingdom to 'default from the rule of law.' The initial offer placed the Social Democratic and Labour Party (SDLP) in a position to 'broker' talks between the IRA and the British government. On the following day, John Hume and Paddy Devlin, both members of the SDLP) held a meeting with representatives of the IRA in Londonderry. At the meeting the IRA representatives outlined their conditions for talks with the British government. The conditions were that there should be no restriction on who represented the IRA; there should be an independent witness at the meeting; the meeting should not be held at Stormont; and 'political status' should be granted to Republican prisoners.

On 14 June, the Royal Horse Guards lost Lance Corporal of Horse Keith Chillingworth (24) in a tragic RTA whilst on duty. Two days later, the UFF killed Charles Connor (32) in another senseless sectarian murder and on the same day John Johnson (59) – who had been wounded on Bloody Sunday – died some 138 days after he had been injured. His family maintained that his premature death was a direct consequence of the trauma he suffered in Londonderry on that day. I suspect that very few people would seriously dispute that assertion.

On the 15th William Whitelaw met with the SDLP and agreed to their terms (see above) and the Provisionals reciprocated with the offer of a ceasefire. Despite the hopeful news, the next day three soldiers from the Gordons were killed in Lurgan. The three soldiers were Sergeant Major Arthur McMillan (37) a married father of one, from Hull in East Yorkshire; Lance Corporal Colin Leslie (26) from the Orkney Islands; and Sergeant Ian Mutch (31), married, from Nairn near the Moray Firth. At the time of the explosion, seven soldiers from the Gordons' search team were inside a house at Bleary, near Lurgan, searching for arms after a tip off which, with the benefit of hindsight, was clearly an IRA 'come on'. Four other soldiers were injured, one very severely.

The following day in Brompton Park, Ardoyne, the RRW lost another comrade when Bryan Soden (21) from Tewkesbury was hit by an armour piercing (AP) round which went clean through the PIG in which he was travelling. Later that evening, the IRA, self-claimed 'protectors' of the Catholic community shot a local man in a club in Leeson Street, then a dirty collection of blackened terraced housing, in a punishment shooting which went badly wrong. Desmond Macklin (37) died of blood loss after an ambulance taking him to the nearby RVH was initially prevented from leaving the scene by the IRA, even shooting at the ambulance as it drove away from the 'Cracked Cup' premises. Later medical evidence proved that he might well have been saved had it not been for the obstructive behaviour of members of the PIRA.

This author accepts that there may well have been some well motivated Republicans within the IRA, but their behaviour, at times evil, certainly ruthless and much of the time bordering on gangsterism, demonstrated that the organisation attracted many with sociopathic and psychopathic tendencies. How those respectable Irish-Americans who funded the murder might have reacted had they seen their heroes' behaviour as Macklin bled to death from a severed artery is open to conjecture!

MAN DOWN ON THE 'MURPH

Corporal 'Tug' Wilson, King's Own Scottish Borderers

We were based at the Vere Foster School in the Ballymurphy estate; The regiment that we took over from had five killed, and three of them were killed in the area of the Bullring to be exact, which was precisely that which we were about to patrol. It was 1972 and the Ballymurphy estate in Belfast was as bad as anywhere you could find in the world. On a bad day it would give Beirut a run for its money.

Out of the gate and turn left into new Barnsley Park on to Springfield Road. Run! Run! Run! Take a quick look and then run again. Don't stop unless you have too. The area was quiet; too quiet as it happened. We would learn in the months to come when it was quiet something was about to happen. From the Springfield Road we turned into Divismore Way and there in front of us was the Ballymurphy Bullring. Corporal Mick Henderson stopped the patrol to let the men get their bearings before taking them into the Bullring proper. No words were spoken; not because of operational reasons but because of necessity. You are too tired to talk and you get by with a series of hand signals. The patrol commander gave a signal meaning 'Lets' go forward and see what is happening.' All the lads were ready to go and as they turned into Glenalina Park, it happened. Crack! Crack! Crack! Everything happened at once. The first thing that the men did was to act instinctively. They shouted 'Take cover! Take cover!' It was the first time they had come under fire in their lives but they knew what to do. Man's instinct is to preserve his life so you tend to keep a grip on yourself even under fire.

The man in charge knew what he must do. First off make a contact report on the radio. 'Hello 3 this is 3/3 Charlie. Contact. Wait out.' When a contact report goes in the company net goes quiet. This allows the man on the ground to assess the situation and report back with the relevant information. At the same time the duty operator at headquarters presses the switch on the intercom to tell the company commander that 3/3 Charlie has had a contact. Another operator will inform battalion headquarters that we have a call sign radioing in with a contact. They in turn will put the medical staff on standby to help with any casualties. Back at the base, the company commander, Major Ian Scallion MC, ordered the stand by platoon to get ready.

Mick's mind was working overtime. This is what he was paid for so it was up to him to get the men out of the situation. As far as he could see the threat was coming from the Bullring so he made the decision to back off for the moment. He signaled to Andy Brown to come over by putting his hand on top of his head. Andy knew what was coming and threw himself forward towards Mick. At that moment the IRA opened fire again and Andy went down on the road like a sack of shit. Mick's immediate response was to shout into the radio 'Hello 3 this is 3/3 Charlie. Reference my last. We have a man down. I repeat a man down. I require back up now, over.' The company commander came on the net. 'Hello 3/3 Charlie this is 3/9. We will be with you in figures five.' Mick knew that the company would be sending help in five minutes but that did not help him now. He could see that his men were returning fire towards the general direction of the gunmen, and that the target of the gunmen was Andy and he ran forward to help his mate.

As Mick went forward to get his mate to safety, the gunmen opened fire with renewed ferocity and he could see the road in front of him come alive with rounds being fired at him and Andy. The tarmac was boiling with the amount of rounds that were hitting it. He was on his way to collecting a military medal but for the moment he did not care. His mate was in trouble and it was his duty to get him to safety. He grabbed him and ran to the nearest cover he could find, a hedge that was about six feet high. He threw Andy over the hedge and tried to go over himself but it was too high. He had lost momentum by stopping to throw Andy over and he could not get over himself. He ran to the first available cover he could find and took stock.

He was a bit away from his men but as far as he could see they were doing well. The whine of an armoured car filled the air and Mick knew that the reinforcements had arrived. The men were pointing to where Andy was and the guys from the armoured car ran out and grabbed him. There was no attempt to nurse him, as one guy grabbed him by the chest and another by the bollocks and threw him into the armoured car. There was no National Health Service on the Ballymurphy estate.

This account continues later, but I am pleased to report that the soldier Andy Brown, although wounded, survived and that Corporal Mick Henderson was awarded the Military Medal.

There was a further meeting – this time in the utmost secrecy – between representatives of the Provisional IRA and officials from William Whitelaw's office. The meeting took place on the afternoon of the 20th in a country house in Ballyarnet, close to the Co Londonderry and Co Donegal border. The PIRA representatives were David O'Connell and Gerry Adams. The officials acting on behalf of William Whitelaw were P.J. Woodfield and Frank Steele (from the British Intelligence agency MI6). The meeting laid the groundwork for a PIRA ceasefire and a direct meeting between the PIRA and the British government on 7 July 1972. 48 hours later, the IRA announced a ceasefire for 26 June and demanded a reciprocal gesture from the government.

The longest day of the year dawned, and with it, the summer of 1972 began, but for the family of Royal Welsh Fusiliers soldier Kerry McCarthy back in Merthyr Tydfil, it was a day which would be remembered for all the wrong reasons. McCarthy (19) was guarding the front sangar at Strand Road RUC station in Londonderry when he was hit in the chest by a round from an IRA sniper. His distraught mother who had lost her husband earlier in the year had had a premonition about her son's death. The IRA had made yet another young widow. No doubt that evening, their 'volunteers' would have joked about 'widow making'.

It was around this time that the Republicans and their apologists in the then opposition Labour Party and the press began to talk about the Army's tactic of 'shoot to kill'. To the men in uniform this comment was met with no little bemusement, having been taught since the first days of weapons training to aim at the largest body mass, the chest. As one former UDR man told the author, 'How do you hit someone with an SLR without killing him?' It would be some twelve years later, in 1984 when a senior British policeman, John Stalker, conducted an investigation into this policy. The following small contribution from a former soldier speaks volumes and encapsulates the author's own thoughts so accurately that further comment is superfluous.

SHOOT TO KILL

Rifleman 'L' Royal Green Jackets

I remember that there was some talk about us shooting to kill at this stage, after a couple of PIRA gunmen had been 'slotted' in Belfast. This occurred at a time when we were cooped up in some Catholic school, saint something-or-other in Andytown [Saint Teresa's]. One of the lads received a letter from some female relative and she thought that it was terrible that we didn't shoot to wound instead! Well, after we had all had a good chuckle at that one, we did feel just a little pissed off that civvies in their nice warm lounges back home, their 'Bird's Eye' TV dinners perched on their laps, sitting in front of their goggle boxes saw things like that.

We was taught right from the first minute that we picked up our SLRs in basic training to aim for the biggest body mass: the chest. The round that it fired was an HV [high velocity] 7.62mm and could punch its way through some metals. What it could do to a human body can only be imagined. It made a small entry wound and then, having smashed up organs and bones would then leave an exit wound the size of a fist. If you were hit by a 7.62mm fired from an SLR – which we called a 'Paddy whacker' – pretty much anywhere then you was dead! Brown bread as we said!

If there was a geezer with a gun and he was going to fire it at you, you didn't have time to think; you either fired first, or it was home in a coffin for Mrs L's little boy. That would have upset my old Mum and I was having none of that. You couldn't shoot to wound, nor could you shoot the weapon out of the gunman's hand. John Wayne and Hopalong Cassidy could, but we couldn't and anyone who claims that we could have done is taking the piss. We shot to kill and so did the IRA and when they killed David Card, they wasn't shooting to wound, nor were they trying to shoot his SLR out of his hands. Civvies never did understand and some of the comments we got back home on leave were not very helpful! The papers didn't help much and the *Mirror* and the *Sun* just printed shit!

Above and opposite: Part of the Army's tactics would be to stop known players or suspected players in order to constantly disrupt their lives and movements. Of course innocent people were also stopped.

On 23 June, the UVF opened fire indiscriminately at a group of young men in the Catholic area of Atlantic Road, Belfast. A young schoolgirl among the group returning from church was badly wounded in the neck, but thankfully survived. Patrick McCullough (17) was not so lucky and died at the scene.

In the very early hours of the following morning, three soldiers, Corporal David Moon (24) from Yorkshire, REME Sergeant Stuart Reid (28) from Hampshire and Private Christopher Stevenson (24) from Birmingham were all killed. The three, all part of or attached to the Army Air Corps, were driving in a Land Rover at Glenshane Pass on the Belfast to Londonderry road when an IRA landmine was detonated. Immediately after the explosion, gunmen opened fire at an RCT driver and two rounds entered his beret, thankfully missing his head!

NO-ONE HAD A CLUE WHAT WE DID!

Sergeant Mick 'Benny' Hill, Royal Anglians

Early one morning sometime in '72 I was told to take my section down to the docks, where we would meet the Liverpool ferry, pick up a civvie, and bring him back to Hastings Street. We met him, and his eyebrows rose a little when he saw that his transport was a Land Rover, and he was to be shut in the back for the journey to Tac HQ. He was installing some kind of equipment in the control room. What it was I never asked, and no-one told me. After breakfast he got to work, and was finished by lunchtime.

I told him that he would have a boring afternoon until we could transport him to the late evening ferry, and he replied that he had another job to do in a hospital in South Belfast, and could someone kindly tell him how to get there! Apparently, his boss, not having a clue about

Belfast in those days, thought that he would save money by sending one rep to do two jobs, rather than sending two reps on different days. My boss had a sense of humour failure, and informed the rep that he had been 'dicked' coming into an SF base, and on no account would they let him into central and south Belfast on his own.

One of the Recce platoon sergeants was ordered to get into 'civvies' and make sure he came to no harm. Later that evening when the rep got back to us, I got talking to the lad, and asked him what he thought of the place. He said that when we picked him up, he thought that we were surly bastards, because no-one spoke to him during the trip to Tac HQ. Now he understood why. When I asked about his trip to South Belfast, he replied that it was no worse than some parts of Manchester, but his escort scared the shit out of him. 'His eyes were never still; if a fly flew past the window, I'm sure he would have seen it; he was like a cat on the hunt, and it wasn't till we got back that I realised why he kept his jacket unbuttoned the whole time and needed to go to the unloading bay. I'm beginning to understand how you guys live, and what it is like here. When I get back I'm going to have a lot of choice words to say to my boss. It has been an experience, but not one I want to repeat.'

He was genuinely pleased when we put him safely on the ferry that evening!

Northern Ireland was a hazardous place for all during the Troubles, even more so if one was breaking the law. Joyriding is a risky business at the best of times, but with armed soldiers manning VCPs during the Troubles it was especially dangerous to be one, or to be mistaken as one. On 25 June, James Bonner (19) a lorry driver from the Falls area, failed to stop at a VCP on the Whiterock Road while driving a car that was not his, although it was not stolen. Soldiers stated that a shot was fired and they 'returned' fire at what they thought was the source. Bonner, who was also drinking and driving, was hit and killed. The Whiterock Road was a particularly dangerous part of west Belfast as its length is the delineating line between the Republican Ballymurphy estate and the equally Republican Turf Lodge. There was more tragedy for the Bonner family as, just over fifteen weeks and over 200 deaths later, James' father Edward (37) was murdered by the IRA in a club near the Falls Road. James Bonner was one of ten people to die in just four days as June ended.

A less innocent man also died that day. UFF man John Black (32) had been shot and badly wounded some five weeks earlier in a confrontation with the Army. Soldiers had been removing barricades in the Castlereagh Road area when they were fired at and returned fire, hitting Black. He died in hospital on the night of the 25th.

On 26 June UDA/UFF member John Brown (29) was killed by fellow Loyalists in a drunken brawl in the Upper Springfield Road area. His family claimed that he had been killed by the IRA and demanded a public inquiry, that is, until the truth came out that he had died at the hands of his fellow terrorists.

The IRA, with a ceasefire at hand, tried to plant a car bomb in Newry. A suspicious officer in the RUC challenged the driver and was shot and killed. Constable David Houston (22) was from England but had chosen to serve with the RUC. His heavily pregnant wife gave birth to a baby only days after the killing. At the same time, two Catholic car dealers were abducted in the Shankill area as they tried to sell a vehicle. Gerald McRea and James Howell were both murdered by Loyalists.

It was the Green Jackets who were to suffer next that day. Rifleman James Meredith (19) from Nottinghamshire was shot twice and died within minutes whilst manning a VCP on Abercorn Road, Londonderry. His killers were later jailed for the derisory term of four years.

Somewhere in the Falls/Springfield Road area, in spite of the morning rush hour, a wary soldier stays alert.

The ceasefire was due to begin at midnight on Monday 26 June and the IRA decided to go out on a show of strength. With only minutes remaining before a cessation of arms, an Army mobile patrol in the Short Strand was fired upon from the direction of Comber Street and Staff Sergeant Malcolm Banks was hit and fatally wounded. The father of two came from the Bramley area of Leeds and was known locally for his superb work with victims of IRA punishment squads. The fatal round actually passed between two soldiers before hitting the Royal Engineers 'Staff'; he died just five minutes into the ceasefire. If there was a single person left who believed that the ruthless Provisional IRA could ever be trusted, his naivety would have been 'cured' by the death of Banks.

STAFF SERGEANT MALCOM BANKS

John Bradley 23rd Engineer Regiment

We called it the 'tour of double duty' the day we arrived, as the advance party. We knew we were in trouble when asked to travel with a search team that had found some old First World War grenades under some floor boards and wanted help disposing of them. We stayed at various places including a school, a church, the Short Strand Bus Depot and Mountpottinger Police Station, which was our HQ. The best accommodation was the triple bunks of good old HMS *Maidstone* docked in Belfast harbour. They removed the internees and put our troop in their place for the last two months of our stay; must admit the Navy cooks were brilliant.

1972 was a tough year and I think the bloodiest of the conflict. We had several bombs to contend with and dozens of shootings but we only lost one man in seven months. Not bad for a bunch of 'engineers playing soldiers', as we were known. Our only loss was a fine chap named Banks, a staff sergeant with 16 Squadron. He was killed whilst out on the final patrol cleaning the streets up at 23.45 hrs just before a-so called ceasefire deadline. His job was to make sure all patrols were off the street and he got topped himself! I was in the Short Strand Bus Depot at the time and had just been pulled in with some chaps from another regiment who had been caught on the wrong side of town.

At about 23.10 hrs we were given orders to come in off the street and head to the bus depot. The brass wanted all of us off the streets early as a sign of good faith I guess. When we pulled into the yard it was packed with lads from all different regiments. We had not been the only ones pulled in; the order was: no troops left out on the street by midnight.

There were about 150 of us in that bus garage when a single shot rang out; you could have heard a pin drop. The buzz on the radio started and then we heard that Banks had got hit and it was bad! The tension was unbearable and many, many lads wanted to get back out into the streets to exact revenge. We got dressed down by our RSM, Mick Turner. He made us all strip off our flak jackets and helmets as a sign of good faith and held us all in that depot until daylight before being allowed back to our bunks on *Maidstone*. Needless to say the political side of things was deemed more important than Malcolm Banks' life.

Despite the ceasefire, the IRA was responsible for two more sectarian deaths on the first day. In the early hours of the last Friday in the month, the UDA began to organise its own 'no-go' areas. Clearly this was a response to the continuation of Republican 'no-go' areas and there were grave fears about the seemingly endless concessions which the British government were seen to be making to the IRA.

The next contribution demonstrates graphically the hatred which the people of the Nationalist communities held for the Army; this was by no means entirely mutual, although the soldiers hated the IRA with a passion, but there were many decent people on those estates. The hatred and suspicion of the soldiers was engendered and engineered by the Provisionals and there were, sadly, some soldiers who let down the British Army. But for every soldier who behaved badly, there were a hundred who behaved with impeccable professionalism. When a soldier has to kill, he does not do with pleasure or enthusiasm; we had a job to do.

GUNMAN KILLED ON THE 'MURPH

Corporal 'Tug' Wilson, King's Own Scottish Borderers

It was just after Andy Brown had been evacuated that the company commander came on the radio. 'Hello 3/3 Charlie this is 3/9; we have picked up your casualty and are returning to base. You will have to withdraw your men and make it back yourselves; over.' Mick Brown acknowledged and had just got the words out his mouth when he heard the sound of two rounds from an army 7.62 rifle.

'Who fired them?' he asked.

'It was me,' replied Don Charles. 'I have seen and shot a gunman.'

'Fuck me,' said Mick, looking at his watch. 'we've been on the streets 28 minutes and already I'm a man down and we've shot a gunman.' The company commander came on the radio and Mick confirmed that we had shot and most likely killed a gunman. After the briefest of pauses the company commander came on the net and told us that our casualty was back safe and being assessed and that they would be right with us. At this stage Mick indicated to his men to move forward to where the gunman was lying.

The locals were now milling around and shouting at the soldiers, calling us 'murdering bastards' and telling us to go back to our own country. Mick was right in his assessment of the gunman; he was dead right enough. You tend to be dead after being hit with a round from a British Army SLR. The man had a small hole in his chest where the round had entered, and a hole about a foot wide in his back where it had come out. It's not like the movies where you can see a man getting shot then saying 'The bastards got me!' When you get it in real life the force of the round throws you about ten feet in the air and knocks you back about twenty feet. If the round hits a bone the bones start spinning through your body as well and that's what causes the big exit wound. The company commander arrived at the scene and took in the situation at a glance. The first thing he noticed was the local priest giving the gunman the last rites. Major Scallion shouted to nobody in particular,

'Right, get that man into the armoured car and get him back to our location.'

'For pity's sake,' said the priest, 'I am giving this man the last rites; have some respect for the dead.'

'He shouldn't play with big boy's toys then,' replied the company commander, looking at the Armalite rifle the gunman had been using.

'This man was fighting to protect his community from the occupying army,' protested the priest.

'Well his fighting days are over,' said the Major, 'he belongs to us now.'

'Can we not wait until the man's wife gets here and gives her husband a last kiss?'

'She can kiss my arse for all I care,' replied Major Scallion to the delight of his men, 'he is coming with us.'

'The last regiment that was here did not treat us with such contempt. They would observe a proper respect for the dead.'

'That's why they had five men killed by your thugs. You will find we don't mess around. Leave us alone and we will leave you alone. Give us stick and we will give you ten times as much back in return. My men only respond to the level of violence shown to them. I can tell you now, Father, that we do not intend to go down in history as the company that took the most casualties in Ballymurphy. Get the message across to the thugs that rule this area. Fight us and you will be killed; leave us alone and we will still do our best to kill them!'

This, of course, angered the local population who were more used to the resident battalion in Ballymurphy being scared out of their wits. If they had had any sense they would have read the signs that were there for all to see and backed off. But you can't educate pork, you have to cure it. Looking around them they could see that a ring of steel surrounded them. The gunmen that had taken on 3/3 Charlie had long gone. The IRA doesn't waste their men and weapons in a no-win situation despite the fact they were sworn to defend the area. The gunmen had been dispersed amongst the sprawling housing estate and their weapons had been hidden. It was useless to try and find them at that moment. The priest had one last try at Major Scallion to try and get him to change his mind.

'Will you not let me take the deceased to my chapel?' He asked.

'Not a chance,' replied the Major. 'If you live by the sword, you die by the sword.'

During the month of June the Army Catering Corps lost Private Roger Kealey (22) from Handsworth in Birmingham and the UDR lost Private George Herbert Elliott (39), both in circumstances unknown. Despite the best efforts of the author, the details are simply not forthcoming from any official source. Both men are included on the full ROH for British personnel during the Troubles.

June ended and the grim toll continued to mount; the year was half over and more than 200 people had been killed. 20 soldiers, 2 policemen, including a member of the Garda Siochana (Irish Police), 13 civilians, 4 IRA and 2 Loyalist terrorists died in June. A ceasefire was in operation and there seemed to be hope at last, but it would not last.

CHAPTER SEVEN

JULY

July was only hours old and the optimism which may have been felt by Edward Heath, his Secretary of State for Northern Ireland William Whitelaw, by every decent citizen of Ulster and the soldiers' loved ones began to dissipate. Slade's 'Take Me Back 'Ome' was number one, a neat summation of the wishes of most of the British soldiers engaged in 'peace-keeping' duties.

On 1 July, the UFF abducted and murdered two civilians. These were Daniel Hayes (34) from the Falls Road area, killed in the Shankill Road area, and Paul Jobling (19) who was a student and had arrived in Northern Ireland from Co Durham, England in order to help deprived children. It is thought that he was 'apprehended' at an illegal UDA VCP where he was taken and shot dead and his lifeless body dumped in the Ballygomartin area of Belfast.

The bloody sectarian killings continued and in retaliation, the IRA – despite the ceasefire – abducted and killed two Protestants who had wandered into a Catholic area and presumably asked that most obscene of questions 'Are you Catholic or Protestant?' On the same day, the UFF escalated further and murdered two Catholics. The next day they killed another Catholic, John O'Hanlon (35) and father of six after he had left his home to buy fish and chips. Tony Clarke in his book *Contact* wrote: 'If you aren't an Agnostic already, a trip to Northern Ireland will make you one. How many evils have been committed in this country in the name of religion? How many have been martyred to a senseless cause? The shadows don't answer and the men can't.' (pp107)

One seemingly sectarian abduction and death was that of Samuel Robinson (19) who was apparently shot by trigger-happy Republican vigilantes manning barricades against possible incursions by Loyalist murder gangs. The following account from a UDR soldier speaks of the incident and goes some way towards explaining the circumstances behind it.

A RANDOM DEATH

Alex B, UDR

This has brought me back to those violent, surreal days in July 1972; I was nineteen years old, working in central Belfast since 4 October of the previous year and witnessing terrorist 'incidents', generally of an explosive nature, on an almost daily basis. A fellow Northern Ireland Housing Executive (NIHE) employee was a Protestant youth from the top of the 'Heel n' ankle' (Shankill). Sam Robinson was a Land Acquisition Admin officer in Progressive House HQ. Almost forty years on, brain-fade has dulled some of the details but I can still picture his always-smiling/laughing face. I think he had a notion of a very attractive female tracer in the same section (as did I), and could often be found at her drawing board rather than his own desk.

From memory, I last saw him on 6 July, a Thursday. In work the next morning and the talk was that someone from HQ had been shot, but it was the tracer, in silent tears at her desk, who told me it was Sam and that he was dead. The *Lost Lives* detail is essentially correct, though they have the date of his death as the 6th, whereas the shooting from which he died a few hours later actually occurred in the early hours of the 7th. The story at the time though was that he'd been out with friends in south Belfast, thus their shortest route home would have been Broadway, Falls Road, Springfield Road, and along either Lanark Way or West Circular Road to Ballygomartin. It was supposedly the decision to avoid the ramps at Springfield Road barracks by turning off the Falls into Cavendish Street that got him killed; hit by a trigger-happy vigilante at the barricade their car drove into. The facts, as I only recently discovered from a now-retired NIHE colleague and friend, were even more poignant.

This gentleman, a north Belfast Catholic, also knew Sam, but in an after-work social context. They were both regular patrons of Pat's Bar in the docks area, a 'neutral' venue renowned for its traditional Irish folk music sessions, with local musicians – from both sides of the 'sectarian divide' – playing mainly fiddles, tin-whistles and even a hammered dulcimer; the jigs, reels, airs and laments common to both Irish and Ulster Scots traditions. Sam was there on the night of his death, together with another Shankill Road friend, J★★ P★★★★★. They'd arrived in J★★'s car and their safest, direct route home would have been via Peter's Hill and on to the Shankill, so what were they doing on the Falls?

A mutual friend of theirs was a Catholic musician, not at the bar that night, who lived in the Iris Street/Iris Drive area – off Cavendish Street! They hadn't been near south Belfast, and on leaving Pat's Bar had decided to call on him, but, with 'drink taken', the first J★★ knew of the Cavendish Street barrier was when he clattered into it. The shots followed immediately, fatally wounding Sam, and the vigilantes hauled J★★ out of the car. They went through Sam's pockets for identification, found his driving licence, had the same result with J★★ and with the Shankill addresses presumed they'd caught two UVF men. The next thing their terrified captive heard was the discussion as to where he'd be taken to be shot. His salvation was mentioning the musician's name as the reason for their presence; one of the gunmen knew him, quickly checked out the story and by the time the Army and police arrived everyone had scattered, leaving J★★ with Sam's body in the car.

All this came from my friend, who also knew J★★ and was given the details by him. Thus the 'avoiding the barracks' ramps' reason for their being in Cavendish Street may have been a cover story from the survivor who still had to live in a Loyalist area, where acknowledging his friendship with Catholics mightn't have been good for his health. That latter thought is my own, but Mr P★★★★★ took the emigrant trail and now lives far from the 'Heel 'n ankle'.

Had they not made that decision to call by Cavendish Street would Sam be alive today instead of being just another name on the Troubles' list? That was the first time that death registered with me, though it was never going to be my turn. It's 38 years on as I write this and I'm now 57. Sam will always be a cheerful nineteen-year-old, just as I was in July 1972. Forever young. Who deals life's cards?

On Friday 7 July amidst great secrecy, then IRA and the British government were involved in clandestine talks with a view to ending the mayhem and murder in the Province. Gerry Adams, commander of the IRA's Belfast brigade had been released from detention for the purpose, on the insistence of Seamus Twomey with whom he would battle for most of the latter's political life. He was part of a delegation that went to London for the talks with William Whitelaw and other Northern Ireland Office ministers in the Chelsea home of Mr Paul Channon, then Minister of State for the North. The IRA delegation included Seamus Twomey, Sean MacStiofáin, Dáithí Ó Conaill, Ivor Bell and Martin McGuinness. These were the first talks between the British government and the IRA since David Lloyd George met Michael Collins in 1921.

Posterity has recorded that the IRA wanted to negotiate only one condition: a timetable for the withdrawal of British troops from Ulster. Naturally, the talks failed and the breakdown of the IRA ceasefire finally occurred because of a dispute over the allocation of houses in the Suffolk area of Lenadoon. In this incident, the IRA and the Army became involved in gun battles in Horn Drive, Belfast. The absolute bankruptcy of sectarianism was ably demonstrated by the unedifying sight of Protestant gangs barricading a street in Lenadoon to prevent a Catholic family's removal van from reaching their allotted house. The UDA clearly did their best to inflame an already tense situation to ensure that Catholics trying to move into homes vacated by Protestants did not do so. The Army, somewhat naively were drawn further into the mess and an armoured vehicle rammed the removal van – which had been organised by the Provisionals – and they were perceived as being even more anti-Catholic. At this point some shots rang out, and whilst the Provisionals were the most likely culprits, it was felt by some that the Officials did the firing in order to force their other wing to end the ceasefire.

Elsewhere in the area a soldier was talking peacefully to a Republican delegation, explaining the Army's role, when he was savagely attacked by a man wielding a golf club and terribly injured; with that, the violence erupted again. The failure of the talks led to chief of staff Sean MacStiofáin stating: 'The campaign will be resumed with the utmost ferocity and ruthlessness.'

There was also another tense stand-off in the north of the city, when the Army clashed with the UDA over the thorny issue of barricades and the 'no go' areas. Loyalists had sealed off a large area comprising part of Woodvale close to the predominantly Catholic Springfield Road. This was in addition to their 'permanent' barriers in the Shankill area where they had driven concrete and metal girders into the roadways. Their argument was that if the Republicans could turn places such as Ballymurphy, Turf Lodge and Andersonstown into 'no go' areas, then so could they. It was at this stage that the Army came close to opening fire on Protestants with the orders coming down that it was permitted if soldiers' lives were threatened.

Negotiations took place between a senior Army officer and the leader of the paramilitaries. After a stand-off lasting over four hours, the Protestants eventually toned down their demands but settled on a compromise with the Army and a permanent but moveable barricade was allowed. This was to be manned by UDA members in the sectarian interface areas. Thus peace was restored in a small part of Belfast, but it was, in many ways, simply a pyrrhic victory.

The sectarian killings continued and five more innocents were killed before the IRA killed a Protestant UDA member in Belfast's Markets area. On 9 July Territorial Army (TA) soldier Staff Sergeant Joseph Fleming (29), attached to the Royal Artillery, was killed alongside two fellow Protestants in a car in Little Distillery Street, Belfast. The Army shot and killed another member of Fianna – the IRA's youth wing –and four people were accidentally killed in crossfire in the Springhill/Ballymurphy area. One of these was killed by the IRA and three other civilians were likely shot by the Army in the confusion of a gun battle where over 800 rounds were exchanged. That period of time is remembered in Republican lore as the 'Ballymurphy massacre'. Republicans have exclusively blamed the Army but the truth is that some of the deaths were caused by sectarianism and some were tragic accidents.

On 11 July the Provisional IRA declared the ceasefire at an end although, given the death toll of the previous fortnight, few were surprised. They then detonated a device in Great James Street, Londonderry and when soldiers followed this up, a sniper, positioned at the top of the street, fired a single round into Bombardier Terrence Jones' back. The married man from the Wrexham area was 23 and was attached to an Army medical unit.

On the same day, the UFF were responsible for three sectarian murders including one which the Belfast Coroner described as the 'worst crime to come before the courts'; he said that the UVF represented 'the lowest levels of human depravity.' The men attacked a Catholic house in the Oldpark area, claiming that they had evidence of IRA membership and brutally tortured a fellow Protestant who was lodging in the house, sexually assaulted the householder, a Mrs McClenaghan, before murdering her fourteen-year-old son, David. The Protestant murder gangs demonstrated that they were prepared to sink to the same sickening levels of depravity as were the Provisional IRA. This was after they had abducted, tortured and killed another Catholic Charles Watson (21) in the same area. 11 July ended with two more sectarian killings, one by either side. The same pattern was repeated the following day and then it was the Army's turn to suffer when a Royal Anglian mobile patrol was attacked in Clonard Street in the Falls area.

ON THE ROOFTOP

John Bradley, 23 Engineer Regiment

So I got to watch the Orange Day Parade from the roof top. We started out by building these monster walls so high that the Catholics couldn't see the Orange Men as they marched. We blocked off every street in east Belfast that looked onto the parade route. Then I got up on this roof that looked all the way down the Newtownards Road to the bridge. I sat up there for about four hours, bored out of my head, wondering what the hell I would shoot at if somebody did something stupid. I tried to remember the firing rules. But when I thought about it, I realised I wasn't given any. Maybe I was supposed to shout three warnings like that bloody yellow card said I was supposed to, but nobody would hear me that high up. And how would I know who the villains were? Lots of silly things went through my mind.

I spent a lot of time on the roof tops after that, mostly at night. Other than that, we just went about our business as usual, getting as much sleep as we could between patrols. We discovered we had a huge vantage point from the roof tops at night and were issued with starlight scopes for our SLRs. Trouble was we only had four between the whole company so we never got them sighted to our personal weapons. They were just for observation purposes, which I thought was foolish. I later learned I thought right. For three nights in a row the 20.00hr patrol was fired at whilst walking near Mountpottinger.

They could not see where the shots were coming from but we could from the roof. It was only about 400 yards away. At 22.40hrs that night a lone gunman reached for his pistol and fired blind at our patrol as they came down the street. I knew that if we sighted him in our scope, one of us could get this guy. I begged a Sergeant to let me do it but he said no. I was infuriated by his stupid decision and decided to expose myself as a target just to get the gunman's attention.

I turned out to be the stupid one. I almost got topped myself, exposed up there on that roof, a perfect silhouette against the night sky. My own guys nearly took a pot shot at me from the alley below. I will never forget the radio chatter after that. 'Baz' who was the squad leader that night, nearly pasted me himself when I came down off that roof. Did I ever feel like an idiot, but that bloody gunman never did get caught and I saw him two nights out of the four he was taking shots. It did make everyone twitchy and it got 'Taff' in a lot of trouble over the yellow card.

He was on patrol one night when someone fired a shot at his patrol. Just one shot, but Taff returned fire with fourteen rounds. He blasted at a window where he thought the shot came from without shouting a verbal warning first. The inquiry that followed cost 'Taff' a lot of money as he was fined. He didn't lose a stripe, but he was put through the ringer as to why he shot so many rounds. This was the frustrating part of being in Belfast. It seemed whatever we did was wrong, conflicting with some dumb rule or regulation. We knew how to get these IRA guys but it seemed like nobody wanted to antagonise them, yet it was ok for them to take pot shots at us. It was frustrating and very nerve-wracking. Now I think I know why. The brass use young men for war, who don't need reasons to be there. They follow orders well and without question while the chess game is played by the war-makers, older chaps with the pips on their shoulders. We were young enough not to be afraid because we didn't know what was coming next. It was a total game.

<hr>

On 12 June Lance Corporal Martin Rooney (22) a native of the Irish Republic was hit by a single shot fired by an IRA sniper and died within minutes of being wounded. Just hours later on the 13th, whilst still in the same area, the same regiment (Royal Anglians) lost Corporal Kenneth Mogg (29) who was shot in Dunville Park near the junction between Grosvenor Road and the Falls Road. The park sits on a crossroads in close proximity to the two aforementioned roads and also the Springfield Road. On the same day the UFF abducted and killed a UDR soldier Private Henry Russell (22) simply on the grounds that he was a Catholic. His body was found in the Sydenham area of north-east Belfast; he had been stabbed, beaten and burned with cigarettes. More soldiers were to be killed over the next 36 hours and in this orgy of bloodletting, a Catholic father of four was caught in crossfire when the Army returned fire at Glenview Street in north Belfast; with all the ongoing violence, his death passed almost unnoticed. The toll of dead RRW soldiers continued when Private David Meeke (24) was shot by an IRA sniper on Hooker Street in the Ardoyne as he was about to enter his unit position.

The month wasn't half way through and, since the breakdown of the ceasefire, in Belfast alone thousands of rounds had been fired and 37 people were dead. On the same day that David Meeke was killed, the IRA killed another Protestant at random, this time at Glengormley in the north of the city; Belfast was starting to resemble a battleground.

On the night of 13/14 July in the area of west Belfast alone, in some of the most intense activity witnessed at any stage of the Troubles, almost 6,000 rounds were expended. Second Lieutenant Robert Williams-Wynn (24) from Shropshire was commanding an armoured vehicle in the Lenadoon area of west Belfast when he was shot and killed by an IRA sniper. Shortly afterwards, Fusilier Kenneth Cranham (24) from England's north-east, was shot and killed, very close to where the cavalry officer was hit.

The scene then switched to north Belfast; there was fierce fighting in the Ardoyne area. Royal Corps of Transport (RCT) soldier Peter Heppenstall, described as 'big, tall lad with blond hair' by his RRW comrades to whom he was attached, was shot and killed on foot patrol on Alliance

Avenue. Very close by, the RRW shot and killed James Reid (26) in Eskdale Gardens. Reid was an IRA gunman and a well known 'player' in the area. Tragically, in the crossfire an innocent civilian – Terence Toolan (36) a father of six – was hit and killed by the patrol. He had only left his house in order to check on an elderly relative who lived close by.

Then, in the same street where Meeke had been killed, just hours later, the IRA killed John Williams. Private Williams (22) a Cardigan boy, was the fifth RRW soldier killed in the space of just eight weeks. The Army then shot and killed two IRA gunmen – Louis Scullion (27) and Edward Brady (30) – in gun battles in the Unity Flats and Oldpark areas of north Belfast respectively. The 14th finally ended when the IRA shot Jane Mcintyre (64) outside her own front door as they were aiming at soldiers; in a period of 24 hours, nine people were dead.

The Unity Flats were built on the site of a Victorian slum and work commenced on a complex intended to house both communities in the late 1950s; it was occupied by the first tenants a mere two years before the Troubles erupted. Predominantly Catholic from the onset, it became a very pro-Republican enclave sited close to the equally fierce pro-Loyalist Shankill and as such, it was a focal point for the hatred of the Protestant mobs. It housed over 300 families in its heyday and is now thankfully long demolished.

Brian Feeney in *Insider* writes of the section of Unity which faced the Protestant heartland over a few hundred yards of waste ground. Loyalist thugs would smash the windows with an assortment of missiles, little caring if children or the elderly got in the way. Most of the time the windows were permanently boarded up. There were allegations – substantiated in some accounts – that the mainly Protestant RUC contrived to help Loyalist thugs attack the flats and looked the other way as the perpetrators were given a free hand. It is small wonder that the Unity Flats quickly became a fertile breeding ground for the Provisional IRA.

The Troubles rumbled on further south, and on 15 July, whilst attempting to defuse an IRA landmine concealed in a milk churn near Forkhill, South Armagh, Captain John Young (22) of the EOD was killed instantly when the device exploded. He came from the Basingstoke area.

The killings in north Belfast continued and the youngest policeman to be killed in the Troubles – Constable Robert Laverty (18) – was shot in the head as his vehicle drove down the Antrim Road. Slightly further north at Ligoniel, close to the spot where three off-duty Scottish soldiers had been lured to their deaths a year earlier, a Royal Marines base came under rifle attack. They returned fire at the gunmen as they ran away and John Mooney (17) was hit and fatally wounded. The Marines stated that he was a gunman and some forensic evidence seemed to suggest that that he had been in contact with weapons, but the IRA has never claimed him as one of their own. The reader must draw their own conclusions on the incident.

The day after, an IRA member was killed in Strabane after being hit by rubber bullets, in, according to Republican apologists, 'disputed circumstances'. Tobias Molloy (18), a member of the Official IRA, was hit in the head and killed at a VCP near the Camel's Hump in the Co Tyrone border town in the early hours of Sunday 16 July. Republicans claim that he was returning from a dance across the Irish border whilst the Army maintains that he was involved in rioting near the VCP. Some 24 years later, an IRA memorial was raised in the area bearing Molloy's name. A spokesman stated that 'Britain must be made liable for its war crimes in Ireland.' The author has always been cognisant of the adage 'one man's terrorist is another man's freedom fighter' but the cant and hypocrisy of the IRA and its apologists knows no bounds.

Later in the day, an IRA landmine exploded along the Crossmaglen to Cullyhanna Road in South Armagh. Inside the vehicle was Corporal James Lee (24) from Otley, Yorkshire and

Lance Corporal Terence Graham (24) from Middlesbrough. Both the soldiers from the Duke of Wellington's were killed instantly by the 150lb device.

Forty eight hours passed before the violence resumed, other than sporadic rioting in Catholic areas. The 'Kingos' lost Kingsman James Jones (18), a Liverpool lad, shot in the neck at the Army base in the Vere Foster School on the Ballymurphy estate. The Jones' family suffered a further devastating blow when James' distraught father committed suicide the following month. Two victims for the IRA for the price of a single bullet! That same day, an innocent civilian was hit by IRA bullets as they fired at an Army patrol close to the Ballymurphy estate. Thomas Mills (50) was a night-watchman at a yard on the Ballygomartin Road and was killed an hour after the shooting of Kingsman Jones. The Army expressed immediate and profound regret for the incident and the loss of Mr Mills who was caught in the crossfire between the Army and the Provisionals.

On the 19th Alan Jack – who was only five months old – was killed when an IRA car bomb exploded near Abercorn Square in Strabane. As usual the telephoned warning was either vague or deliberately misleading and the baby, in the company of his mother and five-year-old brother, was caught in the blast. The IRA issued one of their usual statements of regret and claimed that the RUC were lying about the warnings. An RUC spokesman said 'This is the case of the IRA indiscriminately killing an innocent child and then trying to wriggle out of the responsibility for a horrible crime.' The author will make no further comment here as the RUC spokesman's eloquent comments are sufficient.

Barely pausing for breath, the terrorists then attacked a shop on the Springfield Road in Belfast with guns and an explosive device. They killed Leslie Leggett (54) and shot and wounded his wife. They then machine-gunned Harold Gray (71) minutes later as he tried to stop an IRA member planting a bomb at the nearby White Horse Inn. The Leggetts had been one of the few Protestant families living in Springfield Road and they would be among the last as the area became solidly Catholic.

The fateful day of 21 July arrived and with the day only minutes old, a little after midnight, Catholic Anthony Davidson (21) opened his front door. He was a resident in the predominantly Protestant Clovelly Street close to the Springfield Road. Under normal circumstances no one would have opened the door but the caller used the name of one of Davidson's friends and, lulled into a false sense of security, he opened up. As he did so, a masked UFF gunman shot him. He died shortly afterwards. The day had begun badly, but worse was to come.

21 July 1972 will long live in infamy as one of the blackest days in the tragic history of the Troubles; it will be forever known as Bloody Friday. The IRA set off 21 car bombs, killing nine people and injuring 130 on a Friday afternoon when the streets were crammed with shoppers; a day of utter chaos, confusion, panic and violent death. People were literally fleeing from one explosion right into the next. The IRA bombs killed two soldiers – Driver Stephen Cooper (19) of the RCT and Sergeant Philip Price (27) of the Welsh Guards – and an RUC Sergeant, Robert Gibson (45), father of five children. They also killed six civilians, including three teenagers, and managed to kill two of the very community they claimed to defend. Driver Kevin Wright (Royal Corps of Transport) was driving past in a Land Rover when he saw his friend Stephen Cooper and Philip Price on their way to evacuate an area after a bomb warning. He saw them jump out of their vehicle near Queen Elizabeth Bridge to warn the civilians to move. He saw them engulfed in an explosion and killed instantly; the four nearby civilians were also killed in the blast.

Warnings were allegedly given by the IRA via the local media to the security forces before the bombs exploded with 30 minutes' warning given for the first bombing and around 70 minutes warning for the last bomb. The IRA leader, Seán Mac Stíofáin, claimed that the warnings for the two bombs which claimed lives were deliberately disregarded by the British for strategic policy reasons. He also claimed that accurate warnings were given by the IRA; however, they also called in two more hoax warnings, which impeded the evacuation of the area. As a result, the RUC and Army only effectively cleared a relatively small number of areas before the bombs went off. In addition, because of the large number in the confined area of Belfast city centre, people evacuated from the site of one bomb were accidentally moved into the vicinity of others.

Gerry Adams – who has always denied involvement in the planning and execution of the carnage – had this to say years later: 'I do believe that it was legitimate to resort to armed actions and that it was politically defensible.'

'THAT' DAY

Terry Friend, Royal Artillery

On this particular day, several bombs were set off in the centre of Belfast, including the bus station, where images of policemen using shovels to clear away scattered bits of people were shown on the early evening news. And I think that this was probably the closest that I had ever been to an explosion. At the time I was in a shoe shop in North Street, and the whole building shook

Photo taken near Oxford Street bus station, Belfast, during the carnage of the IRA bombings on 'Bloody Friday'. (Belfast Telegraph)

violently from the force of the exploding bombs. I suspect the experience would have been pretty similar to that of being in a building during an earth tremor, or maybe even an earthquake. I was in the downstairs section of the shop, which had long wooden beams across the ceiling. As things quietened down, I noticed that the floor carpet was covered in long straight lines of dust (looking almost like railway lines) running the whole length of the floor. I turned my gaze from the floor to the ceiling and I realised that the vibration of the building had shaken the dust from the beams, where it had fallen to create those very neat lines on the carpet. Amazingly, not one of the plate glass windows of the shop front had shattered!

Bloody Friday: A Chronology

14:10   A car bomb explodes at Smithfield Bus Station, causing extensive damage.

14:16   A 50lb device explodes in a suitcase at the Brookvale Hotel, having been planted by three armed men. The Army had already cleared the area.

14:23   A suitcase bomb explodes outside the railway station on York Road, causing extensive damage.

14:45   Two devices totalling 50lbs explode at a garage on the Crumlin Road.

14:48   A car bomb explodes just outside the Ulsterbus depot in Oxford Street. Despite the Army's best attempts to evacuate civilians, six people are killed more or less instantly. Driver Stephen Cooper (19) of the RCT, from Leicester and Sergeant Phillip Price (27) a Glamorgan man from the Welsh Guards, were killed as they stood by one of the car bombs. Four employees of Ulsterbus were also killed: William Crothers (15); William Irvine (19); Thomas Killops (39); and John Gibson (45).

14:50   A 50lb device explodes outside a branch of the Ulster Bank in Limestone Road, injuring several people.

14:52   A 50lb device explodes in the railway station on Botanic Avenue, causing extensive damage and a few light injuries.

14:55   A car bomb– estimated at over 160lbs – explodes at the Queen Elizabeth Bridge, causing damage but no serious injuries.

15:02   A car bomb explodes on Agnes Street, causing no serious injuries. Almost simultaneously, a 50lb device explodes inside the Liverpool Bar at Donegal Quay, injuring several people, some severely. A bridge on the M2 motorway is hit, injuring several.

15:03   A suitcase bomb explodes at York Street railway station, injuring several people.

15:04   A 50lb car bomb explodes in Ormeau Avenue, causing light injuries.

15:05   A 150lb car bomb explodes outside a garage in Donegall Road, causing extensive damage but no serious injuries. Within seconds, another device explodes in Stewartstown Road and again, there are no serious injuries.

15:15   A 50lb car bomb explodes outside a row of shops in Cavehill Road, a mixed denomination area where Catholics and Protestants have co-existed despite the Troubles. No warning is given. A mother of seven, Margaret O'Hare (37) is killed and her young daughter is badly injured. Brigid Murray (65) is the oldest person to die on the day, and the youngest victim Stephen Parker (14) dies alongside her. There are also many serious injuries.

15:25   A device explodes harmlessly on a railway line at the Lisburn Road.

15:30   A landmine at Nutt's Corner is detonated as a bus packed with schoolchildren drives by; only the quick thinking and skills of the driver save the lives of those on board as he swerves to avoid the blast. Another device explodes outside a mail depot in Grosvenor Road but causes only slight injuries.

15:31   The Army bomb disposal unit safely defuses a device placed on the Sydenham bypass. It is the final bomb of the prolonged attack and the twentieth in 81 minutes.

The RUC thought at first that eight rather than nine people had been killed, as body parts were scattered across such a wide area and it took time to piece them together. Those watching the evening news saw the terrible images of ashen-faced firemen shovelling pieces of human beings into plastic bags. Several days later, shocked observers watched as Belfast's ubiquitous seagulls screamed down to eat something on top of a building near the shattered Oxford Street Ulsterbus depot. Policemen on ladders were horrified to find a badly burned human torso there where it had been blown.

Under a horrifying front page photograph, the following day's *Daily Express* sub-heading read: 'A mother and father try to calm terrified children while beside them a rescuer gives first aid to a bus-station bomb victim.' Their journalist described it as 'one of the most bloody, horrifying disasters I have ever seen.' An eyewitness said:

> People were scrambling everywhere. In the panic they were getting trampled. I rushed to help. One woman was kneeling over a small child crying and sobbing for help. Her face was covered in blood and the child looked lifeless. Through the smoke I saw torn pieces of bodies poking out from between twisted metal, bricks and shattered glass. I thought: 'Oh my God,' and then I was sick. A soldier grabbed me, helped me to my feet and told me to get out quick.

The *Guardian* newspaper described the carnage thus:

> Girls and men wept openly, hugging each other for safety, in the main streets as plumes of smoke rose around them and dull thuds echoed from wall to wall. It was impossible for anyone to feel perfectly safe. As each bomb exploded, there were cries of terror from people who thought they had found sanctuary but in fact were exposed as before.

The Provisionals deliberately selected public transport depots and stations as their main targets for that day, recognising that on a Friday – the busiest shopping day of the week – they would be focal points for passengers returning from the city centre. Because they would attract large numbers of people wishing to travel, the chances of civilian casualties was immensely high; too high in fact, to claim that all their planning was dictated by intent to avoid death or injury. It was always going to be a massacre, and as IRA man Brendan Hughes later wrote, as the explosions finished and he stood guard in Leeson Street armed with an Armalite to cover the returning bombing teams, he felt despair and horror. Whether or not this was some sort of 'death-bed' confession or whether he was trying to distance himself from the carnage is immaterial. He, Adams and Bell were responsible and no amount of contrition can disguise or excuse that. They had planted bombs at the Abercorn Restaurant and Donegall Street. They had seen what their bombs could do to innocent civilians and yet the three took a calculated decision to continue with a foolhardy and irresponsible mass attack.

Another IRA member, Gerry Bradley, commented in an interview with author Brian Feeney: 'all the work we put in to make sure our people were safe and no-one got hurt. The civilians being killed ruined everything. On the Friday morning I thought "brilliant we're highly organised". On the Friday night I thought disaster.' Ones heart truly bleeds for this IRA man because the deaths of those seven civilians – one assumes that he doesn't mourn Price or Cooper – 'ruined' his Friday. This IRA man and the rest of the Provisionals ruined thousands of people's lives, and not just on one Friday in the year. It is indeed interesting – notwithstanding Adams' belated apologies – that the Provisionals, although cognisant of the terror and carnage which they caused, nevertheless continued to use the bomb as a main weapon of terror for the next 25 years. Clearly, as an organisation and as individuals, they were deeply 'affected' by the trauma.

The IRA claimed that the SF contrived to make maximum political capital out of the appalling attacks in order to ease the way for Operation *Motorman* – the clearing of the IRA 'no go' areas. One of the worst kept secrets at the time was that the Army and RUC had planned to destroy the barricades and restore legitimate authority to the areas under nominal IRA control. The operation was scheduled to take place on the very same date that Claudy (see below) happened; only no-one knew that.

Thirty years after the killings, the IRA issued a hollow statement of 'apology'. It included an outlandish claim which would stretch the imagination of even the most sycophantic of their apologists, that there had been no intention to cause civilian casualties. It is a widely believed though unsubstantiated that the IRA commanders responsible for the planning and execution of the appalling attack were Gerry Adams, Ivor Bell and Brendan Hughes. The British media appear to have only just latched on to the possibility that Adams was the Belfast commander of the Provisional IRA and actions committed by their ASUs had first to be approved by him. The source: a disgruntled former PIRA foot soldier! What a surprise. Thousands of soldiers knew that back in the early 1970s. Gerry Adams had raised the profile of the Belfast IRA to such an extent that the traditional HQ of the organisation – Dublin – was totally subjugated by the upstarts in the north. Indeed 'D' Company based in the Falls area was virtually running the show at one stage with Adams as the OC and architect of the terror, according to Brendan Hughes. Indeed, Adams' former right hand man stated categorically that he (Adams) was the prime mover behind the decision and planning of Bloody Friday.

In Ed Maloney's book *Voices From The Grave*, Hughes talks about his feelings on the day, standing in Leeson Street, listening to the thump of the bombs exploding nearby. He described his thoughts as having come to a sudden realisation that they had gone too far, that they had stretched the Army beyond its capacity to cope. If the plan had been to simply terrorise, to destroy commercial property rather than kill and maim, why didn't the terrorists plan an attack that would just cause chaos?

One other name needs to be brought to the fore here – Seamus Twomey. Born in Belfast, Twomey lived in Sevastopol Street in the Falls district. Known as 'Thumper' owing to his apparently uncontrollable temper and habit of banging his fist on tables, he received little education and was a bookmaker's 'runner'. In 1969, he was prominent in the establishment of the Provisional IRA, and by 1972 he was the OC of PIRA's Belfast Brigade when it launched its bomb blitz on the city, including Bloody Friday. In addition to the Maloney revelations, in a recently-published posthumous memoir, the late Brendan 'Darkie' Hughes alleged that the leadership of the Belfast Brigade of the IRA during the 1970s was largely in the hands of Twomey, Bell, Hughes and Adams, with 'Thumper' as the nominal boss.

Twomey was described variously by several people as being 'uniquely revolting ... crass, ignorant and bullying'. He blamed the British for absolutely everything and anything, citing the perfidy of Albion for each act of violence during the Troubles. He refused to believe that the Ulster Protestants didn't want a united Ireland or that the slaughter at McGurk's bar was carried out by any group other than uniformed British soldiers. He was also described as a man 'indoctrinated in the ways of death, who had repeatedly and casually caused men to be murdered ... whose deeds meant nothing to him' (*Watching The Door* pp90-91).

By the time of Bloody Friday however, according to Hughes' account in *Voices From The Grave*, the de-facto leader was a young Gerry Adams, veteran Twomey having been increasingly marginalised by the three young guns. This, however, doesn't lessen Twomey's responsibility – or enthusiasm – for the bloodshed, not only on that fateful day, but throughout the so-called 'commercial' bombing campaign. Brendan Hughes talks of Gerry Adams' role in the slaughter of that day and rues his former comrade's refusal to acknowledge his IRA past. He mentions Adams' conduct during a riot against soldiers: 'I can't remember if he threw anything but he certainly directed everybody else to do it.'

PIRA member Peter McMullen, a former soldier who had deserted from the British Army gave a detailed account of Adams's involvement in Bloody Friday. McMullen who was in Adams' 'D' Company claimed that Adams attended several brigade meetings prior to Bloody Friday where 'all the details were discussed and all the plans were made out.' McMullen said that at a final meeting the day before the attack Adams said that he was concerned about the routes to and from the bombing. The purpose of Bloody Friday, according to McMullen, was to cripple Belfast and Northern Ireland economically. He has since said that the possibility of loss of life was never discussed at the time. 'The whole operation was discussed afterwards, but I don't think anybody who was there showed any remorse.'

Following Bloody Friday, the *Belfast Telegraph* stated:

> This city has not experienced such a day of death and destruction since the German blitz of 1941. With the callous lack of remorse now so typical of the Provos they audaciously accepted responsibility for what was an operation clearly requiring considerable planning and manpower.

Some years after the event, Tommy Gorman, one of the top IRA bomb makers said: 'It was a terrible, terrible day. A blot on any kind of glory you try to make in this sort of struggle. I am utterly, utterly ashamed.'

Speaking in the Commons on 24 July, Home Secretary William Whitelaw called the bombings 'appallingly bloodthirsty'. He also drew attention to the Catholic victims, and mentioned the revulsion in the Republic of Ireland as elsewhere. The Leader of the Opposition Harold Wilson, who as Prime Minister had sent troops into Northern Ireland almost three years previously, described the events as 'a shocking crime against an already innocent population.' The *Irish Times* wrote: 'The chief injury is not to the British Army, to the Establishment or to big business but to the plain people of Belfast and Ireland. Anyone who supports violence from any side after yesterday's events is sick with the same affliction as those who did the deed.'

Almost exactly 30 years after the slaughter, on 16 July 2002, the Provisional IRA issued a statement of apology in *An Phoblacht* (*Republican News*) which read in part:

Sunday 21 July marks the 30th anniversary of an IRA operation in Belfast in 1972 which resulted in nine people being killed and many more injured. While it was not our intention to injure or kill non-combatants, the reality is that on this and on a number of other occasions that was the consequence of our actions. It is therefore appropriate on the anniversary of this tragic event, that we address all of the deaths and injuries of non-combatants caused by us. We offer our sincere apologies and condolences to their families.

Later that same night, a Loyalist terror gang knocked at the front door of a house in the Oldpark area where a Catholic family – the Rosatos – lived. Unwisely opening the door, Joseph (59) realised his mistake and slammed it shut but his murderers fired through the door hitting and fatally wounding him. Seventy people had now been killed in the worst ever month of the Troubles to date.

The Army was involved in a gun battle with the IRA the following morning in Henrietta Street in the Markets area of Belfast and returned fire using their customary SLR 7.62mms. As any weapons expert will attest, the SLR fires a high velocity round at 2,700 feet per second and a wound from such a round has a devastating effect on its target. Joseph Downey (25) a member of the Provisional IRA was shot with a low-velocity weapon that day and it is highly unlikely therefore that he was killed by the Army. Downey, described as a 'simpleton', was swept along by the waves of support for the Provisionals. With the depraved Loyalist murder gangs terrorising the nationalist areas, murdering at random, who can blame the Catholics for their wholehearted support of 'their' group of murder gangs?

Downey had been unfairly arrested by the RUC on the Short Strand earlier in the year and had been inexorably drawn into the ranks of the PIRA. Armed with a gun and totally untrained, he had been dispatched against the Army or even against Loyalists and had become yet another 'martyr'. There are many similarities between the godfathers of the IRA and the extremist mullahs of Al Qaeda.

That day continued in the same vein when Catholics Patrick O'Neil (26) and Rose McCartney (27) – a well known local singer – were abducted and murdered by the UFF. The same group then abducted another Catholic in the Ardoyne area and savagely beat him and then shot him. His name was Francis Arthurs (34) from the Falls Road area. To reach the Ardoyne from the Falls Road involves crossing the Shankill Road in the Protestant/Loyalist heartland. It was yet another tragic example of being in the wrong place at the wrong time.

On 23 July, off duty UDR soldier Private Robert McComb (22) from the Shankill area was attacked by IRA gunmen near the Crumlin Road and shot in the head, dying shortly afterwards.

During the same evening, Loyalists threw a bomb into a Catholic bar and George Bunning (73) died from a heart attack brought on by the attack; killed by Loyalists as surely as if he had died in the blast. Two more innocent Catholics were killed on the 24th before an IRA sniper shot Kingsman Brian Thomas (20) at the Vere Foster School in the 'Murph. It is thought that a sniper was regularly operating in the area from a high vantage point in the Bullring on the estate and had a clear line of sight into the OP the Army was using.

The IRA killed another Protestant near the Grosvenor Road in Belfast and the UFF retaliated by torturing and murdering three more Catholics. Two of the men were Frank Corr (52) and James McGerty (26); Corr was shot six times and McGerty three. The latter was still alive when the Loyalists set his body alight.

On 26 July the IRA shot and killed Marine Leonard Allen (22) who was serving with 40 Commando in Belfast. His unit was supervising an Orange Order march in the vicinity of the Unity Flats when an IRA sniper, using a German Luger pistol, fired one round which grazed another Marine's head before hitting the Newcastle-upon-Tyne man.

The 27th saw two Catholics killed at random by Loyalists and one Protestant by the IRA. On the 28th, the Army shot and killed a member of the IRA in the New Lodge Road, Belfast after soldiers saw him aim a rifle towards a nearby Protestant high rise block of flats. James Cassidy (22) was described by Republican sources as a member and section leader in the Belfast Brigade of the Provisionals.

Since very early on in the conflict, the Republicans had been sealing off their major areas and excluding the authorities from entering Catholic communities. Areas of Belfast such as the

Sniper on Londonderry's Walls; probably a unique photograph. WO Haydn Davies, Royal Regiment Of Wales, moves to his OP overlooking the Bogside.

Ballymurphy estate, Andersonstown, Turf Lodge as well as some parts of Twinbrook and the Creggan in Londonderry had become 'no-go areas'. The RUC and the Army entered at their own risk and although there were incursions – generally at night – by armed patrols, the Army was content to contain them. There were rent strikes against the local Protestant-controlled city council and 'order' was maintained by armed gangs of IRA members. Generally masked or wearing balaclavas, these men controlled what became known as IVCPs (illegal vehicle checkpoints). There was no rule of law within these areas, only the 'law' the IRA administered. Kneecappings were common as was 'tarring and feathering'.

The Army made several nocturnal incursions and in one such incident, a patrol of the Royal Green Jackets was ambushed and an officer on attachment received dreadful leg injuries, eventually losing the limb. The Heath government rightly viewed the no-go areas as unacceptable and the fact that the rule of law did not apply to certain parts of the United Kingdom could only be tolerated for so long. Amidst great secrecy, the Army's long awaited operation was put into action.

Operation *Motorman* started at 04:00 on 31 July 1972 to retake the no-go areas mainly in the Catholic areas in Londonderry and Belfast but also in some Protestant areas. The operation used almost 22,000 soldiers – 27 infantry and two armoured battalions – aided by over 5,000 UDR soldiers and several Centurion AVRE demolition vehicles; these were the only heavy tanks to be deployed operationally by the Army in Northern Ireland during the Troubles. The tanks had been transported to Northern Ireland on board the amphibious landing ship HMS *Fearless*, and were operated with their demolition guns pointed to the rear, covered with tarpaulins.

OP MOTORMAN

Trooper Terry Maguire, 16th/5th The Queen's Royal Lancers

I think it was around August 1971, when we were sent out to Ulster and we started ops in the Omagh area with armoured cars; Ferrets, Saracens and Saladins. The Saladin wasn't of any great use so we basically parked them up and only used them as a last resort. It was obvious that a 76mm gun would be a little bit of an overkill in this environment!

Our role was in essence provision of border patrols, mobile VCPs, fast response to incidents etc. We had a troop of four Ferrets on immediate notice to move round the clock seven days a week. The Saracens tended to work in pairs with or as a single vehicle attached to a Ferret troop. This would give an extra eight men to support the Ferrets at a big VCP or on culvert clearance duties and at that time we were involved with supporting the Royal Engineers with their border cratering and Dragons teeth placements. Our main areas of operation were County Tyrone and County Fermanagh.

Anyway, August arrived and we got wind of something big. When it all happened, there was very few hours notice to move regarding Operation *Motorman*. I can't remember exactly but we obviously had time to get our gear together and drive from Omagh to Londonderry. What was strange was the sudden influx of sand-coloured Saracens that seemed to appear out of nowhere which we were to use. I was appointed 'shotgun' on the Squadron Leader's vehicle. I sort of remember that we were held up outside of Londonderry at some ungodly hour before being allowed in. What does stick in my mind is that I remember the radio traffic being very busy that day as we waited for the kick off.

As we moved into the Bogside I remember rounds hitting the side of the Saracen and they were just dull thuds. I don't think I was too scared but I was certainly concerned about someone taking pot shots at us. We stopped at one point, whilst I believe one of the 'Cent Dozers' was doing its thing. [Centurion tanks were fitted with bulldozer blades to remove barricades and were the only tanks deployed during the Troubles.] Then we moved off towards the Creggan Estate, where we were to set up an operational base at a school whose name evades me. From this location the Squadron carried out patrols in and around the Bogside with the usual detritus thrown at the vehicles, and in some cases large chunks of concrete from the rooftops. I recall one incident when the crew of a Ferret were trapped inside as they could not open the top hatch due to the damage caused. The crew were forced to withdraw from the area to sort out the problem. Gunshots were fired from a church tower; rounds were returned and someone, not from the military, was injured.

It then becomes a little unclear, but there were small riots and skirmishes to end the day; I seem to have locked the rest out of my mind until we returned to Omagh a couple of days later. We returned to normal patrolling in our Ferrets and back to the rain, cold and mist.

Two youths, one certainly a member of the IRA and the other an alleged member were killed in the Creggan Estate in Londonderry during Operation *Motorman*. Daniel Hegarty (15) died immediately, shot alongside two other men who were wounded. IRA member Seamus Bradley (19) was shot shortly afterwards died of his wounds.

By the end of the day *Motorman* was a success; nowhere in the Province was closed to the Army or RUC. New tactics emerged; schools such as Vere Foster in the 'Murph, St Teresa's in Andersonstown and meeting halls such as Henry Taggart Memorial in New Barnsley were occupied by the Army. The Army also placed fortified and reinforced sangars on many street corners, making it very difficult for the IRA and those who carried their explosives and weapons to move around freely. Unity Flats was virtually sealed off and the one road which remained open to vehicles was the subject of a permanent VCP. This was good news for the SF but tragedy was close at hand.

The village of Claudy in Co Londonderry sits to the west of the A6 road which takes over when the M22 Belfast to Londonderry motorway peters out, six or seven miles from Antrim, and is the same distance from the Waterside which denotes the start of the city of Londonderry or Derry depending on one's stance. Main Street – where the IRA left three car bombs – is a stone's throw from Glenshane Road which then loops back to the main A6.

At approximately 10.22 on the morning of Monday 31 July, the horrors which faced its big brother cities of Londonderry and Belfast were visited upon the sleepy little village. The first device exploded near a petrol station, instantly killing Elizabeth McElhinney (59), Joseph McCluskey (39) and Kathryn Eakin (9). Kathryn Eakin was cleaning the windows of the family grocery store when the bombs exploded. The blast fatally wounded Rose McLaughlin (32) a mother of eight children, Patrick Connolly (15) and Arthur Hone (38); the three died on the 3rd, 8th and 13 August respectively.

Some fifteen minutes later, a second one detonated at the front entrance of the Beaufort House hotel in Church Street. This was the road along which the survivors and uninjured from the first explosion had been directed to apparent safety by RUC officers based in the village's barracks, following the discovery of another suspicious-looking vehicle further down Main Street. David Miller (60), James McClelland (65) and William Temple (16) were killed in this second blast. The latter, who had been helping on a milk delivery, had been slightly injured in the first blast, but had continued to work. The policemen's suspicion of the other car in Main Street was confirmed when it too disintegrated mere seconds later but, with that area having been cleared, there were no further casualties. The nine dead were made up of five Catholics and four Protestants.

Mrs Mary Hamilton owned the Beaufort House hotel with her husband, and had no doubt about the motivation for the bombings. 'I think it was the IRA. They planted bombs outside Eakin's shop, the post office and our hotel. Those were three prominent Protestant businesses in the town. But they denied it because they were afraid of the number of Catholics who had been killed.' The Claudy hotelier, who later moved to Londonderry, said she had vivid memories of the day. She had just stopped work for a cup of coffee with her friend Annie Miller when the bombs started exploding. After the bomb at her hotel, the two women ran outside to find Annie's husband's horribly mutilated body. 'The only way Mrs Miller could identify him was by the buttons she had sewn on his coat that morning.'

Seconds before the hotel blast claimed his life, William Temple had told Mary of his own narrow escape from the first bomb. She told the author that she also believes that had the car at the Beaufort not been parked directly over a main sewer manhole cover there would have been many more fatalities. In her opinion, the manhole chamber and sewer absorbed much of the estimated 250lb explosive's energy.

Both the Official and Provisional IRA denied any responsibility, but as Mandy Rice-Davies once nearly said: 'Well, they would say that wouldn't they?' When I quizzed an Irish Republican as to why Claudy had happened, he simply replied: 'We did make mistakes sometimes!'

Did the Provisional IRA carry out the attacks? I believe that they did, not just through my own sources, but because it bore their hallmark. Could it have been a splinter group, carrying out an independent attack because they felt that the IRA's 'Army Council' was going soft with talk of ceasefires and secret negotiations with the British government? Clearly both are possibilities but I believe that it was an IRA operation and that they intended to devastate a 'soft' target just to give the authorities further evidence of their power. I do not believe that it was their intention to kill civilians that day. It is true, nonetheless, that the IRA and INLA killed more Catholics than the British Army did over the course of the Troubles; shabby work by the so-called defenders of the Catholic community.

I believe that the reason for the shameful murders of innocents on both sides of the sectarian divide in such a place as Claudy was probably more prosaic. The IRA, although guilty of misleading and vague warnings in the past may have tried to give adequate notice but somewhere along the chain of command and among those designated to alert the authorities something went wrong. At the inquest into the deaths, the RUC stated that the bombers had tried to give warnings by telephone, but Dungiven, the area designated to make the calls had only unusable public telephone boxes due to bomb damage at the GPO exchanges. Apparently a sympathiser was then ordered to go into the RUC station in Dungiven to give a verbal warning, but by then it was too late for the nine people killed. Dungiven is about ten miles from Claudy.

To date no organisation has come forward to admit culpability and there is still much controversy over the involvement of a local Catholic priest. A Republican source confirmed the latter's involvement to the author, saying he was in part responsible for the planning and execution of the mass murder. In December 2002, the British *Independent* newspaper revealed:

The British Government and the Catholic Church were involved in an astonishing cover-up to shield a priest suspected of heading an IRA team responsible for one of Northern Ireland's worst bomb atrocities, police said today. Just months after the July 1972 attack on the village of Claudy, Co Londonderry, which left nine people dead, including three children, it has been alleged that the then Northern Ireland Secretary William Whitelaw and Cardinal William Conway, the Catholic Primate of all Ireland, discussed the outrage and the activities of the priest.

The priest, who was never questioned about the murders, was later transferred across the Irish border to Co Donegal before dying of cancer in 1980. Papers obtained by detectives who reviewed the original police investigation have revealed that an unnamed senior officer and the Northern Ireland Office were also aware of the priest's identity, according to Assistant Chief Constable Sam Kinkaid, who ordered the re-examination earlier this year. As he made today's dramatic new disclosures, he refused to name the priest.

But the identity of the cleric has already been revealed as Father Jim Chesney, who at the time was based in south Derry, not far from Claudy, where three car bombs exploded without warning. The Provisionals consistently denied any part in the attack, but the emergence of papers and letters exchanged between the Government and Church have left security chiefs and victims' relatives in no doubt that Chesney and the IRA were definitely involved, and that he was allowed to go free even though he was clearly a prime suspect.

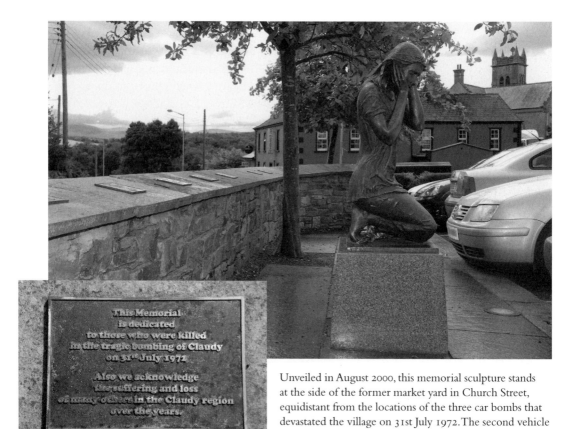

This Memorial is dedicated to those who were killed in the tragic bombing of Claudy on 31st July 1972

Also we acknowledge the suffering and loss of many others in the Claudy region over the years.

Unveiled in August 2000, this memorial sculpture stands at the side of the former market yard in Church Street, equidistant from the locations of the three car bombs that devastated the village on 31st July 1972. The second vehicle had been parked at the front entrance of the Beaufort Hotel, the grey building in the background.

Main Street, Claudy, looking east from the front of Eakin Brothers' garage. The first device to explode was parked just before the entry on the left of the street.

Claudy today. Taken from approximately the same spot in front of Eakin's garage, thought to be a target for one of the three devices. The premises and its staff survived because a tanker was making a fuel delivery when the first car, allegedly driven by Fr Chesney, arrived and could only park farther down the street from the garage, at what is now the gap between the red-brick houses and Dan's Bar – McElhinney's pub, shop and fuel pumps in 1972. The grocery shop where Kathryn Eakin died was on the right beyond the white van and the junction with Church Street. The red building with the clock tower is named 'Eakin's Corner'.

The Beaufort, Church Street and the former market yard with the memorial and its protective wall just visible at the centre-right edge of the frame; and on 31 July 1972 (inset).

At the time of writing, a new report by the Northern Ireland Ombudsman was published. BBC Ireland correspondent Mark Simpson was quoted as stating that: 'the report is expected to confirm that the authorities at the time were aware of the suspected involvement of a priest in the atrocity – but failed to arrest him … instead, a secret deal was done between the Catholic Church and the state to move Father Jim Chesney across the border into County Donegal.' Amongst the allegations was a claim that Chesney drove one of the car bombs into Claudy and actually parked next to the youngest victim, Kathryn Eakin. People of the village itself have always maintained that there was a cover-up and that the families of the dead have been denied justice. The Bishop of Londonderry, Neil Farren, responding to rumours that Father Chesney was a member of the South Derry Brigade of the IRA and may have been involved in the bombings, called him in for questioning.

In 2002, Bishop Farren's successor, Edward Daly, told the BBC that Chesney had denied any involvement with the IRA. However, he did tell his superiors that he had 'very strong Republican sympathies'. If the Ombudsman's report does substantiate the cover up, it will be a major embarrassment for the Catholic Church.

It is further alleged that he (Chesney) was both QM and Ops Officer of the south Derry PIRA Brigade. Some years after the atrocity, and prior to the aforementioned report, on Sunday 22 December 2002, the *Sunday Observer* reported:

Calls have been made for a full public inquiry into the role of clergymen in terrorism after the *Observer* learnt that three more priests were involved with the Provisional IRA at the time of the 1972 Claudy bomb massacre. One of the priests was the IRA's officer commanding the Provos' North Antrim Brigade. He cannot be named for legal reasons.

The other priests who joined the IRA at the beginning of the Ulster Troubles were Father Patrick Fell and Father John Burns. Fell served more than 10 years in an English jail over a conspiracy to cause explosions in Coventry during the early Seventies. He was convicted alongside Frank Stagg and Michael Gaughan, two IRA men who died on hunger strike in English prisons.

On his release Fell, like the priest who bombed Claudy, Father James Chesney, was allowed to serve as a priest in a rural parish in Donegal. In 1972, Burns disappeared from his parish at St Theresa's Catholic Church in the Possilpark area of Glasgow. He fled back to Ireland after Strathclyde police raided his home searching for weapons and explosives. He was given sanctuary by fellow priests but later left the priesthood.

The role of the priests emerged following revelations that the Catholic hierarchy and the British Government colluded to cover-up the involvement of Chesney in the Claudy atrocity. Chesney was a member of the IRA unit that left three 'no warning' bombs in the Co Derry village in July 1972. Nine people including three children were killed. Chesney's involvement in the massacre was discussed at a private meeting in December 1972 between

Looking west along Main Street, opposite the spot where the third device exploded. Eakin's grocery shop was on the left by the white van and Eakin Brothers' garage is the last building on the right at the head of the street.

This view, taken a few yards west of the vantage point in the photo on page 149, gives some idea of the devastation caused by the third device.

the first Northern Ireland Secretary William Whitelaw and Cardinal William Conway, leader of Ireland's Catholics. Documents found by police showed that Whitelaw and Conway were both aware of Chesney's activities. A briefing note was sent by a senior official at the Northern Ireland Office to police headquarters the next day.

Assistant Chief Constable Sam Kincaid – the officer currently investigating Claudy – said the letter states that the cardinal mentioned the possibility of transferring the priest to Donegal. By January 1973 'intelligence suggested he was working there'. Chesney was actually transferred to a parish at Malin Head, in Co Donegal across the border. He died of cancer in 1980. At the time of writing a prominent community activist in Derry has called for the resignation of the Catholic hierarchy in Ireland. Proinsias O'Mianain, a leading figure in the Irish language movement and a Catholic, also demanded a public inquiry. 'These people should have been reported to the police as soon as their murderous activities came to light. But instead the Church just moved them to remote parishes in the Irish Republic … and then engaged in a conspiracy of silence which blocked investigations.' David Trimble, the Ulster Unionist leader, also called for a Bloody Sunday-style inquiry into the Claudy bombing which he said would reveal the role of other priests in terrorism. As this book goes to press, the PSNI's Historic Enquiries Team has announced that families of the Claudy bombing victims are being contacted and asked if they wish to be involved in a review of the case. It follows widespread dissatisfaction expressed regarding the content and findings of the Police Ombudsman's Report released on 24 August 2010, especially its limited terms of reference focusing on the supposed failings of the RUC enquiry and the police force allegedly conspiring in the decision not to arrest Father Chesney.

There is a school of thought that suggests, in the interests of reconciliation, that Gerry Adams and Martin McGuinness and other leading Sinn Féin politicians also be interrogated regarding the atrocity. After all, since they are now alleged men of peace they would have no problem volunteering whatever information they may have. Sinn Féin, incidentally, was an illegal organisation though still the 'public' and political face of the Provisionals. It wasn't until 24 April 1974 that the then Secretary of State for Northern Ireland, Merlyn Rees, saw fit to lift all legal prohibition. Suddenly they became 'respectable'.

July had finally ended, and a total of 97 people had lost their lives in what was the bloodiest month of the conflict; that total could well have been 100, but three of the Claudy victims died of their terrible injuries the following month. The Army lost nineteen soldiers, the RUC lost two officers and the terrorists were hit as well; the IRA lost eleven and the Loyalists lost two. Civilian losses were 62; of those, 35 were killed in purely random sectarian killings, simply for belonging – nominally or otherwise – to the 'wrong' church or living in the 'wrong' area. Loyalist terror gangs killed twenty Catholics and the IRA killed fifteen Protestants.

In all of the carnage and chaos that was July in Ulster in 1972, few, other than his comrades and loved ones, noticed the death of Major Eric Beaumont (57) of the UDR who died in circumstances unknown on 25 July.

CHAPTER EIGHT

AUGUST

During this month, a total of 24 soldiers would lose their lives, surpassing the losses in Aden in June 1967 during the Police mutiny at Khormaksar. Elsewhere the Munich Olympics began; Mark Spitz won the first of his seven gold medals but tragedy was just around the corner as Arab terrorists were plotting a slaughter. In music, Alice Cooper's anarchic 'School's Out' was the number one in the United Kingdom; in Northern Ireland with the school summer holidays in full swing, it just meant more thugs, only younger ones, were out rioting and confronting the squaddies.

The 'economic' bombing campaign continued and Bloody Friday and all the dress rehearsals for the big day had taken their toll. Much of the city centre was a ghost town at night; running a bar or a restaurant was commercial suicide as the locked security gates made entry next to impossible.

The shooting war continued unabated and one battalion commander with its TAOR on the Lower Falls reported that in a 21-day period in August, it had had 21 members wounded by IRA bullets. During this three-week period, the gunmen had fired 2,500 rounds at the soldiers on the ground. The scenarios were almost identical; a crowd of rioters throwing stones or petrol bombs would suddenly part and a gunman would open fire and then the ranks would close again. A sure sign of such an ambush was the sudden ushering of children back into their houses by concerned parents. The call of: 'Sir, they're taking the children indoors' was enough to set soldiers' nerves on edge.

The first to die in August was Private Irvin Bowen (18) of the 'chunkies' (Royal Pioneer Corps) who was killed in an RTA on the second of the month. In the very early hours of Thursday 3 August, a soldier observed Robert McCrudden (19) an IRA gunman near Butler Street in the Ardoyne; he was shot and died at the scene. The IRA man, who received a full Republican funeral, was described as being killed on 'active service'. Yet another young man dead, hundreds more to follow and the end of the Troubles still more than two decades away.

Some hours later, near Strabane, EOD soldier Sergeant Major William Clark (34), a father of four from Scotland was alerted by a unit from the RWF to a suspect device at Sion Mills. Having opened it with a controlled explosion, he went back to examine it more closely; it detonated, killing him instantly.

Opposite: Royal Green Jacket VCP thrown up in a Belfast street. These VCPs were designed to catch fleeing gunmen and halt the movement of arms and explosives around the cities and towns.

JAMAICA STREET SHOOTING

Lieutenant David Ash, Light Infantry

We were out on daylight foot patrols in the Ardoyne when Private Pearson got a bullet in the thigh; he was my first casualty. IRA snipers were clearly still at work in the area, or perhaps there were whole units slowly returning to resume operations, now the dust had settled after *Motorman*.

Our foot patrols were now a bit more business-like than last year and we only went in with a minimum of two sections working in mutual support. I was patrolling south with a section through the waste ground between Etna Drive and Jamaica Street, while Sergeant Spracklen moved with a second section parallel with me down Berwick Road. Suddenly shots rang out somewhere ahead of me; the unmistakable 'crack, crack, crack' of high velocity shots. But in these streets it was impossible to tell where the shooting was coming from. You get rapid weapon reports in one direction, then rapid echoes split seconds later in the opposite direction. The sounds tend to merge, making it impossible to distinguish the echoes from the actual shots. At the same time you get the whip-crack of bullets coming past you. But which way are they going?

It was fairly obvious the gunman was ahead of me on this occasion, and probably firing at Sergeant Spracklen's patrol and I immediately doubled my patrol forward to try and outflank the gunman. Then Spracklen's voice called urgently over the radio: 'Crash call! Crash call! Crash call! Junction Berwick Road and…' I raced across Etna Drive to the location; the shooting had stopped, and young Pearson lay in a front garden, combat trousers dark red with wet blood. A small crowd gathered on the street, and some people were running over with blankets and bandages. A woman said 'The bastard escaped over the wall,' referring to the sniper. Another woman urged people to form a protective barrier around Pearson. 'Gather round so they can't shoot again,' she said. A third woman jeered at Pearson as he lay there and sneered 'Pity he never did the job properly,' and spat at him. A man in the crowd immediately punched her in the face.

Pearson didn't seem to be in pain and said 'Looks like you've lost one of your Angels, sir,' [the platoon called themselves 'Ash's Angels']. His face was completely grey. A black-suited Catholic priest came running over, but Pearson cried out 'Get that fucking priest away from me!' The priest was told his services weren't required. Then a Knights of Malta ambulance turned up and began unloading stretchers. Sergeant Spracklen led the medics over to Pearson. The IRA used Knights of Malta ambulances for their own casualties, and if Pearson was taken away by them he'd effectively be in an IRA ambulance, and there's no telling where he might have ended up!

Eventually, our own ambulance appeared and it transpired that the RMO [Regimental Medical Officer] had got lost trying to find us. Spracklen lost his cool and yelled at me in exasperation: 'Which fucking ambulance, sir?!'

I told him to get Pearson into our own regimental ambulance, and the RMO went to work; the Knights of Malta went on their way. We restored order without drawing any further sniper fire, and continued patrolling.

———————

On the fourth, a foot patrol from 1RGJ was crossing an open field in Andersonstown when an IRA sniper opened fire from a house in Bearnagh Drive. Lance Corporal David Card (21) from Portsmouth and to the author's best recollection, a Pompey fan was hit in the neck and fatally wounded. To his Jacket comrades, pinned down by accurate sniper fire, it was incredibly distressing not to be able to save their comrade's life and he died shortly afterwards.

OLD BEFORE THEIR TIME

Rifleman 'W', Royal Green Jackets

I remember that area so well; the 'Murph, Turf Lodge and of course Andersonstown, or 'Andytown' as we called it. Some of the housing was quite decent and you could see that the tenants had done their best to 'tart' it up a bit, but there were those who really didn't give a damn at all. I remember seeing old Vauxhall Vivas up on bricks, no tyres, just a pile of bricks under each wheel arch, no doubt somebody's pride and joy at some time. No doubt that one day, the owner intended to do the car up but in the meantime, they were beginning to rust.

The people there must have been, at some stage, decent people but years of sectarian hatred, permanent unemployment, kids always in trouble with the 'pol-is', always behind on the rent and the weekly payments to the tallymen had made them old and bitter. We did a check on this woman in the Ardmonaghs just off Norglen Road and I looked inside the pram she was pushing. PIRA used them to move weapons about hoping the squaddie was soppy, or missing his own kids enough to turn a deaf 'un. Anyway, I asked her for her name and DOB, thinking that this was this sprog's Grandma because she looked 60. When she gave it to me, I did a bit of mental arithmetic and worked it out that she was 30-odd. I said something like: 'Come on Mrs, you're 60 or I'm a fucking Chinaman!' I can't remember what she said, but I saw a look in her face, even at 21, I could recognise and still haunts me to this day. It was midway between contempt for me and a sorrow that at 30-odd, she looked like an OAP. Even today at almost the same age that I thought she was, 60, I still feel a pain in my heart and a tear or two will form in my eyes as I remember that look that she gave me. I said: 'Piss off; on your way' and I remember thinking that my mother had never brought me up that way!

There was always trouble on the 'Turf' and Andytown and we lost a lad – Davie Card – there in August. I always remember that the lads who were there were in tears and it was tears of rage because they were trying to save him, but they were pinned down by the sniper and rounds were flying everywhere. Whenever we got one of them bastards, there was always some RC priest kneeling over him, saying all sorts of prayers for his 'eternal salvation' but our lads died with his mates screaming 'Fight it mate' or 'Fucking stay with me mate!'

We would often see men around the shops and that, and we would know from the INT photos that they were known players, some of whom we could lift and others that we couldn't. I was a Rifleman, right on the lowest rung of the ladder and maybe I wasn't that bright, but I couldn't understand why we were told to leave some of them alone; why couldn't we lift them or better, slot the bastards?

Sometimes we would drive up the Whiterock Road from the Springfield Road and we knew that the bricks would start flying at us as soon as we passed the walls of the City Cemetery to our left. The little twats used to hide behind there with a pile of rocks and then jump up and pelt us as we drove past and one day, I saw a mate get hit in the cheek by a piece of house brick or something. He went white straight away before he recovered a bit and started spitting blood and little white chips of teeth out. Someone stuck a shell dressing on his face and he was taken off to the hospital with an armed escort.

Sometimes the bastards would gather on this big patch of grass between the cemetery and the houses of the 'Turf' and they would throw whatever they could get their hands on; rocks, bottles and so on and they always had a steady supply of petrol bombs. Some of the

Photo of Recce Platoon of the Royal Green Jackets at a Belfast base.

lads used to joke that there must be a factory on the 'Turf where they manufactured the bloody things.

I went back recently and nothing has really changed except that they have these professionally drawn murals depicting the fucking IRA as heroes. I saw them close up and personal and I saw what they did to those who either opposed them or they thought opposed them; they weren't heroes, take my word for it. I remember finding this lad of about seventeen or eighteen in a cut-through between houses and he was crying and his jeans were down around his ankles and there was blood everywhere.

One of the lads ran over to him whilst me and a couple of others took up defensive positions. I kept looking around, fascinated by the sight of all that 'claret' as the London boys called it. The medic was trying to get a dressing on the front where the knee had been but all there was bloody, jagged flesh where the knee cap had been. Some twat, judging by the wound, had stuck a pistol behind his leg and just fired, blowing off his kneecap. The wounded man, his ballroom dancing days over as one of the lads joked, kept shoving the medic away, telling him 'You'll just make it worse for me if the Provies see ye!'

Maybe I was a bit naive but later I asked a Sergeant why the lad's jeans were round his ankles. He told me that it reduced the risk of gas gangrene if no fragments of clothing were embedded in the wound. He almost made the PIRA sound like a caring organisation. They were bastards; take my word for it.

The day after David Card's murder, the *Daily Express* kept Ulster on the front pages as news from the Province jostled for importance with the on-going Dockers' strike. Under the headline '47 More Freed in Ulster' Cyril Aynsley and Norman Luck discussed the recent release of some Republican internees following pressure from Gerry Fitt's Social and Democratic Labour Party (SDLP). Of the murder of David Card – or even the reporting of the death of an un-named soldier – there was no mention. However, they did see fit to mention a human interest story from the USA concerning millions of grasshoppers that caused the postponement of a baseball match in Texas! Clearly of more concern than the killing of a British soldier on British soil.

TARGET PRACTICE, OLDPARK ROAD

Corporal Roy Davies, RRW

Private Williams and I were on sentry duty in the attic of the school, and we were bloody knackered from lack of sleep and from being constantly on the alert. Trouble had been brewing all day and the 'Bone' was bloody hostile. We were in a sangar and someone kept shooting at the shop dummy which we sometimes left in position and moved about while we lay down on the floor. It seemed strange that the firing was coming from the centre of the road; perhaps

Members of a Black Watch 'snatch squad' pull one of their wounded officers away.

from a manhole cover. But we had just received a new innovation – a 'Starlight scope', an American gadget that gave you a green image of a half lit scene up to a hundred yards or so to your front. The scope was handed up to us from the ladder below while the intermittent fire from the street continued.

With the scope we saw that the gunman was being pushed quickly from a house doorway and towed by a rope fitted on a large child's pram; he was being pulled very quickly from one door opposite and into the passageway of the house the other side of the narrow terraced street. The pushers and pullers were out of sight. They had been doing this for some time, but now we were onto him. 'Bloody moving target practice,' I shouted to Williams. We waited for a few more minutes and then Williams emptied a full magazine down onto the pram. There was crying and screaming and lots of shouting and then a howl of grief that could have only come from a relative of the gunman. We found much blood on the road and a bloodstained coat, but we never found a body.

On 9 August a leading Provisional – Martin Meehan – was arrested in a bedroom of a house in Jamaica Street, Belfast. He was described as one of Ireland's most wanted men and his capture was a real coup for the Army, particularly the Royal Marines who 'lifted' him. Having received a tip that Meehan was back in the Ardoyne area, more than 100 soldiers managed to hem him into Jamaica Street, located between Brompton Park and Oldpark. He was visiting a leading member of the Ardoyne republicans – Mrs Mary McGuigan – when he was spotted entering the house and the SF moved to arrest him. In the *Daily Express* an eyewitness reported: 'I was standing in the hallway when Martin ran past me. I knew the troops were after him. As I ran away, shots were fired into my house by the soldiers. Martin could not escape through the back door because we had nailed it up.' An officer was reported as saying: 'Commandos came under fire from the house and they returned shots. They entered the house and found a wounded man in a room on the ground floor. Then they found Meehan hiding behind a bedroom door.'

MEEHAN'S ARREST

Lieutenant David Ash, Light Infantry

We got the codeword to go in on *Swordfish* [operation to arrest Martin Meehan] in the Ardoyne. There were several additional units from outside the Battalion involved, including Royal Marines. My platoon task was to provide the inner cordon at 19 Jamaica Street, where Meehan was supposed to be.

We roared in by Saracen, burst out onto the road, and deployed fast into doorways along the street. There was immediate panic and uproar and IRA lookouts ran off in all directions, long hair streaming behind them. Women screamed and others stood frozen to the ground, crossing themselves and praying aloud. Sergeant Spracklen immediately saw Meehan run out of the McGuigan house at number 19 and dash into number 32 across the road. We re-directed the arrest team – a troop of Marines – and they ran up the middle of the street to number 32, which was the Mullens' house, another well known IRA family. Gunmen opened fire which the Marines returned and then went straight in. Minutes later they came out with Meehan and doubled him away.

We then had to fight our way out of Jamaica Street and get back to Flax Street Mill on foot. Missiles rained down on us from all directions: paving slabs, stones, and bottles. We skirmished back, firing baton rounds and sporadic sniper fire started again. I flung myself down in a fire position amongst bomb rubble and fired two rapid shots at a gunman near the junction of Herbert/Butler. He didn't fall, but disappeared and I think I was too out of breath to get a hit. Once back in the safety of the mill yard, I followed the arrest team as they led Meehan inside. His arms were tied behind his back with plasticuffs. Base-rats leaned out of top floor windows to get a look at Meehan and hissed loudly as he walked below them; classic, shabby behaviour of men not involved in an operational role on the streets. Meehan remained totally silent and emotionless.

The platoon had a few casualties from crowd action; bad bruising, cuts needing stitches, and so on. They were in good order nonetheless, and it wasn't a bad do.

In the six weeks following the introduction of internment in August 1971, six soldiers from the Green Howards were killed by the IRA in the Ardoyne area of Belfast. Subsequently, as a result of his involvement in at least some of the killings, Meehan became one of the most wanted IRA men in the area. After his arrest, he was imprisoned under the Special Powers Act in Crumlin Road Jail. Later, Meehan and two other IRA members – including the notorious 'Dutch' Doherty – escaped from prison on 2 December 1971. The men covered themselves in butter in order to keep warm, and then hid inside a manhole for six-and-a-half hours before scaling the prison walls using ropes made from knotted blankets and sheets. Doherty was subsequently arrested in the Republic where the Northern Ireland authorities appealed unsuccessfully for his extradition; there were no surprised faces in the British Cabinet at that decision.

Meehan escaped across the border to Dundalk in the Republic and on 27 January 1972 he was arrested by the Garda along with seven other IRA members following a four-hour cross-border gun battle between the IRA and soldiers from the Royal Scots Dragoon Guards. Meehan told reporters 'We pasted them. You could have heard them squealing for miles,' but despite over 4,500 rounds of ammunition being fired, the only casualty was a farmyard pig. The IRA men were arrested in possession of an anti-tank gun, a carbine and seven rifles, but as a consequence of collaboration, or at best, downright leniency, they were acquitted at their trial the following month due to lack of evidence.

He was sent to Long Kesh after his arrest in the Ardoyne in August 1972 and was released on 4 October 1974. At the end of his sentence he was re-arrested and interned. On 5 December 1975 he was the last internee to be released. Meehan died in 2007.

CASUALTIES

Sergeant John Black, RAMC

I remember some of the soldiers who died in our hospital or who were brought in dead. Kingsman James Jones was just eighteen years old and was shot one night in Andersonstown. He was from Manchester, and a couple of years later I read that his father never got over it and had committed suicide. Lance Corporal David Card was in the Royal Green Jackets. He was shot in the head one summer's morning as dawn was breaking. The field surgical team at Musgrave Park Hospital made heroic efforts to save him but to no avail. In 1977/79 when I was an undergraduate at Bristol University, I befriended a young lady who lived on the same estate in Cosham, Portsmouth as David Card, and knew the Card family well. The family had to live with their tragic loss for the rest of their lives without respite, as did hundreds of other families.

On 6 August a new Loyalist terrorist group, the Red Hand Commando, abducted a late night drinker, Terence Hennebry (17) as he was walking home. The fact that he was a Catholic was enough for these cowards – described by the Belfast coroner as 'monsters' – and they shot him and dumped his body in the street.

The 7th brought heartache for the Royal Artillery when a mobile patrol at Lisnaskea, Co Fermanagh was hit by an IRA landmine. The quaint town in the western part of Northern Ireland is predominantly Catholic and very close to the border with the Republic. As the Army vehicles passed over a culvert about three miles from a tiny hamlet called Forfey, a landmine exploded and two soldiers were killed instantly by the blast which left a massive crater in the road. Lance Bombardier David Wynne (21) from South Wales and Gunner Leroy Gordon (21) from Jamaica did not stand a chance. Both soldiers were married with kids and their deaths caused much anger amongst soldiers who had warned about the dangers of mobile patrols in the area.

Just hours later, Trooper Geoffrey Knipe (24) from Bradford, West Yorkshire was driving a Ferret armoured vehicle, one of two, when it was attacked by a mob, numbering several score, throwing rocks. The attacks at Drumarg Park, Armagh were intense and a missile smashed through the observation slot and hit the soldier from the Royal Dragoon Guards in the head and, having lost consciousness, the vehicle crashed violently and he was killed. Even when an ambulance was summoned, the mob, mostly teenagers, continued to hurl bricks and stones, even as the dead soldier's body was taken away.

Amongst all the mayhem and carnage there were occasional moments of humanity when the sight of a prostrate blood-soaked soldier did not invoke a wave of cheers or derision. George Prosser, after the killing of Lance Corporal Andrew Webster (20) on 19 May 1979 spoke of the tears of a young woman, a resident of the Turf Lodge, at the death of a young soldier. Webster was killed instantly by an IED in the 'Disco block' – a three storey building in Ardmonagh Gardens – and George was on hand at the scene. A distraught local woman collapsed into his arms in a flood of tears at such a senseless killing. No doubt the local Provisional commander popped around to remind her just whose side she was on!

The day ended as badly as it started and a fourth soldier was killed before the stroke of midnight. Lance Corporal Harry Creighton (27) a part-time soldier in the UDR and a librarian had just returned to his home at Drumrainey, close to the Irish border from his shift at Newtownbutler. Masked IRA gunmen had lain in wait outside his house and shot him as he approached his front door; he died at the scene.

ANOTHER UDR MAN KILLED

Keith Williams, Royal Regiment of Wales, Att: UDR

The tragedy occurred on 7 August when Lance Corporal Harry Creighton of our 'C' Company died after gunmen opened fire on him near his home at Magheraveely, near Clontivrin which was only 500 metres from the border. He was well aware he was a PIRA target and had been very concerned that in accordance with general instructions issued by HQNI, his personal protection weapon was changed from an SMG to a .38 revolver. Shortly before he was murdered I can remember him telling both the Training Major and me that in his particular circumstances a .38 revolver would be almost useless if he was attacked. So it proved!

UNDER ATTACK IN BANDIT COUNTRY

Jim, Argyll and Sutherland Highlanders

I still break out in a sweat thinking about arriving in Crossmaglen and landing on the playing field behind the police station. We jumped out with all our gear to the screams of our sergeant telling us to hit the deck. I thought we were under attack or something as he threw ammunition at us and we frantically tried to load our magazines. Nothing was actually happening; this was simply a way of introducing us to the next four months. We had to realise, quickly, that it was no longer an exercise or a game; it was the real thing.

We were on a patrol a few miles from base [at Cullaville] when we were approached by a woman telling us about a burning lorry down the road to Dundalk. Our sergeant had us running down the road towards this incident; Christ that got the adrenalin going. As we got near to where the incident was we left the road and went up the hillside to get a better look. We could see the smoke but no sign of activity so we made our way slowly down to the lorry. It had been a butter lorry and the stink was hellish. We could have been walking into an ambush or booby-trap, but we were hyped up and alert. Luckily there was nothing but a burning lorry.

We were at the Dundalk road/Moybane junction and tried radioing base, using A41 radios; these weighed in at 18lb 8oz with the battery and a range a 1.5–3 miles, but couldn't get through. Looking at the map there was a single track road, heading to the Moybane road nearby which was a quicker way back to the base so we headed for it. We found a burned-out car blocking this road. We still couldn't get through on the radio, so we decided to head back to base along the road anyway. It was a very warm afternoon and we were hot and tired. Almost at the other end of the road we found a 45-gallon oil drum in a ditch by the roadside; then someone shouted that it was a bomb. We scattered, getting maybe 120 feet from it when there was an almighty explosion.

Everything stood still; we were on the deck watching this cloud of dirt and rubble slowly rising – it was quite a sight. Then it all came back down a lot faster. A falling rock snapped the pistol grip of one rifle and one man was knocked unconscious. We got up and stood around, shocked and confused. Then the ground started kicking up around us and the sergeant shouted that we were under fire. At one point someone shouted for me to follow him and I did so automatically. We went down a wall towards the general direction of the firing, but couldn't see anything so came back. The shooting stopped as quickly as it had begun and for some reason the radio worked and we got the standby section down to help us reorganise but the gunmen had already disappeared back over the border.

Internment was introduced on 9 August 1971 and, twelve months on, the Republican mobs decided to 'celebrate' the first anniversary with widespread riots in Twinbrook, Andersonstown, Turf Lodge, Ballymurphy, Falls, Ardoyne and New Lodge in Belfast. There were also mirror riots on the Creggan and Bogside in Londonderry. A year on from that event, the repercussions and social and military fall out from botched intelligence was still being seen. The Army had been equipped with obsolete lists of suspects, containing the names of dissidents and Republicans from the 1940s and the abortive border campaign of 1956 to 1962. Men were being interned incorrectly, often the family members of suspects; the lists were so out of date that the 'young Turks' of the Provisional IRA were being ignored and their grandfathers who were no longer any threat were being dragged from their beds. This served to further alienate the very community that the Army had gone in to help and gave the IRA a major recruitment boost. Notwithstanding this, it singularly failed to recognise the Loyalist threat and gave more ammunition to the Catholics who felt that they were carrying the can for the crimes of their sectarian enemies.

ARTISTIC ENDEAVOURS

Mike Sangster, Royal Artillery

One of the lads – called 'Stitch' – got fined £100 on orders for defacing public property. Late one night, he was in charge of a foot patrol in the Bogside. He got hold of a pot of paint and wrote on the Rossville Street entrance of the Rossville flats: 'You are now entering the biggest shithouse in Europe. Built by Paddies for Paddies.' A local saw him do it and reported it. Poor Stitch; it cost him any chance of being awarded his LSGC [Long Service Good Conduct] medal but he thought it was worth it. We thought it was hilarious and made a collection to help pay his fine. Even some lads from the DWR sent some money when they heard about it.

On the 9th, an IRA 'own goal' resulted in the death of Colm Murtagh (19) when a bomb that he was planting in Newry exploded prematurely. His three injured accomplices managed to escape. The ranks of the IRA were further culled two days later when another premature explosion caused the deaths of Anne Parker (18) and Michael Clarke (19). The pair was en-route to attack a warehouse close to the Army base in North Howard Street, Belfast as part of the 'economic war' and to display their bravado in

One of the 'milder' forms of PIRA punishment. This man has either sold drugs (which 'stepped on the toes' of PIRA themselves) or is a thief, as indicated by the placard, they made an example of. The same fate befell women who dated soldiers.

front of the British Army. Thankfully, neither was achieved and the pair were refused entry at the target and got back into their van. Somewhat piously the IRA announced that the pair had decided to withdraw in order to avoid civilian casualties.

On the 10th, an Argyll's VCP on the main road leading south from Crossmaglen to the Irish Republic was heavily attacked by IRA gunmen from two positions just north of the border. Using classic infantry training methods, the Argylls managed to almost outflank the terrorists. One IRA team withdrew over the border to the protection of the Gardai Siochana but an Army helicopter closed in on the other team. It came under fire and was forced to withdraw and a car was then observed driving from the direction of the border to collect the gunmen who had been firing from a derelict house. The car was forced to retreat and the three gunmen were seen to escape, like the other team, into the safety of the south, on foot.

BARRICADES ON THE FALLS

Alan Lengden 14/20 King's Hussars

It was standing orders that we would always carry a wet blanket stowed behind the turret in case anyone was petrol bombed or on fire from other causes. Many times we went down to Belfast on patrol and might end up down there for four or five nights because of the situation and we worked alongside 'Angle Irons', Jocks, Green Jackets and many others. One night, Lieutenant Scott directed me up the back streets to the top of the Falls Road, telling me that the Paras were having a bit of trouble. I turned into a street and saw either a 'Sarra' or a PIG in the middle of the street with a Para near its front wheel.

Nothing seemed to be happening, so we stopped for a fag and, looking at the Para, I thought that he didn't look worried. Then we were ordered to mount up and crash through some barriers which the locals had assembled as the Paras wanted to go through and take a look. Now, down inside the vehicle you can't always hear what is going on outside, especially with the headphones on and with the noise the engine makes. So, towards the barricade we headed and people started throwing all sorts at us; at this moment, I could see that they had piled up all sorts of rubbish including a park bench, old armchairs, beer kegs and the like and I was hoping that we wouldn't get 'bellied' when we hit it. When the rioters realised that we weren't going to stop, they began scattering. When we hit the barricade, we must have been doing 50/60mph and I felt something underneath the Ferret, so I ran it up onto the kerb and stopped and a beer keg came rolling out, spurting beer all over the place.

We were ordered back for a second smash through but when we went through again, I saw 'Smudge' had stopped his vehicle and I asked what was wrong, why had he stopped. He shouted that he had wanted to grab a keg of beer and was most upset when ordered to leave it! We carried on for a few hours, doing back street patrols and then back to the mill for some kip where my 'bed' was an old armchair with a broken arm.

Next morning, with reports of foot patrols being stormed coming through, we were ordered back to the Falls. Just as we arrived, a bottle was thrown at us and what a good shot it was. It came through the battle hatch and bounced off my left ear but the headset protected me. I looked behind me and Scotty was standing on the seat and I grabbed at his leg to get him to sit down but he was annoyed because he couldn't fire the machine gun at the rioters! We drove around for a bit and we came to an open area behind a big block of flats and he jumped out and went to grab some bricks. Just then, there was a crash and a terrible smell of petrol and I looked at my shoulder and it was covered in grey paint and petrol. Then I saw the bottle, broken at the neck with a bit of rag hanging out of it; it was a petrol bomb but thankfully it hadn't exploded. We then went back to the riot where Scotty, now armed with pocket-sized rocks, enjoyed himself immensely, throwing them at the rioters! I kept the flak jacket – my good luck charm – for the rest of that tour!

Another time we were called to a riot and we were confronted by a mob that had broken into a frozen goods factory and the bastards were throwing frozen chickens at us. Afterwards, we went back to our 'luxury' portacabins and we took some of the frozen chickens with us. Our cap badge is the Prussian Eagle and some other mobs called us the 'skipping chickens' so we shaped the chicken – by now thawed – into the shape of the badge and wired it to the front of the Ferret. Later that day, we were stopped in a side street and some women came out and saw what we had wired to the front. One of them said: 'That's disgusting, having a chicken on the front; some of the kids around here haven't had chicken for months!' I told her that she should have been with us the night before, then she could have got as many as she wanted for free!

Over the coming days two more innocent Catholics were murdered for purely sectarian reasons by the UFF; Frank Wynne (37) and Thomas Madden (48) were killed and their bodies dumped in north Belfast. One wonders what the supporters of the UFF thought when it emerged that Thomas Madden was stabbed 116 times. This was the behaviour of psychopaths and not dedicated 'defenders of the Protestant community'.

Casement Park, Andersonstown was the site of an Army base and on 14 August the Royal Engineers and REME were tasked with erecting a series of anti-sniper screens to shield the base. An IRA anti-personnel device had been concealed close to the path which the soldiers took and it detonated as two soldiers walked by. Royal Artillery Major David Storrey (36) father of three from Ascot in Berkshire was terribly wounded, dying in hospital. His comrade Craftsman Brian Hope (20) of REME from Aylesbury, Bucks was killed instantly.

The same day, the Army was involved in more firefights with the IRA in the Ardoyne area and soldiers of the Light Infantry took casualties from gunmen firing from Jamaica Street. A Sergeant, having spotted a comrade who had been badly wounded in a garden in Brompton Park, rushed to the aid of the fallen man. A gunmen opened fire, but missed the soldier and instead hit Charles McNeil (68) a pensioner and resident of the area. He died shortly afterwards.

On 16 August in what one can only surmise was an internal feud, UVF gunmen went into the Loyalist Long Bar pub on Shankill Road, clubbed William 'Billy' Spence (31) to the ground and then calmly shot him as he lay defenceless. It is thought that the same Loyalist group was behind the murder of one of Spence's friends, Thomas Boyd (28) eleven days later for reasons connected with the original killing.

Three more car bombs exploded the next day and two soldiers from the King's Regiment caught in one of the explosions on the Falls Road were horribly maimed. One of the wounded 'Kingos' was Roy Christopher who lost both legs in the attack. Shortly afterwards, an IRA sniper fired a shot at a foot patrol of the Royal Anglians and fatally wounded Lance Corporal John Boddy (24). The patrol was walking along Selby Street, close to the Grosvenor Road when the soldier was hit in the head. Despite frantic efforts by the staff at the nearby RVH, he died of the wound.

Photo of the dilapidated and boarded-up shops on the Republican Derrybeg Estate in Newry.

The same area featured in the deaths of two more soldiers on the 18th. First to be killed was another 'Kingo' Rennie Layfield (24) from Burnley, shot whilst he manned a VCP on the Falls Road. Within hours and not more than a thousand yards away, Private Richard Vercoe Jones (21) Light Infantry was shot dead by an IRA sniper. He was in a vehicle driving along Roden Street, just off Grosvenor Road when he was hit.

Two more sectarian killings followed, one by either side, and then nine more people were killed on Tuesday 22 August by an IRA bomb. A four-man IRA team carried a 50-pound bomb into the Newry Customs Clearance station on the Dublin Road and either dropped it or were arming the device when it exploded prematurely and killed four customs officials, two innocent lorry drivers and three IRA men in the blast.

The customs officials were Frank Quinn (30) from Hilltown, Co Down; Patrick Murphy (41) father of three; Marshall Lawrence (33) father of five; and Michael Gillesse (32) from Armagh City. The two lorry drivers – ironically both Catholics from Armagh – were Joseph Fegan (28) and John McCann (60). The son of one the dead bombers, Patrick Hughes (41) was himself killed in 1974 when he was shot by the Army on the notorious Derrybeg Estate in Newry.

On the same day but many miles further north, the IRA 'executed' a known leader of one of the Loyalist paramilitary groups, killing James Johnston (40) near Grosvenor Road, Belfast. The IRA then turned their attentions to the Army and no fewer than nine soldiers were killed over the course of the next week.

In the late morning of the following day, an explosion occurred at Dungannon, Co Tyrone and it was observed that a mechanical digger had been blown up. A passing patrol from 8 UDR called in the incident and a patrol of the Queen's Own Highlanders (QOH) was sent in to investigate. As a two-vehicle armoured patrol from the QOH arrived, a second explosion occurred as they neared Donaghmore. The vehicles drove through the falling debris and then stopped further up the road. As they did so, an IRA gunman opened fire but the rounds bounced harmlessly off the armour and he ran off, narrowly being missed by an aimed shot from one of the soldiers. The main water supply to Dungannon was badly damaged and the crater was later measured at 15 by 10 feet.

THEY KNEW US

Sergeant John Black, RAMC

The Andersonstown local IRA shooting team used to zero their weapons in our direction particularly on Saturdays before embarking on their murderous campaign. To spare us the agony of being defenceless we were provided with a .38 pistol, but no ammunition. The 'cowboys' in Andersonstown began their shooting match, as we were conveniently placed and could not return fire. Living in a community with hundreds of civilian staff, the IRA would have known this; I bet they knew our names, ranks and serial numbers too! I don't know whether or not it was intentionally aimed at us, but it sure was close.

———◦◦◦◦———

Fusilier Alan Tingey (23), father of two from Warwickshire, Royal Regiment of Fusiliers was shot by an IRA sniper in Kenard Avenue in the Andersonstown estate on 23 August. The day after, whilst patrolling the Shantallow estate in Londonderry, a foot patrol of the Light Infantry came under rifle attack. Sergeant Arthur Whitelock (24) on his third tour of Northern Ireland was hit and killed instantly. He was killed on his wedding anniversary and was buried in the same church where he had married in 1968.

The many tentacles of the IRA were demonstrated as further south, at Moybane near Crossmaglen in South Armagh a landmine exploded just as a mobile patrol, consisting of a Saladin and a Ferret of the Royal Scots Dragoon Guards drove by. The device which was detonated from across the nearby Irish border fatally wounded Trooper Ian Caie (19) from Aberdeen. The car was thrown about 60 feet and caught fire when it landed, crushing Trooper Caie. The young soldier was rushed to hospital by helicopter but his wounds were so severe that he died shortly afterwards.

The UDR was the next regiment to suffer when it lost two soldiers who were checking a suspiciously abandoned car at Cherrymount close to Enniskillen. The stolen car had been booby-trapped by the IRA and it exploded in what the dead men's comrades described as a 'blinding yellow flash' (*Lost Lives* p255). All the men in the patrol were injured, but Jimmy Eames (33) and Alfie Johnston (32) were both killed instantly by the 150lb device. The explosion also rocked a passing mobile patrol of the Royal Artillery.

CHERRYMOUNT DEATHS

Keith Williams, Royal Regiment of Wales, Att: UDR

James Eames and Alfie Johnston, Lance Corporals who had both recently transferred to 4 UDR from the local TA company lost their lives when they went forward to examine a suspicious car near an electricity sub-station at Cherrymount. The bomb hidden in the car was detonated by remote control killing them both instantly. I still have great regrets about this as I had actually been involved in enticing them to join the UDR and because of their previous military TA experience may have allowed them to short circuit some training requirements. Why they both went forward to inspect the suspect car is not known as standard procedure was to report it and await the results of the checks made on the vehicle.

⎯⎯⎯◦◊◦◦⎯⎯⎯

Two more IRA men were killed in another 'own goal' explosion at Downpatrick, Co Down. Shortly afterwards John Nulty (26) and his friend Patrick Kelly (26) were abducted by the UVF whilst walking back from a night's drinking in the Oldpark area. They were taken away, systematically tortured – one had an ear cut off, both were kicked and stabbed and one had a symbol of the Irish flag carved into his arm – before finally being killed.

THE NIGHT I BECAME 'HAN SOLO'

John Bradley 23rd Engineer Regiment

Another memorable night was when I was out on patrol with the RSM and I spotted a guy on the most wanted list by the name of Sean Flynn going into a pub called the Britannia Bar [since blown up]. Some Brigadier gave me a pat on the back for that when we got back to Osnabruck. I got some laurel leaf [Mentioned in Dispatches] for my GSM but didn't think much of it at the time.

It was always fun being out with 'Mick the Nick', as we called him; Mick Turner was our RSM and he was of Irish decent but hated the Micks. He would get a couple of us poor lads at night to go with him into the back alleys and wait for curfew dodgers. Most of these were just screwing some other guy's wife but we arrested them anyway; lots of night patrol fun.

No-go areas were without a doubt the most hectic of the tour, as tartan gangs and civilians on both sides started to riot and turn over cars, lorries, milk carts and rubbish trucks, you name it. They used them to block off streets, and one night we were ordered to stop any activity on a main road (I don't remember the name of it) but our CO, Colonel Cholerton himself gave us the order to make sure nobody blocked that street! So Corporal 'Taff' Phillips took charge and when a group of rioters took a rubbish truck and started driving down our road he ordered me to stop and seize it before they could tip it over. From about 50 yards away 'Taff' and Sammy Salmon fired their rubber bullets at about 100 teenagers, and there I was with my SLR and all the gear hanging off charging down the street towards those kids. To my surprise they started running away!

It was like the scene out of *Star Wars* when Han Solo chased the storm troopers until they realized that he was all alone. I was 50 yards down the street, screaming my head off, when the mob turned towards me and started back in my direction. Without even thinking I jumped into the rubbish truck front seat, there was a red light on the dash and I pushed the button; screw me if the engine didn't start in gear no less. Shocked, I grabbed the steering wheel and wrenched on it to drive the truck out of harm's way with bricks and bottles flying all over the place. I drove it off down the street and 'Taff' and Sammy hung onto the sides with over 100 angry kids chasing us. It was a blast I can tell you. We pulled up and about faced, got out every rubber bullet we could muster, called for support on the radio and started to blast away. Fortunately, we had some 'penny assisted bullets' and that seemed to do the trick although we didn't like using them on the Protestant 'Micks'.

Colonel Cholerton came to the scene and thanked us and told us to give the truck back to the city blokes. Can you believe it? After all that we handed over the truck and they gave it right back to the frickin' kids! I was pissed off for days over that because I risked my neck getting the truck away from these madmen only for some bloke to give it back to them. Anger and frustration soon turned to sheer exhaustion. It all died down after 36 hours straight and I slept for two days.

On 27 August the IRA shot and killed Sergeant Anthony Metcalfe (28) of the Coldstream Guards at an Army OP on the Creggan estate in Londonderry. The soldier, from the Hull area, and his wife were shortly due to adopt a baby.

The next day, in Newtownbutler, Co Fermanagh, an IRA landmine intended for a passing Army patrol exploded and killed farmer William Trotter (57) as he walked around his land. The same day, a foot patrol of the Light Infantry (LI) was attacked as they patrolled the Beechmounts close to the Falls Road. Corporal Ian Morrill (29) of the Royal Green Jackets attached to the LI was hit by a single shot and died at the scene. At the time of his death he was serving with 3 RGJ whom he had joined from the 3 LI in February 1972. He was from the Southend-on-Sea area. Later that night, in the same area, the Army were involved in a series of fierce fire fights with the IRA, and the soldiers alone fired over 600 rounds.

In any army there have always been incidents involving that terrible oxymoron, 'friendly fire'. 'Blue on blue' is the modern expression and it is a seemingly necessary tragedy of warfare. In a month, in different parts of Belfast, three soldiers were shot and two died as a result of friendly fire.

In the first incident, on 28 August, Private Ronald Rowe (21) Light Infantry from Cornwall was on patrol in the Ardoyne when he was mistaken for a gunmen and shot by a soldier from another regiment. He had served in 1 LI for over three years and was a member of the Battalion's Support Company; he left a wife and baby daughter. He died at the scene and six days later, a Royal Marine was killed under similar circumstances.

With August drawing to an end, an IRA sniper opened fire on a foot patrol of 3RGJ who were in Odessa Street, in the Falls Road area. Rifleman David Griffiths (20) from Liverpool was hit in the chest by a single round aimed by the gunman who was at the junction of Clonard and Odessa Streets. The sniper, it later transpired, fired through a hole in a house wall made by removing a single brick and designed for shooting at the precise spot where Griffiths was kneeling on the street corner. Yet again, the troops on the ground were easy targets as a well concealed sniper, often some 500 yards away with the latest American-financed arms, was able to pick them off with impunity. As one soldier said to the author, 'It was like shooting those fairground ducks!'

In the last week of the month, in what later became known as the 'Battle of Broadway' the Army and the IRA exchanged several thousand rounds in what was a five-hour running gun battle. The Broadway runs from the Falls Road, passes the southern entrance to the RVH and in 1972 crossed the Donegall Road near what was then the end of the M1 motorway. The gun battle raged along Broadway but there were no reported fatalities. A section from 3RGJ was manning an OP and was in serious danger of being overrun by the concerted IRA attack.

THE BATTLE OF BROADWAY

Alex B, UDR

Monday 28 August 1972. I remember that night so well and finished work as usual at 17.00 and went to my 'digs' for dinner, then out to meet friends for a couple of pints. My memory of the battle started when I left the Students Union at the junction of University Road and Elmwood Avenue c.23.30hrs to walk the three-quarters of a mile back to Chadwick Street, off the Lisburn Road. The warm glow of five or six Bass beers couldn't erase the unmistakeable intimidating crack of high velocity gunfire – a normal nocturnal sound at that time – but this night was very, very different.

Instead of the occasional single round or short burst breaking the silence every five or ten minutes, the noise was continuous and loud. By the time I reached the Lisburn Road it seemed that every rifle in Belfast was firing, apparently from just beyond the City Hospital. I wasn't too far out in my estimate, with Broadway roundabout at the end of the M1 motorway being directly beyond that medical facility; though by about half a mile! At the top of Tate's Avenue, with the wind-borne racket now seeming to be only yards away, I was cold sober and glad to reach the security of the house. Up to my room, where for the next couple of hours I sat by the unlit open window, awestruck at the intensity of what was clearly a full-scale fire fight. It gradually slackened, reduced to the odd report every minute or so, then ceased for what remained of the night.

During that latter period two virtually spent rounds whirred past me, lapwing-like, to glance off the rear of a building on the Lisburn Road with low-pitched whangs. This was almost certainly someone's double tap. As confirmed by an OS map, I was a full 1,200 yards from the action, thus definitely not in anyone's sights so they weren't meant for me. Glad neither connected though. Wonder whether they were .223 or 7.62? If the latter, very poor marksmanship that man! [The 7.62mm round was standard British Army and the .223 favoured by the IRA in the early days.]

Though I'm recalling this event 38 years on, when the landlady told me the following morning that, 31 years earlier, in May 1941, she had stood at the same bedroom window with her father and watched fires blaze across Belfast from the Lower Falls to the Castlereagh Hills as the Luftwaffe's second major raid devastated large areas of the city, leaving almost 1,000 dead from the two attacks; her story seemed like ancient history. However, that wartime destruction didn't knock the place out, so how PIRA ever imagined they could do it with individual IEDs and Armalites beats me! What a waste. I know now, as she did then, just how quickly the years flick past. Looking back, 1972 is only a blink away.

'WE SHALL NEVER KNOW'

Colour Sergeant Ken Ambrose, RGJ

The loss of Cpl Morrill [see above] was part of a chain of events which culminated in the biggest single battle of the Battalion's tour. It is hard now to discern cause and effect, but interesting that even before the shooting in Beechmount Avenue there had been an unusually high level of sniping at 'R' and 'A' Companies' joint base on the Broadway from a variety of different positions, as though the opposition was firing its sighters.

That evening 'A' Company turned out in force, leaving only the guard platoon in base, to tour the Beechmount streets gathering information on the Cpl Morrill incident and distributing leaflets exhorting the inhabitants to help the Security Forces. Within a space of about fifteen minutes there was suddenly a stream of hysterical complaints through police 999 calls, community leaders, and direct to Battalion H.Q. that 'the military were running amok and smashing up every house in the Beechmount.' The Second-in-Command was actually on the telephone to a local resident when, just before 2330 hours, the latter's voice was drowned by the first burst of gunfire outside his house and the whole of Beechmount erupted.

Within two minutes the shooting had spread across the Falls Road and heavy fire was opened at the Broadway base from half a dozen different places. In the next two hours about 1,000 rounds were fired at the base and something like the same number returned. Major Christopher Dunphie from 'R' Company Ops Room described it as 'like the Somme'. A particularly fierce battle built up round an isolated 'R' Company OP on the Clarence Engineering building at the north end of the M1 Motorway. In spite of very heavy fire by the Section and considerable cool-ness and leadership by the Section Commander, Cpl Mann, it seemed possible at one time that they might actually be over-run and it was decided to pull them back.

An expedition was mounted under 2nd Lieutenant Simon Blake consisting of an empty Saracen APC escorted by a section and a troop of Armoured cars from the 14/20 Hussars. The OP was duly withdrawn without casualties covered by Browning machine-gun fire and smoke. Perhaps our summer diversion to train for conventional war had not been in vain after all! One other curious feature of the battle was that, before its withdrawal, the OP reported firing from the east, from the direction of the Protestant 'Village' district, into the Republican Rodney area from which they were being attacked. At one time a stream of tracer from a machine-gun was seen. In spite of some corroboration the next day, the exact truth of this third-party intervention was never officially admitted.

After two hours the firing died down and 'A' Company was able to get back into its base. No casualties were suffered by us. We shall never know what IRA losses were. Claims ranged from

The RUC were subjected to nightly attacks by rioters in virtually every Republican area of the province.

a probable twelve hits as seen through our Starlight scope night-sights to propaganda claims by the IRA; first that they were not involved at all and later that a total of six gunmen suffered one minor wound between them.

***

Earlier that month on the 18th Kingsman Roy Christopher (20) had been injured in an explosion in Clonard Street, off the Falls Road. A source from the King's Regimental Association told me that both his parents were flown by their home in Chorley near Manchester to be at his bedside and were with him when he died of his wounds on the 30th. He was the seventh member of the regiment killed in Northern Ireland in a three-and-a-half month period.

The UFF killed two more Catholics as August ended. Eamonn McMahon (19) was abducted and murdered and his body dumped in the River Bann in Portadown. The other murder was truly sickening and even hardened RUC officers were shocked at the torture and death of Patrick Devaney (27) a former British soldier. Devaney who lived near the Ormeau Road in south Belfast had been invalided out of the Army where he had served with the Royal Ulster Rifles. Loyalist terrorists had beaten him, hung him upside down from a roof beam, tortured him and then shot him in the head. Later they stashed his body inside a cardboard box and abandoned it like so much household refuse.

There was no backlash against the sectarian killings in either community just so long as the dead were of the 'other' faith. Sectarian murders were not simply the province of the Loyalists – the IRA were not backward in coming forward in the senseless tit for tat – but the Protestants did it with a particularly savage gusto. They were happy to torture and kill any Catholic too drunk or to naive to consider that their route home from work or the pub might lead to their deaths. Kevin Myers in his *Watching The Door* describes how they also targeted children:

> Broken bottles – presumably intended to castrate their victims – were routinely sunk into the sand of the long jump pit at a Catholic school in north Belfast. Razor blades which would have filleted a child like a trout were often embedded in playground slides used by young Catholics.

BRITANNIA BAR BOMB

John Bradley, 23 Engineer Regiment

A bomb at the Britannia Bar on our own turf was a movie all in itself: *The Good, the Bad and the Ugly*. It was good we got cases of Harp lager from the cellar of the bar after it blew up. It was bad that one of our lads was blinded by the blast while in a sangar across the street from the pub. And ugly was the bloody mess we had afterwards. From what we were told, an Austin 1100 had pulled up outside and the driver went in for a pint. He must have had one too many because the bomb went off while he was still inside and the place was leveled. That was the first time I ever had to pick up body parts. It wasn't a pleasant job, going through that wreckage and smell. We were given face masks but the smell was awful.

HEAVY RETALIATION

Alex B, UDR

I have an extremely accurate rounds-counter somewhere in my brain, though on that Battle of Broadway night it was completely overwhelmed, but one other incident from that mad year stays with me.

In Chadwick Street bedroom, late o'clock, sitting at desk doing stuff for the following day's tech classes, day release at Millfield. The republicans in Rodney Parade/St James Park had been agitating all evening with single-round sniping across the motorway at their Hun neighbours. Not heavy stuff, just 'harassing', with long periods of silence between times. Prod patience eventually snapped some time around midnight, with the longest sustained burst of individual machine-gun fire I've ever heard. At this remove I can't be certain of the exact number, but the figure 57 comes to mind; at any rate the counter clicked with every bang and I had the total recorded. Thing was, the rate of fire was the slowest I've experienced too. Low-velocity 'dak – a– dak – a – dak – a'. You get the picture and the image that immediately sprang to my mind was of a First World War water-cooled Vickers MG at an attic window somewhere in the Village. Why did I think that? With a burst of such duration it wasn't magazine-fed; could any air-cooled barrel have stood up to the punishment, and a Jimpy ripped off rounds much faster? [GPMG: General Purpose Machine Gun.]

Go back a further 50-odd years and imagine half a dozen mad Belfasters coming off the boat from France in December 1918, with all the bits of a 'liberated' Machine Gun Corps tripod-mounted Vickers – and a belt of 57 .303 rounds – distributed among their kitbags! 'Yez never know when it might be useful lads!'

The following morning's BBCNI news carried the report that a large number of shots had been fired across the motorway into Rodney Parade. Not a word of the nuisance fire that had preceded it all evening. Myself? I just thought: '57. Am I the only one here who can count?' Oh yes, the response had the desired effect on the snipers as well. Silence for the rest of the night.

During the month, three other UDR soldiers died, again in circumstances unknown. They were Corporal Albert Johnston (35), Private William Hamilton (30) and Private Kenneth Twaddell (36). Although listed on the ROH at the National Arboretum, the author has no further information.

August was over and Northern Ireland moved into the last few weeks of summer. The toll was again grim; 24 soldiers, 28 civilians, 9 IRA and 1 Loyalist terrorist were killed. 62 dead as the year marched on. Of the civilian deaths, at least twelve were random sectarian murders; Loyalists killed ten and the IRA killed two.

CHAPTER NINE

SEPTEMBER

As the month began, Rod Stewart's 'You Wear it Well' was number one in the British music charts. He was soon to be replaced by Slade and the sickly sweet David Cassidy. On the 5th, terrorist group 'Black September' seized and held hostage several members of the Israeli Olympic team. It ended bloodily with eleven members killed in a shoot out following a failed rescue attempt.

The death toll was already over 350, the worst year for the British Army since the Korean War. There was always a hint of a ceasefire, but much of it was talked up by the UK press, hopeful as ever.

Start them young. A Loyalist paramilitary 'mini me' stands guard with his older UDA comrades in the Shankill area of Belfast. (Belfast Telegraph)

September began with a bang quite literally when the Provisionals detonated a device out-side the HQ of the Ulster Unionist Party (UUP) in Glengall Street, Belfast. The device killed no-one but it did cause extensive damage to the building. There were complaints from the politicians about 'protection' from the SF, but the Army and RUC were simply not able to cover every single building or 'target' in the Province.

Rioting continued unabated and the soldiers on the streets were weary of the daily sight of young men and even children, their faces masked to protect their identities and slow down the effects of CS gas, armed with bricks and stones, waiting for a patrol to come their way. The older people would often have vinegar-soaked rags for the faces of those caught by the gas as it helped alleviate the discomfort. Hundreds of soldiers were injured during this year, often suffering burn injuries from the massive numbers of petrol bombs thrown. Many squaddies joked that they were most surprised that Belfast and Londonderry weren't suffering a petrol crisis given the amount that was being thrown at them. In addition to the 'normal' burns, the rioters sometimes added sugar to the petrol, which solidified upon ignition and stuck to the clothes and bare skin causing more severe injuries.

One favourite tactic was to skim jagged-edged roofing slates along the street at ankle level caus-ing some very bad foot and shin injuries; indeed, some soldiers resorted to pushing flattened tin cans down the front of their puttees in order to minimise the injury. Some of the rioters would fill their pockets with small stones and carry around Hurley sticks (an Irish game similar to hockey) and then place the stones on the ground and propel them towards the troops with well aimed strikes.

Under constant attack, soldiers were often frustrated by the fact that when they shot a gunman they could rarely find the body. When one was seen to fall the soldiers could not advance imme-diately for fear of back-up gunmen hidden from view or in position to fire when they broke cover. IRA snipers would lie on blankets so they could be dragged away if hit; by the time the soldiers reached the firing position the gunman was long gone. His weapon was also disposed of, often into the mobile IRA armouries. These were generally stolen cars which could be aban-doned as capriciously as they were stolen. If the gunman was only wounded then he might be spirited away across the border to a doctor or hospital sympathetic to Republicanism. The IRA also had supporters in the medical profession in their own communities who would either treat their casualties through choice or through intimidation. The Knights of Malta – a Northern Ireland equivalent of the St John's Ambulance Brigade – would administer rudimentary first aid until more professional medical help could be reached.

In 1972, there was a perceptible shift in the way the Army's different units 'policed' their areas, a tactical change which was ordered from HQNI and above. In the early stages of the Troubles, the troops had come in to 'aid the civil power'; the RUC had lost control and had understand-ably retreated to their barracks, leaving a power vacuum which the Army had to fill. For many years, the RUC would not venture into the Republican heartlands without a military escort and it would be some time before they would be become initiative-led. For the time being, the Army had to be policemen and do their best to contain terrorism whilst also maintaining civil law.

Company commanders would be briefed by the outgoing unit's equivalent officer on just who was who, who needed to be under observation and which known 'players' were in their TAOR. It would be the incoming company commander's role to identify the terrorist structure of the area. Their role was also to recruit intelligence on the ground – to 'turn' locals and reward them for informing on the Provisionals. In particular, they had to be aware of the locals who might have a grievance against the IRA and be weak enough to be pressurised to become 'touts'.

At around this period, the Army had accepted that they were in Ulster for the duration. Specialised urban warfare training centres were established, one in Germany ('tin city' at Sennelager) and another on England's southern coast under the auspices of NITAT (Northern Ireland Training). They were no longer simply soldiers on peacekeeping duties; they were rapidly becoming professional urban warfare specialists. This training and a bit of luck would keep some alive, but not all.

A BIT OF LUCK FOR A JOCK

Soldier, Scots Guards

On the 5th sometime in the afternoon, one of our patrols was moving along Cable Street, Derry, not far from Lecky Road and Guardsman Spinks was back marker. As he turned left into Drumcliffe Avenue, I heard a shot ring out. The round as we later found out was an AP [armour-piercing] and it hit Spinks in the middle of his back and he was thrown about 20 feet or so along the pavement. He was one lucky boy and all he got was bad bruising but he was really shaken up. We had a few casualties over there and Spinksie should have been one of them; thank Christ he wasn't. The sniper's round had hit his riot gun and then fragmented on contact with his flak jacket. He was out again later on all kitted out with a new flak jacket and a replacement 'dildo gun.' You ken why we called them that? Because the wee ladies of the Bogside used to take them home for their bedrooms for 'personal use' whilst their hubbies were away in the 'Kesh or suchlike.

Spinksie was lucky but a couple of weeks later, we lost John Van-Beck shot very close by on Lecky Road and, not long after, George Lockhart died of his wounds after he was also shot in Derry. Derry was a nasty, nasty place, especially up on the Creggan, and the bloody Bogside was no better. The local youth known as the DYH (Derry Young Hooligans) were an evil bunch and they had no respect for law and order and they hated us. They were totally lawless and for people so young, so full of piss and hatred; I hadn't witnessed anything like that as a wee lad despite coming from a poor background.

I ken that they wanted to be Irish, but as I used to say, the border with the so-called 'Free State' was only a couple of miles away; why didn't they piss off over it and take their fucking tricolours with them?

The second 'blue on blue' of the Troubles occurred on the 3rd when the Royal Marines accidentally shot one of their own men. Two foot patrols in Stratheden Street in Belfast's New Lodge came into contact from separate directions and in the confusion Gunner Robert Cutting (18) was shot twice and killed. At the time of his death he was attached to the Royal Marines. The Manchester boy was part of a foot patrol in the New Lodge Road approaching Stratheden Street. There was some confused shouting and an eyewitness recalled a cry of 'Who the hell are you?' before several shots were fired. A Royal Marine from the patrol in Stratheden Street saw a man whom he thought was a sniper and fired and hit him and then hit him a second time as he attempted to crawl away. Tragically, the man was Gunner Cutting.

On the 4th, a car bomb was planted outside a Catholic bar in Portadown and, although no terror organisation ever claimed responsibility, it is widely believed that it was the work of Loyalists. The device exploded just as UDR Lance Corporal Victor Smyth (54) was driving past.

His car was wrecked and he burned to death as it caught fire, trapped inside. An RUC patrol opened fire on two suspects running from the scene but they managed to escape. A piper played a lament at Smyth's funeral as the coffin, draped with the Union flag, was carried from his home in Jervis Street across Portadown to Seagoe Cemetery with several thousand people lining the route.

The UFF then threw a bomb into the house of a local Republican councillor in Cedar Avenue, close to the Antrim Road in Belfast. The intended target was not in the house at the time, although three children were. The device exploded and killed Bridget Breen (33) who lived nearby. The following day, Samuel Waring (20) who had possible links to the IRA was shot near La Salle Drive just off the Falls Road. He had recently been released from the prison at Long Kesh and was a budding professional footballer. It is thought that he was killed by Republicans and his death was certainly not claimed by Loyalist terror groups.

The following day, after severe rioting between the UDA and the Army in the Shankill area, two Protestants were shot dead, allegedly by the Army and very possibly in the crossfire between soldiers and Loyalist gunmen. The dead were Robert McKinnie (49) father of five and Robert Johnston (50); there is no evidence to link either of them to the paramilitaries.

PARA SHOOT OUT

Kevin Myers, Journalist

That autumn, there had been intensifying friction between the local Protestant paramilitary Ulster Defence Association and the Parachute Regiment. One evening, I got a phone-call from a taxi driver, warning me that serious trouble was brewing on the Loyalist Shankill Road. He suggested I go to the Matchett Street area, and I immediately drove there, not having the least idea what I would I do once I arrived, but anxious to do it regardless.

Well, I had seen IRA men in action, many, many times, and I knew how they had honed their street-fighting skills. But a UDA ambush was a sight to behold, straight out of the textbook marked 'Loyalist caricature'. A car was parked in Matchett Street with its boot open, and a uniformed UDA man was distributing guns – Sterling sub-machine guns and SLR semi-automatic rifles – to other uniformed UDA men, who, being good Protestants, were queuing politely in their brand new, wife-ironed combat-fatigues.

Once armed, the various UDA men took up position at street corners, waiting for some obliging paratrooper patrol to walk wide-eyed into this rather sportingly ostentatious ambush, no doubt then to be obligingly slaughtered by the loyal sons of Ulster. With about as much wit as the would-be ambushers were themselves exhibiting, I got out of my car, and sauntered up to the quartermaster as he was instructing a pot-bellied warrior in army surplus clothes how to fire his rifle. There is, I suppose, no more propitious time to learn the rudiments of firearms-drill than in those final few seconds before open warfare with the 1st Battalion, the Parachute Regiment.

Flashing my press card, I said: 'You lads look as if you're planning a bit of action.'

The quartermaster looked around in wild alarm.

'What gev ye that idea?' he yelped incredulously. I nodded around me, at the various ridiculous creatures hammily imitating what they imagined to be a soldierly mien.

'Oh, you know, this and that.' He paused, before succumbing to – what must have seemed to him – my almost irresistible intellectual acuity.

Above, left: A 'C' Coy 1RGJ foot patrol heading for the exit gates of the joint RUC/military base at Castle Hill, Dungannon. Closed several years ago, the derelict buildings remain today as a reminder of these scenes.
Above, right: 'Not sure I like it here Mam.' A pensive squaddie on the railway bridge at Beech Valley, Dungannon. At the time this was taken, the line – from Portadown to Derry – was ten years closed with the station buildings on the trackbed below him long-demolished. The White Heather Club, where Scottish balladeer Andy Stewart often starred, forms the backdrop.

'Aye, there's going to be trouble all right, and I tell you what, we'll be teaching them there Para fuckers – excuse the language – a lesson they won't be forgetting in a hurry.'

'You're going to ambush the Paras like this?'

'We are, aye. Why? Anything wrong?'

'No, no. But you know it's very fucking dangerous taking those boys on?'

'It is for them – right lads?' A couple of neatly-uniformed UDA men obediently waiting for their guns, chuckled in agreement, and exchanged knowing smiles. 'Now here young fella; you better get offside before the lead starts flying,' the quartermaster advised me in an avuncular way. 'Go on. Fuck off wi' ye.'

I didn't always take such wise advice, but from the manner of these grotesque and bumbling infants, it was very likely something horrible was soon going to happen, so I promptly left. I'd only gone a few hundred yards when a cacophony of gunfire announced that the ambush had been sprung. It was – as I had anticipated – both inept and bloody. No soldiers were hit, but at least half a dozen people were shot, and two middle aged and apparently innocent men – Robert Ritchie McKinnie and Robert Johnston – were killed, presumably by the Paras, for that tended to be the latter's way. Some months later, one of the ambush party told me what had happened, deeply indignant at the way the evening had gone.

'They come round the corner, and we opened fire at them, and fuck me, then they started firing all over the fucking place. At us'ns! And we're fucking British, for fuck's sake.'

On the 10th, an IRA landmine, thought to have been around 500lbs and the largest seen at the time, exploded as an Argyll and Sutherland Highlanders mobile vehicle drove over it just outside of Dungannon. Lance Corporal Duncan McPhee (21) from the Glasgow area and Private Douglas Richmond (21) from Clydebank were killed at the scene and Lance Corporal William McIntyre (23) a married father of one from Aberdeen died of his wounds the next day. On the same day, the RGJ lost Lance Corporal Ian George (25) in vague circumstances. Sources from the regiment close to me confirmed that he was shot by an IRA sniper in east Belfast.

On the 13th a Loyalist murder gang walked into a Catholic bar on Springfield Road, Belfast and shot Patrick Doyle (19) who worked there; another senseless and random sectarian murder. The next day – a Wednesday – a member of the UFF was shot by an RUC officer in the Newtownards Road area of Belfast as he attempted a robbery. The policeman was off duty at the time and was hit first by Robert Warnock (18) but managed to fire back and killed the Loyalist terrorist.

MEASURING ME FOR MY COFFIN

Lieutenant David Ash, Light Infantry

We were on foot patrols with two sections on the ground, mutually supporting each other when we came under erratic sniper fire. Fortunately we had no casualties and did not return fire. Unfortunately, we weren't able to identify specific firing points. People in those streets seemed to pay little heed to shooting. I suppose they knew that they weren't the targets and felt quite safe, as long as they didn't get in the way of crossfire. But I still found it a bizarre sight. A patrol could be pinned down under fire in one street; eight terrified men on the edge of life and death in a desperate firefight. In the next street parallel to it, mothers with toddlers in push chairs could be seen walking down the pavement quite normally on their way to the shops; it felt weird!

On this particular day, two women began to follow behind me at the bottom of Jamaica Street and I could hear them discussing how tall they thought I was, deciding what size coffin I'd need! 'Six feet tall, so your man is,' one of them said. 'Aye, six feet should do it,' the other one said. 'It'll be a six foot box for him. Six feet long; six feet down! That's where you belong right enough, fucking soldier you!' They went off chanting my coffin dimensions, hooting and cackling with shrill voices. Then the shooting started again: Crack! Crack! Crack! Loud high velocity whipcracks of bullets coming and going from somewhere; but where? You can never tell. The soldiers dived for cover and looked at me for orders, faces gone completely white.

On the 14th, a UVF car bomb left outside the Imperial Hotel in north Belfast exploded, killing a passing taxi driver –Andrew McKibben (28) – outright and fatally injuring two others. Martha Smylie (91) a resident in a nursing home and Anne Murray (53) died over the next two days. Two of the three were Protestants.

Nearly a month earlier, Corporal John Davies (22) had been shot whilst on foot patrol in the Bogside in Londonderry. The soldier from the RRF died in hospital of his wounds on 15 September. On the same day, Staff Sergeant John Gardener Craig (39) of the Royal Artillery was killed in a RTA whilst on duty.

Over the next few days both the UVF and the IRA lost members when Sinclair Johnston (UVF) was shot by the RUC in Larne, Co Antrim and Michael Quigley (IRA) was shot by the Army on the Creggan Estate, Londonderry. Quigley was killed in what Republican apologists describe as 'disputed' circumstances. A soldier had been shot and a gunman had been observed behind a wall on the Creggan Estate. The soldier, Guardsman John Van Beck (26) of the Scots Guards died in Altnagelvin Hospital in Londonderry on the 18th after being fatally wounded by an IRA sniper whilst on foot patrol. The Army stated that as the gunman stood to fire another round a soldier shot him dead. Quigley – whose name, tellingly appears on the Republican Roll of Honour – it was claimed, had merely been standing to see if the firing had stopped. If he was involved and indeed no weapon was found as was claimed, then his death was a tragedy. However, it was not unknown for the locals or IRA dickers to spirit weapons away. It made the Army look like murderers; it was more recruiting done for the Provisionals and another 'Irish martyr' claimed for the terrorists.

What should be noted, irrespective of the circumstances in which Michael Quigley was killed, was that the Provisionals had yet again chosen a residential area, where civilians would be going about their lawful activities, because even on the Creggan there were still some decent, albeit probably alienated people going about their everyday business. They had taken that area and turned it into a battlefield, cynically believing that they could use children or housewives as cover and that the Army would not fire back. For all that they accused British soldiers of being murderers, they were also aware of the Army's discipline and restraint and their reputation for fair play. The author accepts that this was not always the case, but those who sullied the reputation of the British Army were few and far between.

On the same day that both Quigley and the Scots Guards soldier died, Private Frank Bell (18) of the Parachute Regiment was shot and fatally wounded during an IRA attack on the Ballymurphy estate in Belfast; he died three days later. The UDR lost another member when Private Andrew Nelson Simpson (36) was killed in an RTA; circumstances and place unknown.

On the 19th Private Tommy Stoker (18) died of wounds received on 27 July in a friendly fire incident. He had only been in Belfast three days when he was placed in an OP on Berwick Road, some 600 metres from his base in the Flax Street Mill. Whilst he kept a watchful eye over the area of Alliance Avenue, a colleague was in an adjoining room, fitting an IWS (individual weapon site) to his SLR rifle. The soldier had a round chambered – one 'up the spout' as squaddies say – and the safety catch must have slipped off. As he caught the trigger a round was discharged into Stoker's back. He died in the RVH with his distraught parents at his bedside.

The IRA lost another gunman when Joseph McComiskey (18) was shot in the Ardoyne area by the Army shortly after another soldier was badly wounded by gunmen using a rioting mob as cover. The UDR was targeted again as killers from the IRA burst into the Killynick, Co Fermanagh home of UDR soldier Private Thomas Bullock. The Bullocks farmed a large property close to the border hamlet of Aghalane near the Enniskillen-Belturbet Road and as such were in an extremely vulnerable position. A group of nine IRA gunmen in two cars crossed the border and attacked the house as the UDR man and his wife watched television. Mrs Emily Bullock was gunned down in the hallway as she answered the door and then the gang burst into the lounge and murdered Private Bullock (53), shooting him several times in the head. John Potter in his *Testimony To Courage* reports that the farmhouse remains empty to this day.

The other car belonging to the same IRA gang which murdered the Bullocks then raided the home of another UDR soldier living nearby. Private Darling, a member of 4 UDR, was out at work, but they found his sister home and threatened her with death unless she revealed the whereabouts of her brother's service weapon. When she refused, they threatened to take one of her children outside and shoot him; she continued to resist and, after wrecking her furniture, the men drove off empty-handed. The cars met at the border and fired shots at the local Post Office before crossing back into Eire loudly cheering and sounding their car horns.

A further sectarian murder took place in Belfast and then on the 22nd the IRA ambushed a joint Army-RUC patrol in the border area around Crossmaglen. In the ambush, second

With what appears to be the cordoned aftermath of an IED attack on the footpath behind them, two soldiers (thought to be Cheshires) proceed west along Madrid Street at its junction with Lisbon Street in east Belfast's Short Strand.

Lieutenant Stewart Gardiner (23) of the Argyll and Sutherland Highlanders (ASH) was killed and an RUC man was badly injured. The young subaltern was the fourth ASH soldier to die in 1972; there would be four more. A further tragedy took place the next day, when the wounded RUC officer's distraught mother collapsed and died at his hospital bedside from a suspected heart attack.

THE DEATH OF STEWART GARDINER

Jim, Argyll and Sutherland Highlanders

Information came in that a bomb had been planted on Moybane Road, close to the border and we had to check it out. We were helicopter in two groups of four to a hill overlooking

Drummuckavall. As we made our way downhill to the road, I found a length of wire. I told the Colour Sergeant to come down and have a look and we followed it along the side of the road. I thought we would walk into a bomb but there was nothing attached to the end of the wire. We then retraced our steps in the opposite direction. At one point the wire crossed the road in a cleverly concealed groove. The other side of the road was over the border so we had to call up the Gardai. When they had checked it out – no bomb or control point – we stood at the side of the road talking. I said I'd go and start rolling up the wire and walked maybe fifty yards when there was a burst of gunfire. Bullets pinged past me as I dived for the ground. I thought it was me that was the target, but it was the other group. I shouted to check if they were OK and began crawling back down.

When I got back our platoon commander was lying on his back with blood spurting out of a hole in his side. We put a bandage pack on the hole and the blood came through; another bandage and it still came through. We used about four although we knew that more than two and it was pointless. He was in deep shock, not registering anything. His face was draining of colour and it was as if he was clenching his teeth, breathing hard through them. I called in a report as the radio operator had been shot as well. We were told to get out of the ambush area before help could come. We moved up the road a bit and called for help again. We were told no again by the company commander. It was too dangerous for vehicles to come down. We decided to get our own transport and stopped the first car that came along and dragged the driver out. I got in the back with the platoon commander on my lap and we sped off for the base, two miles away. The others stopped another car and followed us shortly after. The platoon commander was all but dead. I had his head in my lap. A rifle had been lost at the ambush site and 2 RUC police officers volunteered to go down to have a look for it. Both were shot.

≈≋∘≈∘≈≋≈

The killing switched to the north again and on the 25th an armoured vehicle of the Royal Anglians was attacked and Corporal John Barry (22) was shot in the head and died instantly. The attack took place near Cyprus Street in the Falls area. A young Catholic civilian was then shot and killed by plain clothes soldiers operating in the Falls Road area; it is unlikely that he was an IRA member but rather the victim of a tragic misunderstanding. Daniel Rooney (19) was shot whilst on St James Crescent; further details are not known.

On the 26th Guardsman George Lockhart (24) of the Scots Guards, who had been shot whilst on patrol in Londonderry's Bogside area, died of his wounds in the RVH. The same day a UVF bomb attack on a Catholic club in Upper Library Street in Belfast resulted in the fatal wounding and later death of Daniel McErlean (48) a waiter at the club. The following day, the UFF abducted and killed a young Catholic, James Boyle (16). The bloody tit for tat continued and the IRA shot dead a Protestant Alexander Green (45). They rounded the day off with the murder of Paul McCartan (52) who was shot by Loyalists at his home in Park Avenue, Strandtown in Belfast.

Another murder took place hours later when the UVF shot Edward Pavis (32), a Protestant, after he was suspected of selling arms to the IRA. *Lost Lives* reports that the killer of Pavis was none other than Lenny Murphy, a member of the 'Shankill Butchers'. Murphy was a killer at the age of twenty, and for the remainder of his life excelled in the 'art' of the bloodletting. Like 'Doctor Death' Steenson, it is likely that he would have been a killer even without the smoke-screen of the Troubles. The Shankill Butchers were a group of UVF men who became infamous for their Loyalist paramilitary activities in Belfast. They specialised in late-night abduction, torture and killings (often slashing the throats of their Catholic victims) although they also killed many Protestants as the result of feuds and personal grudges. The police found it impossible to obtain many leads on the men due to the wall of silence in the Shankill community. The group operated beyond the remit of the leadership of the UVF and their reign of terror caused even that hardened murder group acute embarrassment.

The gang brought a new level of paramilitary violence to a country already hardened by death and destruction. While most of the members were eventually caught and received the longest combined prison sentences in British legal history, Murphy and his two chief lieutenants escaped prosecution. He was later killed in November 1982 by the IRA. Intelligence circles believe that the Republicans were told how to find Murphy by his fellow Loyalists; he was as much of a threat to his own side. As one Belfast resident said of him: 'The guy was not someone you would desire to meet. Murphy's thirst for blood and in particular his pathological hatred of Catholics was astonishing.'

On the final Monday of the month, a four day conference was held at Darlington, on Teesside in northern England to discuss the issue of devolution and power-sharing. The Darlington meeting consisted of the Ulster Unionist Party, the Northern Ireland Labour Party (NILP), the Alliance Party of Northern Ireland (APNI), and William Whitelaw, Secretary of State for Northern Ireland. The Social Democratic and Labour Party (SDLP) refused to attend because of the thorny issue of internment. Some hard-line Unionists also refused to attend. Although many previously 'taboo' subjects were discussed, no agreement was reached on the shape of any future Northern Ireland government. At the same time, there were semi-formal talks between Prime Minister Heath and Jack Lynch, *Taoiseach* (Prime Minister) of the Irish Republic.

On the 29th, the IRA lost two more of its members at the hands of the Army. In the first incident, Jimmy Quigley (18) was lying in wait in a shop in Servia Street, Falls area to shoot at an Army patrol. He was observed on the roof of the shop by troops, possibly from the Royal Anglians, and shot dead. An American- manufactured Garand rifle was found close to his body. A fierce gun battle broke out between the 'Angle irons' and the IRA, and a lone soldier from 3RGJ shot and killed Patricia McKay (20) of the Official IRA. Republican apologists complained that she was unarmed and taking no part in the gun battles raging around the Falls Road area. She is almost eulogised in both the main text and the Brendan Hughes interview in Ed Maloney's *Voices From The Grave* (pp84/5), although Hughes says that he took the Armalite from her, at which point she had her hands on a rifle, so was clearly not unarmed. The fact that she was then killed, whilst tragic for her family, does not excuse her actions. That Hughes later spoke at her funeral implies a guilty conscience for getting an impressionable girl killed in an urban battle of his and the IRA's making. The following is the account of the soldier who killed McKay.

RIFLEMAN, ROYAL GREEN JACKETS

Death on the Reservation

We were halfway through a very busy tour of duty. The battalion had already suffered two dead and countless wounded; one of the dead being from our own Company. Based in North Howard Street Mill, I was employed as a radio operator for 'B' Company Commander. Virtually on a daily basis the Company Commanders were required to attend briefing sessions with the Commanding Officer who was based in Tactical Headquarters at Springfield Road [approximately a mile away]. The quickest, but not the safest route was to drive down the Falls Road and take a risk that as long as we didn't set a pattern we would get away with it.

Approximately mid morning, the Company Commander informed his mobile team that he was required at Tac and that we would do the 'dobbie dash', the term used for taking the more dangerous but quickest route to Tac. We drove out of the Mill and onto the Falls Road; almost immediately we saw that our path was blocked by a hijacked double decker bus. Simultaneously we heard a large amount of small arms fire, although the gunfire at that time was not being directed at us. The Falls Road was also the Battalion boundary and it appeared that the neighboring unit had run into some serious grief. This was the start of a gun battle that was to last all day and well into the evening. 'B' Company had to deploy into their neighbouring unit's area and one of its platoons was virtually cut off and unable to extract a casualty.

Our vehicle was an open-topped Land Rover which offered no protection; on board were four men, including myself. Upon seeing the bus we immediately exited the vehicle and took cover along a row of shops, a distance of some ten metres. The firing by this time had intensified and we knew that many gunmen had come out onto the streets. The call had gone out for the immediate reaction platoon to come and support us. To try and identify where the firing was coming from I informed the Coy Commander that I was going to get into the roof of one of the shops. I entered it – a sewing shop – and explained to the old lady behind the counter that I was going into her attic. I soon discovered that I had view of approximately seven streets and that the height I was at gave me a good view of all the area; we had nicknamed the area 'the Reservation' owing to its hostility on our previous tour in 1971. The firing at this time was intense and I witnessed a Saracen armoured car move from right to left engaging with his Browning machine gun at targets I could not as yet see.

I knew that I probably had one of the best views of the area and had a strange feeling that I would witness something. I remember feeling very calm. Within a minute or so of my arrival in the attic the firing slowly stopped until all guns were silent. From experience I knew that the IRA would try to move their weapons out of the area so I began to scan the empty streets through my optical sights (the sights had only recently been issued and gave us an incredible advantage). After a few minutes I saw a door open and a male head pop out and looked left and right; it went inside and closed the door. This was the only activity that I had seen and decided to keep my scope on the door. A few minutes later the door opened once more and a man and woman exited; the woman was wearing a large maxi coat which she held closed with one of her hands. They made their way across the street towards an adjoining road which would have placed them out of my sight, but halfway across the road her coat came open and I had clear sight of a rifle barrel pointing downwards under the women's arm. I instinctively knew that I had to fire at the woman; I also knew that I only had seconds to react before she disappeared round the corner and out of sight.

The distance was about 200m although through my optics she looked very much closer. I had used my firearm on the previous tour of duty but this time it was very different. Having a scope on the weapon brought the situation to an entirely different level; it was if I didn't need to fire, I could just as easily trip her up with my rifle. Blocking all other thoughts out of my mind I took the first pressure on the trigger and then slowly squeezed and the bullet was released. I had aimed for the bulk of the body; as soon as I had fully engaged the trigger the woman fell to the ground. My attention immediately turned to the weapon, which had also fallen to the ground. The man ignored the woman, grabbed the weapon and began to run. I fired further shots at him in quick succession; sadly I did not manage to stop him although I hit him in the arm and he had to have it removed.

The woman was still on the road not moving, but a few seconds later I saw a pair of hands sneak out from the corner and tried to fasten onto her feet in an attempt to recover her. I fired further shots and the hands disappeared. I decided to rejoin the remainder of the group, and within a few minutes I was briefing the Company Commander about the incident. He then received information from our Battalion Headquarters that a woman had been admitted to the Royal Victoria Hospital with gunshot wounds. We quickly drove to the hospital. On arrival I saw the female just prior to going into theatre; it was then that I realised just how young she was. There was nothing further we could do at that moment so we rejoined the company.

Following our withdrawal later that evening we received further news informing us that the young terrorist had died. There were no shouts of joy, no 'well done'; we knew by then that the man I had shot was the girl's partner and our thoughts were of anger at him. Why had he placed her in such a position that she lost her life; what a waste. Later the IRA admitted that the woman was one of their members but they stated she was unarmed at the time; I don't think so. She was buried with full military honours.

In the same fighting, both wings of the IRA attacked the Anglians and Private Ian Burt (18) from Essex was shot and killed close to Servia Street. The Army stated that up to a dozen gunmen were involved and in addition to the two killed at least one other was wounded.

CAR TROUBLE IN BELFAST

Mick 'Benny' Hill, Royal Anglians

I much preferred working alongside and with the Royal Marines. They were much more efficient and really laid back. 'Course we all feel that our own mob are the best and I am no exception when it comes to talking about the Royal Anglians, but the Marines were a top bunch.

I remember vividly when three of my mates, in plain clothes and on undercover ops in Belfast, broke down on the Grosvenor Road, close to the hot spots of Leeson Street. and the Lower Falls. This was not a healthy part of the world, especially if you had a 'Norf Landun' or Leicester accent! One of the blokes walked to Mulhouse Base, and explained the problem to the Ops Officer of the Marine Company based there. He got no stupid questions, no time wasting, just a PIG rapidly dispatched. The two blokes were realistically 'arrested' so as not to arouse suspicion amongst the locals. They must have been pissing themselves in that area with Dickers and other suspicious people about. The locals recognised strangers and would be on the lookout for plain clothes soldiers or police or even Loyalist murder gangs.

The Marines had the car towed into Mulhouse, and the only questions they were asked were 'Do you need privacy to use the phone?' and 'Do you want to make arrangements about the car?' Top blokes!

As the month ended the UVF and UFF were involved in three more killings. On the 30th they shot and killed a fellow Protestant, Thomas Paisley at Straid Road, Ballyclare, Co Antrim, during an attempted robbery. They then abducted Francis Lane (23), a student. He was tortured and shot and his ravaged body was found dumped on Glencairn Road in Belfast. The district is to the north-west of Belfast but conveniently close to the Crumlin Road and an easy escape route for the Loyalist killers. Finally, after a bombing attack outside a Catholic bar in Belfast city centre, they killed Patrick McKee (24) and fatally wounded James Gillen as they watched television in the crowded drinking area. James Gillen (21) died of his injures almost three weeks later. The murder gang had planted a stolen car packed with explosives outside Conlon's Bar in Smithfield, just a short half-mile car dash to the safety of the Shankill Road.

On the same day tragedy struck the Rudman family for the second time. The Rudmans from Hartlepool in the north-east had already lost one of their soldier sons the year before, killed by the IRA in Dungannon. John Rudman (21), Light Infantry was shot and killed on 14 September 1971. A year later, his brother Thomas (20) was shot and killed whilst on foot patrol in Ladbrook Drive in the Ardoyne. His twin, also serving with the Light Infantry, was immediately air lifted out of Northern Ireland and the Army stated that he would not serve there again.

As the final month of summer drew to a close and autumn beckoned, a soldier on patrol in the Andersonstown area had a negligent discharge and John Kelly (44) a father of five was shot dead. The Army claim that the weapon was accidentally discharged when civilians grappled with the soldier for possession of the rifle; Republicans claim that the soldier deliberately fired into the crowd. The author is not so naive as to believe that every soldier who served in Northern Ireland was an angel and there were those who did lose control. In this instance, my gut feeling is that he acted under extreme provocation and that the discharge was a tragic and avoidable accident. In any case, whatever the truth of the matter – and only the soldier concerned and those in the immediate vicinity really know – the Provisional IRA and Sinn Féin would be sure to 'milk' the tragedy for all the propaganda they could. In a dozen Irish bars up and down the eastern United States, the 'fascist' British Army would again by demonised by hundreds of Irish-Americans.

For many years Republicans and their sympathisers in both the Irish and British press have maintained that there was collusion between the Army and the Loyalist murder gangs. Whilst this author gives no credibility to these stories, it would be remiss not to at least bring them into the frame of the accounts of 1972. An undercover and very secretive Army unit that I cannot name and its predecessors were accused by Sinn Féin/IRA of collusion in some sectarian murders in that they 'paved the way' for some attacks to take place. Specifically, the British Army was alleged to have secured restriction orders banning troops and patrols from certain areas at certain times. This it was alleged would be to facilitate safe passage into and out of Catholic areas in order to carry out random sectarian killings. Some families of those murdered stated that regular Army patrols failed to materialise or that soldiers disappeared 'as if by magic' shortly before a sectarian attack. This implied that HQNI, the RUC and the British government either had tacit prior knowledge of an attack or actively agreeing to requests from the UDA/UFF, UVF and Red Hand Commandos. I believe that there may have been some collusion between members of the UDR deliberately placed by Protestant terror groups, but the vast majority of the UDR were decent and professional soldiers. Consequently, this author dismisses this out of hand as Republican propaganda.

September ended with the deaths of 50 people. These included 17 soldiers, 27 civilians, 4 IRA members and 2 Loyalist paramilitaries. Of the civilians killed, seventeen were killed by Loyalists in either outright sectarian murders or in bomb attacks; the IRA were responsible for two sectarian murders.

CHAPTER TEN

OCTOBER

David Cassidy's 'How Can I Be Sure?' was playing on the radios. In Paris the Americans and North Vietnamese were talking peace. A passenger plane transporting a rugby team crashed in the Andes. Rescuers came on the 20 December but the survivors had resorted to cannibalism.

One of the worst kept secrets of the Troubles, viewed with the invaluable weapon of hindsight, was the Army's ingenious undercover plan that created an apparently bona-fide mobile laundry service, with the explicit aim of infiltrating Republican areas to collect forensic evidence. The Four Square Laundry was set up in 1972 and involved a mobile laundry collection and delivery service in Belfast. The delivery vans also allegedly contained concealed compartments to allow undercover operatives to secretly observe the goings on in the heart of IRA territory.

Laundry was collected – the Army having shrewdly undercut local rivals – washed in Army premises having first been tested for evidence of arms or explosives handling, and then returned in the same open manner. The turnaround from collecting, examining, cleaning and returning had to be fast so as to not arouse the suspicions of the customers; if items were retained for longer than usual, it wouldn't take much for the opposition to smell a rat and the whole operation would have been blown. Therefore the timing had to be exquisite.

During the laundry's lifetime, two IRA members or sympathisers had been 'turned' by INT and were privy to the operation. The two men are thought to have been Seamus Wright and Kevin McKee, known in Army-speak as 'Freds'. 'Freds' were selected from PIRA men arrested in the swoops. They were taken to barracks, plied with offers of money and women or simply cajoled and threatened into becoming informers. However, under interrogation from an IRA torture team, Wright and McKee confessed all and the game was on for the Provisionals to kill the Army operatives.

At approximately 11:30 on Monday 2 October, unaware that they had been rumbled, one of the vans containing Lance Corporal Sarah Warke (WRAC) and Sapper Edward Stuart (20) of the Royal Engineers, drove into the Twinbrook estate in south-west Belfast. As they parked outside a house in Juniper Park, Sarah Warke approached the front door whilst Edward Stuart remained in the van. An IRA team in a stolen car drove by and attacked the two with machine gun fire. Twenty shots hit the van and Sapper Stuart was very badly wounded, but Lance Corporal Warke escaped into the house, pulled the startled 'customer' inside and locked the door, shouting that it was a Loyalist attack.

Totally convinced that it was, the woman and other local Catholics shielded her from the IRA until help arrived. Sapper Stuart was clearly dying and two local men including a Catholic priest, also suspecting a Loyalist attack, jumped into the van and drove in the direction of a local hospital, later flagging down a passing ambulance. Sadly it was too late for the undercover soldier and he died en route. Lance Corporal Warke was rescued by a joint RUC/Army patrol and was quickly shipped out of the Province; she was one incredibly brave and resourceful woman. She was also incredibly lucky.

At the same time as the laundry operation, Army INT had also been running a massage parlour – a 'knocking shop' in local parlance – and had female operatives listening in to the pillow talk of local players or any other Republican with loose lips and a story worth hearing. It is thought that during the course of the operation the identity of one of the three IRA men who had killed three Scottish soldiers in Ligoniel the previous year was revealed. Patrick McAdorey was considered to be one of the three gunmen who ambushed the Scottish boys after they had been lured, unarmed to a supposed 'party' whilst they were drunk and off duty and shot them down in cold blood.

The parlour – the Gemini Health Studios – was located above a house at 397 Antrim Road in north Belfast and this information was revealed to the IRA during the 'interviews' with Wright and McKee. At the same time that the Four Square Laundry van was being hit, the Provisionals also attacked the massage parlour and an assassination team entered the house and began creeping up the stairs. Fortunately for the undercover Army operatives, one of the terrorists tripped and, proving that the IRA can have NDs too, fired a burst of machine gun fire into the steps and walls. At this, the Provos panicked and ran out of the building leaving the INT operators rumbled but still alive. A client in a waiting-room was shot and injured as the IRA gunmen fled the scene.

That was the end of the Four Square Laundry and the Gemini Health Studios; even more alert, the IRA made it doubly hard for the Army to mount such undercover operations. Seamus Wright and Kevin McKee were taken away and it is believed that they were taken to South Armagh and shot; their bodies were never discovered. They had been held and interrogated by the Provisionals – McKee broke after two solid days of brutal questioning – and then allowed to go free. The men returned to their homes but this was an elaborate ploy by the IRA to ensure that if Army undercover troops were observing the houses of their two 'Freds' their suspicions would not be aroused. The two were then called in for further 'questioning' once PIRA had ascertained that their information about undercover operations was correct. They were immediately handed over to the 'nutting squad' who killed them in separate locations. Kevin McKee was the nephew of Billy McKee, a founder member of PIRA and McKee's actions in informing on his bosses were a major embarrassment for that iconic Republican family. It is believed that his 'executioners' were Jim Bryson and Tommy Tolan, both later killed. Bryson was shot on the 'Murph by Green Jackets in August 1973 and Tolan was killed in an internal feud with the Officials in 1977.

In the aftermath the Provisional IRA released a press statement claiming that they had 'executed' no fewer than five undercover British soldiers, typical overblown Provisional propaganda. It has been said that the former customers of the Four Square Laundry often complained that other cleaning companies didn't have the excellent service the Army had provided. It was also rumoured that the Army was running a third undercover 'sting' operation in the area of College Square in Belfast, but the author is unable to substantiate this and on this occasion, will save the MOD's censorship department some black ink. All I can state with any certainty is that the unnamable Specialist Army unit had 'evacuated the premises' by the time that the Provisionals arrived.

The following account of the Four Square Laundry was sent to me and permission to use it was given on the condition that the writer was not identified. I reproduce the soldier's words here without further comment.

THE FOUR SQUARE LAUNDRY

Anonymous Soldier

A couple of years before I arrived, Army Intelligence had literally been taking in the IRA's dirty washing, with spectacular results. One of the Belfast units of the a specialist Army unit that I cannot name had dreamt up the Army's most secret and successful intelligence operation. The members of the unit which included a couple of Army girls had been through background rehearsals and elocution lessons until they could pass themselves off as Belfast locals.

They were given their secure flat in Belfast and a small business office near the city centre, where they ran the Four Square Laundry. The laundry business was a smash hit from the beginning. One undercover soldier drove the laundry van while another spied from a concealed compartment above the driver's cab. The girls went from door to door in the most hardline terrorist housing estates of west Belfast, handing out leaflets introducing their new service. There was a special cut-price deal on dry cleaning gents' suits, trousers and casual jackets. 'Rock-bottom prices for a limited period only; hurry, hurry, get your bargains now!' And the housewives of Belfast handed in their men's clothes at the beginning of the week and got them back, immaculately laundered and pressed, 48 hours later.

It was a service with more than a smile; the secret owners of the Four Square Laundry could hardly keep from laughing out loud. Each laundry bag was neatly tagged with the owner's name and address. Back in the central Belfast office the bags were re-labelled with fake names, switched to an unmarked van and driven to Aldergrove Airport. Every item of clothing was 'paraffin-tested', a swift and simple chemical test which can show up traces of gunpowder and explosives residue on anyone who has fired a weapon. The clothes were then loaded into an RAH Hercules and flown to an English base. Then they were delivered to a commercial dry-cleaning company, who were told that they were being given a trial contract for servicemen's family laundry. The clothes were beautifully cleaned, on over-time rates, and air-freighted back to Belfast.

A week or so later, the proud owners of newly cleaned jackets which had shown traces of powder were being arrested at bus stops and Social Security offices and pubs. And they never twigged. Terrorists were being targeted at an enormous rate and, given the lack of business overheads on their official accounts, the Four Square Laundry was turning in a healthy profit.

But it all came to a grisly end. It was inevitable that the Provisionals should start to take an interest in the flourishing operation. Not because they suspected it was an intelligence front but because it was a promising looking business and it wasn't paying protection money to the IRA. Republican patriotism in Ulster is one-tenth politics and nine-tenths straight money-making gangsterism for the big boys in the movement. Every pub, club, taxi and building site had to pay them protection money,

The laundry would happily have handed over its entire income in protection money. But round about the same time, an informer, a tout who knew about the operation, slipped away from his Army minders and blew the secret to the Provos. When the van went out on its next run, it was ambushed. One IRA man shot the driver and another let a burst from an automatic into the bodywork above the cab. It was a warning to us all about the dangers of ever trusting a tout.

———◦◦◦◦———

It was clearly a major setback for British Intelligence but in terms of loss of life, other than the tragic loss of Sapper Edwards, it could have been much worse. For the British, however, an intelligence coup was just around the corner with the 'turning' of Eamon Molloy, Quartermaster of the Belfast Brigade of the Provisional IRA. He was the highest profile member of the IRA – officially – to be recruited in those early days of the war with the Republicans. He was passing high grade information which led not only to arrests of major players but also the discovery of arms and ammunition dumps, including his own.

He gave the British Army a massive amount of incredibly high grade information, some of which led to the arrest of at least seventeen leading Provisionals, including Gerry Adams and Brendan Hughes in 1973. Some sources estimate the number of men 'lifted' as a result of Molloy's information may be as high as 25, and the damage caused by Molloy's informing was so great that the IRA had to call a ceasefire in 1975 to recover their strength. This allegation has never been officially confirmed by the IRA. Molloy (21) was abducted from his home in the Oldpark area of Ardoyne, North Belfast in 1975 after being accused of being a British informer. While is it not known when exactly he was taken, the speculative date of 1 July has been adopted as his date of death. Sources from within the Provisionals say that he was tortured and then tried before an IRA 'kangaroo' court before being shot. His body was the first of the 'disappeared' to be recovered after the IRA issued their list of victims in May 1999. Within 24 hours of the statement's release, his skeletal remains were found in a coffin in a grave yard at Faughart, Co Louth. Local Republicans denied that the 21-year-old had been originally buried in the area but that he had been recovered from elsewhere and transported to the remote graveyard by the Provisional IRA.

Another top Provisional who was also working for British Intelligence in 1972 was Dennis Donaldson, a convicted bomber and a hunger striker, who was not publicly uncovered until late 2005. Gerry Adams announced at a press conference that Donaldson had been a paid informer for British intelligence. Incredibly enough, Donaldson confirmed this himself soon after in a broadcast statement on the Irish State Television station (RTE). He admitted that he had been recruited after compromising himself during 'a vulnerable time in my life.' He had operated largely in the Republican heartland of west Belfast and was a well known figure in Republican circles. He had initially joined the old IRA several years before the Troubles and joined the fledgling Provisionals sometime around 1970 or 1971.

Jim Gibney, writing in the *Irish Times* described Donaldson's 'hero' status after his actions during a major battle in the Short Strand area in 1970 when he took part in the IRA's defence of St Matthew's Chapel in the face of an armed Loyalist attack. A recent article by Liam Clarke (March 2010) suggested that the 'battle' might have been somewhat contrived by the Provisionals, in order to appear as protectors of Catholic communities. The Protestants claim that they were 'lured' into the Short Strand and that Donaldson actually shot an IRA member, Henry McIlhone, albeit accidentally. Republican legend disputes this of course.

In March 2006, several months after the revelations, Hugh Jordan, a journalist for the *Sunday World*, tracked Donaldson down. He was living in an isolated cottage near Glenties in County Donegal. Once this had been discovered by the Republican movement, it was only a matter of time before their particular brand of 'justice' caught up with him. Barely a month later, on 4 April 2006, Donaldson was found shot dead inside his cottage. His death was condemned as a barbaric act in a statement by Northern Ireland Secretary of State Peter Hain. Simultaneously, Irish Prime Minister Bertie Ahern also condemned the 'brutal murder' of the former informer.

The Provisional IRA issued a terse statement saying that it had 'no involvement whatsoever' with the murder. It was also condemned even less convincingly by Gerry Adams. Finally, just over a week later, on 12 March, the 'Real IRA' claimed responsibility for his death. 'We always intended to claim the operation, but we wanted to wait until we had first executed Crown forces personnel. That was secured at Masserene.' This was a reference to the murders at Masserene Barracks of Sappers Mark Quinsey (23) from Birmingham and Patrick Azimkar (21) from Wood Green, North London on 8 March 2009.

It should be noted that the year of 1972 was the first year that the IRA tactic of 'disappearing' people first became evident. The bodies of victims were usually dumped somewhere public as a warning to others as to the consequences of informing. Occasionally, as in the case of McKee and Wright (Four Square Laundry) where untold embarrassment would be caused to dynastic Republican families or other prominent supporters, the bodies vanished.

The final postscript of the Four Square Laundry fiasco was that the IRA was clearly rattled and they hastily shot and killed Geoffrey Hamilton (23) in the Lower Falls Road area. His 'crime' was to have escorted photo-journalists to the site of a bombing. They had lost much face because of the tout's betrayal.

NORTH HOWARD STREET MILL

Guardsman Mike Firth, 2nd Battalion Coldstream Guards

It seemed like I was going to help my kind; Irish Catholic where my roots are, with half my family being from County Cork. That was a big mistake.

There was an incident in Belfast when guns were found being carried in the dress and pram of a Catholic woman. I decided to run my metal detector over her dress and pram but when I got back to base I was taken in the office and given the hard word. Boy did it hurt; I was confused. We were at war weren't we or was this all a game? Well as far as I was concerned it was 'big boys' games'. The Company Commander didn't like my forthright attitude but there you go. More important was that we were hit fairly regularly by PIRA from the Falls Road; sniping, ambush and RPG. I was very lucky on all three incidents. Just sooooo lucky. My section had been deployed on the Black Mountains to look after the signals equipment on the hill. The attachment was seen by all at NHSM [North Howard Street Mill] as a bit of R&R. It snowed a lot that week and we played in it, knowing no one could hurt us. We were due back at a certain time on a certain day but missed the appointed time because we couldn't get off the hill.

Back at the Mill, on my way up the steps, I heard sustained gunfire from way outside on the Falls Road. I opened the window and poked my head out for a look. I could hear the sounds of a machine gun and Armalite rifle in the near distance then nothing; complete silence. A minute or so later there was a cry over the tannoy for the ready platoon to go downstairs and the medics to deploy to the Falls Road. It transpired that several men had either been killed or were seriously injured in this incident and once the Land Rovers had been cleaned of their body parts we had to use them complete with chalked bullet holes and still bloody. I had just come down off stag from the roof of the mill, and reached the ground floor to clear my weapon when a shot rang out; sniper on the Falls Road. Minutes later I was told to go back on the roof to replace Guardsman Malcolm Rounding who had replaced me minutes earlier. I saw him at ground floor level on a stretcher and he levelled some choice words in my direction: 'Why couldn't it have been you? Bastard.' He had been shot in the side and back; not fatal but not helpful.

On the same day as the Four Square Laundry attack – 2 October – the IRA shot Edward Bonner (37), a resident of the Falls Road and subsequently accused him of being a 'tout'. In the aftermath, the Provisional IRA released a press statement claiming that they had 'executed' five undercover British soldiers, a wildy inaccurate claim.

TOUTS

Jock 2413, Royal Artillery

To the various government intelligence agencies, they were agents. In army parlance they were sources. But to the population of the Republican areas of Northern Ireland, they were touts. Some were ordinary people living in those areas; others were members of the different terrorist organisations operating there. So what was it that made those people do what they did when, if caught out by PIRA and its like, would almost certainly face torture and death? It has been said that a paedophile stood more chance of forgiveness than the tout and the stigma of having had a tout as a relative stayed with that family for generations.

Why did they do it? Most of those who were classed as low level sources were just normal people living in the area that were fed up with the daily grind of the Troubles. They would pass on little snippets of information to troops on patrol or at checkpoints. If the information panned out, further contact with the person would be casually initiated by one of the regimental intelligence operators using flattery and the inducement of payment to get the source to work for us on a regular basis. If he/she agreed, contact points would be arranged, usually in a safe area where the source could divulge whatever had been learned since the last meeting. If it was a 'hot' tip that needed immediate action, the source would be told to turn up at an Army checkpoint and cause himself to be arrested by the soldiers. When he was taken in, the source could then be debriefed at leisure. Most at this level did it for the money although there were some who were genuinely sick of the Troubles and thought that the best way to end it was to help the security forces. The main problem with this level of contact was the fact that the regiments rotated every four months and the source had to be passed on to the next unit. This sometimes caused problems if he/she did not take to the new handler and became reluctant to work with him. Extra money would be offered, but if that failed and money had been accepted in the past, then the 'dirty' part of the operation would be brought to bear. Blackmail using the threat of exposing him to his own people was a tool that was very often used. This became counterproductive as the information that was then produced would be suspect as it was obtained under duress.

Another source of information was obtained using what could be classed as the Army's version of the 'honey trap'. Most soldiers looked young, fit and healthy; attractive specimens to the female population whose menfolk were often not exactly perfect specimens of manhood, and often in jail or on the run. Furtive assignations were quite commonplace especially in areas such as the Strand and City in Londonderry. Many a casual relationship developed between lads of the local unit and ladies from the Bogside and Creggan. Once the lady's name and address was obtained, regimental intelligence would check this out and if she lived near a known player, the soldier would be briefed on how to cultivate the lady in question for useful information in regards to the movements of said player, and visitors who called to his home.

It was found that the soldiers best suited to this task were married men as it lessened the chance of attachment to the lady. The most suitable targets, for lack of a better word, were women in their mid to late thirties whose children didn't need babysitters and whose husbands were typical specimens of the times; unemployed, drunken wife beaters. Lots of sympathy and a willingness to listen to their problems was sometimes all it took. Again, most info obtained was of a low level, but it all went to build up the big picture. I have to say, at this level at least, that this was not official policy but the chance of a bit of intelligence, however obtained, could not be ignored. The majority of contacts were on a casual basis but sometimes it went a bit further.

In Derry, there was this lad from the battery INT cell who used to spend most of his time in uniform at the various checkpoints in the Strand, keeping a check on the players entering and leaving the area. He developed a relationship with a female who lived next door to a well known player from the Creggan and she was more than willing to pass on what he was up to. She used to turn up late at night at the checkpoint which guarded the approach to the rear of Strand Barracks and ask for, let's call him 'Brian' who would go round there and talk to her in the privacy of the sangar. One night I was dropping off some photographs at the Strand unit's regimental INT cell, when this lady turned up at the checkpoint asking for 'Brian' who happened to be on R&R at the time. Rather than put her off, I volunteered to go and talk to her.

Borrowing a combat smock and flak jacket and armed with a pocket tape recorder, I was escorted round to the checkpoint. The lady was waiting in the sangar and I explained to her that 'Brian' was away and that I was a good friend of his. She accepted this, and in the privacy of the dark sangar she related what she had to tell, which was, actually, pretty mundane stuff. When done, I gave her the usual spiel that what she was telling us was extremely valuable and that we were very grateful etc and cautioned her to be careful. She then surprised me by asking if I was 'flush' as she'd had a good win on the horses. I said I was fine and that she should use her winnings to buy her kids a nice present. I then noticed that she had unbuttoned her coat, and when she started to hoist up her skirt the penny dropped. NO, I DIDN'T! I made an excuse that I had to have a word with the checkpoint commander and got off my mark sharpish reminding myself to have a word with 'Brian' about his taste in women. Queen and country didn't extend to 'sangar bangers'.

The most fruitful sources of high grade intelligence were the terrorists themselves. By various means they were either blackmailed or coerced into working for the security forces. It usually came about following the arrest of the person for some low grade offence such as rioting or car theft. He would be told that he was in for a long jail sentence but if he agreed to work for us, something could be arranged. If he was a known player, it would be better all round if the potential source was passed up the chain to one of the agencies better equipped to handle such a person. But in the early days, inter-service rivalry was such that units tended to hold onto a prize for their own use. Commanding officers were keen to gain kudos for their regiments by means of weapons finds and arrests. Unfortunately, this sometimes backfired on the security forces as, although in the early days PIRA didn't have experienced counter intelligence people, it didn't take a genius to work out who knew what and that spelt doom for the source.

Kidnapped at home or lured to a meeting, he would be taken somewhere safe and quiet and interrogated by a team of his own people. Torture would be used, although not always, to obtain a confession. Sometimes this was recorded or written down and signed by the unfortunate person. The result would be passed up the command structure and a verdict handed down; inevitably it was a death sentence. The convicted person would be taken, bound and gagged to a quiet place like an alley, hooded and executed by having two shots fired through the back of the head. Often a sign was left explaining why he was shot or occasionally money was put in his dead hands signifying that he had been a paid informer. As a final ignominy, sometimes a suspicious parcel was placed under the body to make it look like it was booby trapped. This ensured the final insult because for safety's sake, the dead body would be towed several yards by an armoured vehicle. In a lot of cases, the agony for the family didn't end there because as soon as the locals found out about the 'betrayal' by one of their own, the family home would be attacked, family members beaten and in a lot of cases, forced to leave the area altogether.

Whatever your opinion of these people, the bottom line was that they saved lives, very often at the cost of their own. The 'secret war' as it has been labelled was fought mainly without the knowledge of the normal soldier who patrolled the streets. Hundreds of weapons were seized and countless casualties avoided due to the efforts of the informer. High grade agents like Raymond Gilmour and Sean O'Callaghan were the lucky ones. They survived the war to write their memoirs. Others like Wright and McKee did not and ended up buried in secret graves somewhere in the green fields of South Armagh.

Loyalist murder gangs were responsible for four more killings in as many days. They cornered and savagely beat James McCartan (21) in a Protestant hotel close to Belfast's Markets area. He was beaten to death in full view of a watching mob and despite his desperate pleas to a hotel employee no-one lifted a hand in his defence. His cowardly killers then dumped his body in Mersey Street, Belfast. They then attacked a Catholic family living in Portadown and threw a hand grenade through the window of their house. The explosion killed Patrick Connolly (23) and the next day a UFF bomb attack on the Capital Bar in Dublin Road in Belfast's city centre caused the death of John Magee (54), a local Protestant.

RPG STRIKE

Guardsman Mike Firth, 2nd Battalion Coldstream Guards

On one occasion, I was sleeping during daylight hours in my pit on the top floor of the mill, when 'Wham!' We had been hit by a shoulder-mounted RPG from somewhere on the Falls Road. The projectile had hit the corrugated roof of the building in front of my floor and exploded causing debris to fly everywhere. Windows were shattered and others rattled. I rolled out of bed and for a short moment was indeed under the bed, then up and pushing my rifle out of the window hoping for the lucky shot. It never happened, but boy did my young heart race and was I scared. At that time no one except the Prods liked the British Army. It was indeed pointless being nice, so in our ignorance we were not nice people to know. We gave the Catholics a hard time but in all fairness they gave as good as they got. I was probably very brash in my dealings with everyone, but I was making sure I didn't go home in a coffin.

On the 6th, an Army patrol was attacked in the Bosnia Street area of the Falls in Belfast and moments later an IRA gunman Daniel McAreavey (21) in nearby Raglan Street was observed by troops; they opened fire and killed him. Unaware of the carnage still to come in Dublin over the course of the next two years – or mindful of the need to be shown to be strong – the Prime Minister of the Irish government Jack Lynch closed down the city's Sinn Féin office.

The following day, a UVF car bomb was planted outside a Catholic Bar in Leeson Street, just off the Falls Road, and close to where it meets Divis Street. Olive McConnell (23) heroically pushed her young baby away and was tragically killed by the blast. On the same day, the UDR were involved in two tragedies. In the first, they shot and killed a young boy who was innocently walking home in Newtownstewart. Alex Moorhead (16) was deaf and when he was observed at the rear of a cinema following an earlier explosion he was called upon to stop. Alex was unable to hear the warnings and continued walking and was shot dead.

On the 10th Colour Sergeant John Ruddy (50), father of nine children and a part-time soldier in the UDR was targeted by the IRA. He was walking from his home to his place of work in Newry and had only gone a few paces when masked gunmen shot him dead. Ruddy had spent over 30 years in both the Regulars and the TA. His distraught wife watched him being killed from her front doorstep and two of his children were only yards behind their father on their way to school. He was the fifth Catholic member of the regiment to be targeted and killed.

That same day, an IRA bomb-making team were assembling a device in a house in Balkan Street, close to the Falls Road. The device exploded prematurely and three terrorists died. John Donaghy (18), Patrick Maguire (24) and Joseph McKinney would not make any more bombs. Locals desperately broke down the door to the bomb factory but were beaten back by the flames and yet again the all-pervading smell of roasted flesh wafted across the city. As usual, their supporters turned out in the hundreds for a hallmark IRA funeral with masked men in berets firing volleys of shots over the coffins.

OCTOBER IN THE ARDOYNE

Lieutenant David Ash, Light Infantry

We had a gun battle at the Ring on 11 October and it was a running battle with the platoon out on the ground. There should have been casualties. At the time I thought that I was far too thick for this job whenever it really counted. I was standby platoon back at the mill. As usual, a bomb exploded inside one of the Ring shops, number 100 Alliance Avenue, and we had to roar off in Saracens to deal with the thing again. The building was severely damaged this time, and a fierce fire was blazing in the ruins. There were crowds in Alliance Avenue, as well as at the north ends of Jamaica Street and Etna Drive, when we arrived. We came in from the east past the Fort.

I dropped off 1 Section east of the Ring, deploying them on the south side of Alliance Avenue and left them to cover the waste ground and the east end of Stratford Gardens. I took the remaining two Saracens on to the open ground in the middle of the Ring, and de-bussed the rest of the platoon there. Why on earth did I do that? I tried to tell myself afterwards that I had to dismount there to move the crowds back from the burning, bombed out shop. But the truth is the crowds had been rapidly dispersing of their own accord anyway, and there was no need for me to put the platoon in such an exposed and vulnerable position. Naturally, the IRA gunmen were waiting for me to do exactly what I did. They opened fire on us with automatic weapons from what seemed like numerous different positions simultaneously. The entry alley between Stratford Gardens and Eskdale Gardens was one of them. We ran across the open ground towards the Ring shops. The Browning gun on 1 Section's Saracen opened up to give us immediate covering fire. One of the troops, Private Grimes tripped and fell into a barbed wire entanglement as he ran. 3 Section's Saracen also began firing its Browning. We pulled Grimes off the wire and made it to a position of cover.

Another soldier, Private Mahony took cover behind Young's burnt out garage. He climbed onto the flat roof and settled into a fire position with his sniper scope. The IRA was quick to spot him and we observed patterns of red brick dust erupting as bursts of fire were directed at him. He began returning fire; just steady, aimed shots. He was, I recall, a very cool young man. We re-grouped north of the shops in the alley behind Sloane's newsagents and the IRA's main position seemed to be based around the south end of the Etna/Jamaica waste ground. I decided to put in a right flanking attack on the position, using covering fire from 1 Section, the Ring OPs, and 3 Section's Saracen. I gave quick orders over the radio. Alex [the Company Commander] was on the net, but behaving perfectly, just keeping quiet and letting me get on with it with no unwanted waffle or 'advice'.

I took the assault group across Alliance Avenue via the alley behind the bombed shop and meanwhile the fire blazed furiously behind us. We formed up and made the dash down Etna Drive at full sprint. The Saracen Brownings opened fire noisily, with further rapid fire coming from the Ring OPs and 1 Section. All shooting stopped as we turned into the waste ground through the Etna Drive gap. Reports came over the radio that the IRA had bugged out, so we carried out a sweep, moving well spaced out, but there was no opposition. We went firm again at the north end of the waste ground and I called one of the Saracens down to our position for extra firepower and protection.

We came under fire again, this time from the east end of Stratford Gardens and rounds struck the side of the Saracen. I ordered 1 Section to mount up and do a mobile down Etna Drive, Berwick Road and Stratford Gardens. The mobile would give us the initiative and put a stop to any further movement of gunmen; it worked. There was no more shooting after that and 1 Section found two abandoned cars blocking off the west. Water cannon arrived to deal with the fire. We provided cover for ATO, and set about restoring the area to normal. A TV team turned up and I made a brief appearance on the evening news, seen talking into my radio. They wanted to interview me in front of the cameras, but lowly platoon commanders like me weren't allowed to do that. We might say something naughty! The platoon claimed several hits during the action but we found no blood trails or bodies. The IRA was very skilled at removing casualties and traces of casualties.

The following morning, the Glenard post office in Alliance Avenue at the Ring was held up and robbed. The OPs told me they saw nothing of it, and it was thought the raid was carried out by four armed men. There were more gun battles with the IRA during the night at the OPs; repeated attacks with single shot and automatic small arms fire. I had all three OPs manned with a good team in each position. Sergeant Spracklen was in the northern OP, firing the GPMG himself and I had the centre OP. There were several close hits around the fire slits at both the northern and centre OPs throughout the night. The IRA was using a variety of firing points, including the bombed ruins of the shop at 100 Alliance Avenue and it was there that Private Graver got an IRA gunman. He watched and waited for just the right moment, saw the man for an instant and immediately fired four rapid shots using his starlight scope. The gunman's legs seemed to buckle under him and he fell backwards out of view. During a lull between attacks, a woman appeared with a bucket and mop, washing blood off the street. That was always the sign of a confirmed hit.

There was a 'blue on blue' of sorts when an off duty RUC detective was shot by soldiers from the Prince of Wales' Regiment at a VCP in and around Queen Street, Belfast. The policeman's car failed to stop and a soldier opened fire and the policeman was killed, with alcohol later being suggested as the reason for his failure to stop. Two more UDR members died in duty-related RTAs as the toll for that regiment continued to mount. Private Robert McKeown was killed on 13 October and three days later, Major John Munnis died in similar circumstances.

Loyalists targeted another Catholic soldier in the UDR, abducting Terence Maguire (23) in east Belfast. He was then shot and his body dumped in the UFF's customary manner. Catholic members of the UDR were rarities and they faced murder at the hands of their fellow Catholics in the IRA and their Protestant terrorist counterparts in the Loyalist murder gangs. Not content with this, the UFF attacked an off licence in south Belfast and shot and killed Leo Duffy (45) and Thomas Marron (59) and wounded another member of staff.

Death was no respecter of age. John Doherty (4) was shot and killed in the Republican Turf Lodge area of west Belfast; only the IRA were in the area and the blame lies at their door.

On the 14th, Colour Sergeant John Morrell (32) of the South Staffs Regiment, a married father of three, was badly wounded in south Armagh by an IRA booby trap during a routine search. The Cheshire man died in hospital ten days later. He is listed on the National Arboretum's roll of honour as belonging to the Prince of Wales Own Regiment of Yorkshire and it is thought that he was attached to the Staffs.

On 16 October four terrorists were killed, two from either side. William Warnock (15) and John Clarke (26) were killed in separate incidents in Templemore Avenue, Belfast, in incidents involving Army vehicles. Warnock's brother was killed the previous month by an off-duty RUC officer. The IRA lost two members when Hugh Heron (38) and John Mullen (34) were shot by the Army at a VCP in Mullahitra, Co Tyrone when a rifle was pointed at the soldiers.

In September, Marine Anthony David (27) was badly wounded on the Falls Road by an IRA sniper; on 17 October the Glamorgan boy died of his wounds. On the same day, the UFF were responsible for shooting Eleanor Cook (32) a mother of two from Belfast. That night, soldiers were involved in the clear up after rioting in the Shankill area when they came under fire. They fired back and a UDR soldier, Private John Todd (23) was killed. Because he was also a member of the UFF, I have taken the decision not to include him on the UDR's roll of honour.

Another member of the SF was shot and fatally wounded that day when a RUC patrol pulled over a suspicious car in the Belfast area. The car contained several members of the UFF and in a confused situation one of them shot Constable Gordon Harrison (32). The man was tried the following year and was convicted and sentenced to death. Although the death sentence was abolished on the mainland during the 1960s, it still applied for capital murder in Ulster. The sentence sparked days of rioting in Loyalist areas and even the 'saintly' Ian Paisley was involved – in my opinion, a man whose bigotry and intolerance was as culpable as his Republican counterparts – and eventually the sentence was commuted. On 21 October, Constable Harrison died of his wounds.

On the 19th, William Craig, then leader of 'Ulster Vanguard', spoke to a meeting of right-wing MPs at Westminster. He said that he could mobilise 80,000 men to oppose the British government, stating: 'We are prepared to come out and shoot and kill. I am prepared to come out and shoot and kill. ... I am prepared to kill, and those behind me will have my full support.'

One of the major sources of irritation to both the British government and the SF was the impunity with which the IRA could attack and kill soldiers and policemen alike and then melt away across the border to the safety of the Irish Republic. There were dozens, probably hundreds of instances when terrorists detonated bombs or fired fatal shots from across the border, or immediately fled there after a murder. Amongst those particularly vulnerable were not just Army/RUC border patrols, but also UDR members, many of whom worked the land in border country.

One of those vulnerable part-time soldiers was Private Robin Bell (21) whose family farm was at Lough Erne, Drumquillagh in Co Tyrone. On the 22nd, he was in a car with his father and brother when they were ambushed by the IRA and both Private Bell and his father were hit. Fire was returned by Bell's brother, also a part-time soldier, but the terrorists escaped and the young soldier died on the operating table in hospital later the same day. The murderers sped off in a stolen car, abandoning it close by before escaping in a boat across the River Erne and into the Republic. *Lost Lives* (p285) quotes a leading Unionist politician John Brooke who demanded that the Irish Government give permission for British soldiers to be allowed to cross the border and destroy the IRA in their safe bases. 'Because of the failure of the Dublin government to stop these murder gangs on the border, the British government must … give our troops the order to seek and destroy the IRA.' To the troops on the ground a collective 'we wish' must have been heard on their lips. As a former soldier, the author can attest to the frustration soldiers felt at not being able to follow the terrorists across an arbitrary border in the countryside.

On Monday the 23rd, Loyalist paramilitaries carried out a raid on an UDR/TA base at King's Park Camp in Lurgan, County Armagh, and stole 85 Army issue SLRs and 21 Sterling submachineguns. The camp guard stated that they were overpowered by the armed gang. Within a few hours of the raid, 63 SLRs and eight SMGs were recovered close to an abandoned Land Rover. There was a further theft of UDR weapons on 30 October 1972. On 21 July 1973 one of the Sterling SMGs was recovered in the possession of Loyalist paramilitaries in Belfast. A confidential report later indicated that this weapon alone had been used in at least twelve Loyalist attacks which resulted in one civilian being killed and in seven attempted killings.

The month was drawing to an end, the clocks had gone back and the nights were getting longer and darker. It was ideal cover for the murder gangs' lethal trade. On Arundel Street – some reports state that it was Naples Street – which used to be sited between Grosvenor Road and Roden Street, Belfast, the Royal Anglians lost Private Robert Mason (19) when he was shot by an IRA gunmen and died shortly afterwards. He was from Cambridgeshire and which wing of the IRA shot him, a point of debate at the time, was of little interest to his grieving family in England.

The day after, two soldiers brought great shame to the uniform of the British Army when they murdered two Catholic farmers at a farm on the Co Fermanagh/Irish Republic border. A four-man patrol called at the farm with information – spurious or otherwise – that Michael Naan (31) was connected to the IRA. Two of the soldiers – convicted in 1979 for the murders – brutally stabbed both Naan and Andrew Murray (23) to death with pitchforks whilst two other soldiers looked on. Of the two that took no active part, one was found guilty of manslaughter and the platoon commander of withholding information. The men's regiment had lost several comrades in the area and had seen several others terribly injured. They were later deployed to the Lisnaskea area where one of the first tasks was to escort the funeral of UDR soldier Frank Bell. That said, despite their frustrations and anguish, there was no justification for the brutal slayings.

The Scots Guards were based in Londonderry during that month, and on the 28th, IRA gunmen attacked one of their mobile patrols in the Brook Street area and a round entered one of the vehicles, passing between two soldiers before hitting Lance Sergeant (Corporal equivalent) Thomas McKay in the head. The Edinburgh man and father of two small children died very soon after being rushed to hospital.

Loyalist murder gangs were again in evidence and on the last Sunday of the month two young Catholics walking along Cliftonville Avenue in Belfast were attacked with gunfire from a passing car containing UVF gunmen. A volley of shots was fired, slightly wounding a 15 year old but fatally wounding Michael Turner (16) who died later that afternoon in hospital. Neither teenager had any links with the IRA or other Republican groups; they were targeted because they were deemed to be Catholics walking through a Catholic area close to the Antrim Road. The point where the attack took place is approximately midway between Sacred Heart Boys' Primary School and the Holy Family Nursery School.

Another random sectarian killing occurred the following Tuesday when the Loyalist murder gang the Red Hand Commando killed a young Catholic petrol pump attendant. The gang shot James Kerr (17) at his place of work on the Lisburn Road, Belfast. One of the murderers – Stephen McCrea who was 20 at the time – was shot and wounded by a passing RUC patrol and was sentenced to life imprisonment the following year. Having served sixteen years, he was released only to be killed in 1979 by the IRA.

Some three or four hundred yards from the scene of Michael Turner's murder, the Army was involved in extensive search operations in the Republican New Lodge area. The Queen's Regiment were involved and one of its foot patrols was fired upon whilst on the Antrim Road. Private Richard Sinclair (18) from Lincolnshire was hit and died at the scene; he had only been in the Province for two weeks.

On the final day of the month the UFF were involved in the sickening murder of two small children when they exploded a car bomb in the Belfast docks area. They left a car packed with explosives at Benny's Bar – a known Catholic watering hole – in Ship Street. It was Halloween and there were many children playing in the narrow terraced streets. When the car bomb exploded close to a burning bonfire, Paula Stronge (6) and Claire Hughes (4) were killed and many other children were blown off their feet, buried in the rubble and injured. Paula Stronge's parents tried to dig her out of the debris but she was already dead.

Eyewitnesses later testified that the UVF gang could not have failed to notice the children playing nearby. And yet their spokesman claimed that they had not realised that there were children and apologised for the girls' deaths. In 1982, three UVF men were jailed for the murders and told that their crimes would haunt them for the rest of their lives.

In that month, three more UDR men died in circumstances and from causes unknown. The men were Private Thomas Olphert (30) from Co Tyrone, Private Edmund Simpson (34) and Sergeant William Calderwood (56); all are noted in the National Arboretum's ROH.

Winter was around the corner and a cold November beckoned; October had claimed 47 more lives. The dead included 15 soldiers, 22 civilians, 2 RUC officers, 6 IRA members and 3 Loyalist paramilitaries. Loyalist terrorists were responsible for thirteen sectarian deaths through random murders or bomb attacks; the IRA was responsible for four civilian deaths. Three of the civilian deaths were men 'executed' by the IRA for being informers.

CHAPTER ELEVEN

NOVEMBER

In the US, President Nixon won the presidential election, beating George McGovern, but the Watergate scandal would soon gather pace and bring him down. The month was played in by Lieutenant Pigeon's 'Mouldy Old Dough' and Gilbert O'Sullivan's 'Clair' as the days turned noticeably colder. Gangs of mainly Catholic youths with their 'mullet' hairstyles and tartan turn-ups, hatred etched across their faces, threw rocks and bottles at the soldiers and RUC. Then

On the extreme right is Colour Sergeant James Struthers, killed by an explosion along with Capt. DW Watson while investigating a farmhouse on 20th November, 1972. Also pictured are Jim Chestnut and Jim Taylor. Taylor was wounded in the same ambush.

from behind them, older youths lit milk bottles full of petrol and hurled them from behind the front rows of rioters. Then, like the Red Sea parting, the crowd would open up and concealed gunmen would fire at the soldiers. After a shot or two, the front rows would re-form, safe in the knowledge that the Army, whilst not averse to firing baton rounds at them, would not open fire. The gunmen would then slink away into a dozen or so safe houses, their weapons disposed of by willing helpers, and then jump into a waiting bath, still clothed as they attempted to wash away the forensic evidence.

SQUADDIE ON FIRE

Bob Luke, Royal Corps of Transport

It all started like a normal mobile patrol; we set off from our base at Vere Foster School, for a roaming stint of about four hours. Our duty was to patrol streets in the 'Murph and we were out looking for suspects and any other possible terrorist activities.

About 40 minutes into the patrol, as we were heading into a bad area, we saw a number of youths gathering and by their actions, it looked as though they were going to confront us head on. Our section commander, who was travelling in my 'Jumbo' [Saracen], contacted base for back up. At this stage I started to batten down; all side ports and the main trap which was in front of me were all closed and all that I was left with was my small vision block at the front slightly ajar and ready to close if needed.

We moved forward slowly with both Jumbos moving abreast in the road and the commander told the second vehicle that we would apprehend any of the crowd that came at us, at this time approx 40+, which, for this area was relatively small. Any captives would then be taken to Black Mountain School for screening. At this stage, we were approximately 50 yards from the main group, when missiles started to rain down on to our vehicles.

At about 30 yards from the 40–50 people, the commander ordered the deployment of our sections, and, as was the practice, my co-driver manned the 30 cal in the turret. This would give extra cover if needed. At this moment I saw a flamer [petrol bomb] coming our way. Just as I closed the hatch I heard the unmistakable crash of glass on the outside and noticed almost straight away that petrol was leaking in through the main hatch. Before I could do anything there was a whoosh as the fuel ignited. My legs were covered in fuel and all I could see were the flames jumping around on my legs and abdomen area. It did not take more than a second to realise that the main fuel tank was beneath me and I could fry at any moment. I shouted at my oppo in the turret to get the extinguisher and put me out. He casually looked down and said: 'Who is going to sign for it?' Squaddie humour to the last!

At this point all I could do was to keep my hands away and lean back and let the extinguisher do its job. I shouted 'Get out' and I followed my mate out, but my main concern was that the fuel tank could still go up. We both left the vehicle rather sharpish, not like you see in the movies, as we dived/fell into a heap outside and scrambled away.

The section commander came over and asked what we were up to; as if we did not have enough to be getting on with! We moved back to a safe area and we could hear the back up more or less arriving at our location. Our thoughts now were that if the crowd surged forward they would have control of our vehicle and of course the 30 cal. After a couple of minutes we moved back to the vehicle and felt the floor to see if it was hot and, as there was no flames or smoke inside, we mounted and give the section commander the ok. We could all smell petrol, and there were a few more flamers that came our way but none that caused us to worry.

We were part of the team again and moved forward to the crowd and 'lifted' about eight people, most of them teenagers. They were taken to Black Mountain School and we then returned to our location. On arrival we cleared most of the debris from the outside of the vehicle and while the team checked the vehicle, I went to the med centre and got some cream for my legs and privates and of course was told that I was not bad enough to be taken off the road. I went to the stores next and exchanged my burned combats, and of course I was made to feel humble that I got away without paying for the new ones.

While I was otherwise occupied a message came in that one of our lads had been killed, as it turned out he was not from our Squadron, but I did know him. He was Driver Ronald Kitchen. Later, we thought about Ronald; it so easily could have been one of us. The long days and nights were starting to take their toll on all of us and there seemed little or no light at the end of the tunnel.

Driver Ronald Kitchen (20) was shot whilst manning a VCP on the Oldpark Road on 10 November. The Ballymurphy estate saw nineteen British soldiers and two RUC men killed by bomb or bullet during the Troubles. Although the 'no go' areas were a thing of the past, the Catholic enclaves were still extremely dangerous places for the SF and the RUC were not likely to enter any of them without Army protection. Almost every dwelling was pro-Provisionals and anti-Army and daily attacks on the SF were the order of the day. There were many allegations against soldiers that they used brutality and carried out indiscriminate and wanton vandalism in searches of the Unity Flats. That many IRA men lived there is not open to discussion, nor is the claim that weapons and explosives were regularly stored there and moved around by willing helpers. If soldiers were compelled to search these places on a regular basis in order to help others stay alive, then the author sees full justification.

Until the seventh, there had been no troubles-related deaths but on that Tuesday as the Army searched houses on the Turf Lodge housing estate in west Belfast a Catholic mother of ten was to die. The Turf Lodge lies immediately to the west of the Ballymurphy estate and, like its sister on the other side of the Whiterock Road, it is fiercely Republican. Soldiers were searching a house in Norglen Road and the occupant, Mrs Margaret Cunningham was confronting soldiers when the situation became all too much for her and she collapsed and died from what was thought to have been a heart attack.

Then it was time for the IRA's preferred method of operation; a soft target. On the Thursday of that week they lay in wait for a UDR soldier out on a domestic errand. Second Lieutenant Irwin Long (29) was driving through the town of Lurgan en-route to collect his young daughter when he was attacked by gunmen. He was fatally wounded and died soon after in hospital.

ZOMBIES

Starlight, Royal Army Medical Corps

As I said earlier, I was injured shortly after the Abercorn Restaurant bomb. Following a period of rehab at Chessington I returned to NI at the beginning of October as a Crash Team Commander/

Medic with 1 QLR [Queen's Lancashire Regiment]. This was a dreadful tour, as we lost five killed and some twenty or more suffered major life-changing injuries. We had two RPG 7 attacks on Saracens; both resulted in death and many injuries. During one of them the young RCT driver, although injured himself and with blood obscuring his vision, drove his damaged Saracen to the RVH casualty. This selfless and unrewarded action undoubtedly saved lives.

To provide the best possible medical support, we had a three 'crash teams' in Saracen ambulances, who responded to each contact on a rotation basis. They monitored the Command Net [Radio] and on hearing: 'Contact, wait, out' moved into the Company TAOR of the C/S involved. This was tiring and many of the 'shouts' came to nothing. But in those involving casualties it allowed us to be with an injured soldier within five minutes of him being wounded; this was all that mattered, it was part of a covenant that no soldier would bleed to death. We had many black days during that tour at the tail end of 1972. On reflection, many of us were suffering from battle fatigue as the tempo of ops and call-outs was relentless; we were virtually zombies. My 'crash team' had to treat injured civilians as well as soldiers. Even today, 38 years later, many of those 'shouts' still haunt me.

We frequently went unarmed as our issue weapon the SMG was a useless hindrance whilst treating a badly injured casualty. Added to this was the constant fear that the normal rent-a-mob would steal it. So we just rode our luck and left the weapons in the Saracen. We were very far down in the pecking order for pistols and needless to say, the Red Cross armband was just another target. We also bought our own Entenox [nitrous oxide] as it had fewer side effects than morphine when casualties arrived in hospital. I liberated one of the stretchers which were normally fitted on the small Army Air Corps Sioux helicopter, before the Gazelle; it was body shaped, slightly hollowed and covered in chicken wire, and quick release straps secured the casualty. This was a real godsend in Divis Flats and other confined spaces.

The next day, two members of a Loyalist terror group boarded a bus in Castlereagh Street, Belfast and immediately confronted Joseph Kelly (45) and fired a volley of shots at him, killing him instantly. Kelly's crime? He had the temerity to be a Catholic working in a Protestant factory. Over the course of the next four days, the UFF and the Red Hand Commandos, a synonymous and interchangeable Loyalist murder grouping killed two more Catholics. In the first attack, Joseph Kelly (50) was serving in his shop on Upper Crumlin Road, Belfast in the presence of his young daughter. Two men made a purchase and then calmly fired eight rounds into his body in front of the terrified child. Then, as he returned home from work, Joseph McCrystal (28) was gunned down by the UFF in Newtownabbey, Co Antrim. His wounds were severe and he died shortly afterwards in hospital. He did have links with the IRA but was not a member, nor was he, apparently, involved in any terrorist activity.

NO FIRING AT PIRA

Guardsman Mike Firth, 2nd Battalion Coldstream Guards

Another op was on the peace line between NHSM and Springfield Road. There was four of us with Lance Corporal Danny Wildeman in charge in the roof space of a derelict house. Three PIRA came down the road, arms full of blast bombs which they threw over the peace line, duly

Looking north along Downshire Road in Newry – before the bypass the main road from Dublin to Belfast. The fortified base across the road was originally the town's TA Centre, but became the 3 UDR Newry Platoon's facility after the Regiment's formation in 1970, with the Coy HQ in Rathfriland. Note the Castrol sign half-hidden on the right, outside –

McCullough's BP garage and petrol station. The view towards Newry from outside the entrance. Today, the former military site is an expensive apartment block, and the garage lies derelict.

exploding. They just walked away and we had them in our sights. We called for the mobile section but they were tied up at the police station so I asked for permission to shoot, but it was refused and even if we got a kill we wouldn't be able to get out until we had transport and that meant a real risk of death. I was just young and foolish. So we stayed and later on got out quietly.

My time in the province with 2CG was relatively quiet in my eyes but I lost a good mate in Mal Pearson the following February. He was from Leeds too and a good egg.

Guardsmen Robert 'Mal' Pearson and Michael Shaw were both shot and killed by IRA snipers on 20 February 1973. The two Coldstream Guards were on mobile patrol in the vicinity of Panton Street and Cupar Street in the Lower Falls area of Belfast. The patrol was struck by automatic gunfire and Robert Pearson (19) was struck six times and died immediately. Guardsman Shaw (23) was hit a dozen times and died at the scene. A third member of the Coldstreams was hit by a blast bomb thrown simultaneous to the gun attack and was seriously wounded. The Belfast Coroner condemned the IRA for using children from the Falls area – some as young as thirteen and fourteen – to 'spot' for them and alert them to the presence of the Guards' vehicles.

The following piece relates to a soldier, who having served in the Troubles, left the Army but returned to live in Belfast with his young wife. He realised that he was still *persona non grata* in his own country and, as the IRA were killing former members of the SF, still in a highly dangerous situation. He speaks here of one terrible night and the violent sights which he witnessed as a resident of Belfast.

'Call yerself a soldier? Get yer bleedin' 'air cut.' The familiar cry of RSMs/CSMs in (nearly) every regiment clearly hasn't reached this lad as he takes cover at the entrance to the former Newry High (before that, Newry Grammar) school – again on Downshire Road.

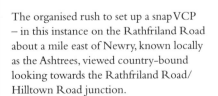

The organised rush to set up a snap VCP – in this instance on the Rathfriland Road about a mile east of Newry, known locally as the Ashtrees, viewed country-bound looking towards the Rathfriland Road/ Hilltown Road junction.

Back towards Newry with the checkpoint operational. Unless the area was cordoned, ten minutes would normally be the maximum duration for one of these spot searches.

BELFAST WAS A SHITHOLE

Terry Friend, Royal Artillery

It was one of those heavy, damp and dreary late autumn nights, where no matter how well you wrap up; the chill still gets right through to the bone! My girlfriend Jeanette and I were making our way through the city, from where we had been babysitting her newly married elder sister's house, and were just approaching the inner city end of the Shankill Road. As we were just passing some shops, a gang of youths dressed in the typical yob uniform of the day – denim jackets, denim trousers and Dr Martin's boots – suddenly tore out of a side street just in front of us, which led to a Republican area known as Unity Flats, and hurtled straight towards us. My heart leapt into my throat, for this was Belfast in 1972, and who could ever tell what the next few minutes would spring upon you in such a place! There were about eight people in the small crowd that approached us, and what happened next occurred in less than the time it would take to tell the tale!

It was only when they had caught up with us that it dawned on me that it was, in fact, one poor fellow being chased by the others. One of the yobs had this guy by the hair and had forced his head downwards and was mercilessly sticking the boot into his victim's stomach and groin area. The rest of them went tearing past, skidding on the pavement, sparks flying from their boots, as they realised that their quarry had been caught. By now their victim was on the ground lying in a foetal position, his back against a brick wall. Instantly he was surrounded, some of them faced him; some had their backs to him, all the better to lash at him with the heels of their boots.

As all this was unfolding beside us, my girlfriend turned her tear streaked face to me. 'Terry!' She blurted out. 'We've got to get the police!' Survival instinct took over, as these people were so close to me I could have reached out my hand and touched them. I really didn't fancy being their next victim! Grabbing Jeanette's hand we took to our heels pretty sharpish. I was literally stunned by the look of sheer hatred on the faces of those administering the kicking, and I briefly wondered if their victim might possibly have been an undercover soldier or policeman. After all, they had appeared from a staunch nationalist enclave.

We ran up the road with that poor man's screams ringing in our ears. It was a terrible sound and there was nothing human about it at all. He sounded more like an animal in torment. I had never heard anything like that before in my lifetime, and I never want to hear anything like that ever again. It made the blood run cold in my veins!

A couple of minutes of sprinting later and we encountered a policeman. He was on his own, and I noticed that he seemed quite old and had grey hair, but I could plainly see the pistol on his belt. I told him what we had just seen and he slowly drew out his radio and began speaking into it. 'What the fuck are you doing?' I yelled. 'There's a man being kicked to death back there, you've got a weapon get down there and deal with it!' He never made a comment or moved an inch! Thoroughly disgusted I pulled Jeanette away and we ran off into the gloom of the night. Fuck this place! It really was time to get out before I too joined that poor sod on the pavement. The next day I pored over the *Belfast Telegraph*, searching for anything about the incident; there was nothing! Perhaps it was considered too minor even to be mentioned. It was just another nasty little incident in that dirty, rotten, violent shithole of a place.

On the 12th the Argylls lost a soldier when Private David Harper (18), whilst on sentry duty near a railway line, wandered too close to the line and was struck by a passing train. He was from Paisley in Scotland. Many of the soldiers were permanently exhausted and rarely had sufficient sleep for the long, demanding hours of fighting. If weariness indeed killed young Harper, he was as much of a victim of the Troubles as surely as if he had stopped a sniper's bullet.

That same day, the Army came under fire from a car near the Falls Road and when they returned fire, they hit Stanislaus Carberry (34). Carberry was a member of the IRA and had just hijacked the car in the immediate vicinity. After they came under fire, soldiers fired back and killed him and wounded another man who escaped. The propaganda machine of the Provisional IRA accused the Army of a 'cowardly murder.'

Before the day was out, the IRA had 'retaliated' by killing a soldier in the notorious Unity Flats in Belfast. A four man 'brick' from the Queen's Regiment was searching a house in the area and soldiers were questioning a man. A soldier was searching inside a cupboard when an armed man approached the window. The gunman fired a single round which fatally wounded Private Stanley Evans (19) who was standing only inches from the householder and his babe in arms. The gunman used the same Luger which had allegedly been used in the murder of Marine Allen in July. The Provisionals issued a statement which used the killing of IRA member Stanislaus Carberry as an excuse for Evans' murder. One member of the Queen's Regiment told the author: 'When did those cowardly bastards ever need an excuse for killing one of us or a copper?'

Then it was the Loyalists' turn as the UFF attacked George Doherty (32) in his house on the Upper Newtownards Road, Belfast. He wisely refused to answer a knock at the door so the gang tried to scare him into coming out. When he again refused, they fired through his front door, hitting him in the stomach; he died on the way to the hospital.

The IRA was the next to strike and they planted a bomb underneath an RUC officer's car in Enniskillen. The UVBT (under vehicle booby trap) detonated as the off duty policeman drove away, killing him instantly. Reserve Constable Joseph Calvin (42) was only a part-time policeman and two more lives were devastated by Republican terrorists; he left a widow and daughter.

On the 20th a search team from the Argylls was inspecting an old building close to Cullyhanna in South Armagh on 20 November. They were there as the results of an anonymous phone call and because of their suspicions, the search was called off until first light. However, and inexplicably, Captain William Watson (28) whose wife was pregnant and Sergeant James Struthers (31) re-entered the house and seconds later an explosion killed them both instantly. Captain Watson was from Edinburgh and Sergeant Struthers from Midlothian.

BORDER FIGHTS AND TWO ARGYLLS ARE KILLED

Jim, Argyll and Sutherland Highlanders

The IRA on the border were supposed to be the most experienced and together group in the whole of Ireland and we were put up against them, young and inexperienced. It was decided to bring others in to support us. A heavily armed platoon was sent out to live on the border. We were then set up as a sort of duck-shooting gallery in an area where incidents happened. We spent a few hours walking up and down the Moybane Road wanting something to happen but hoping it wouldn't. We had just given up when there was shooting over where our ambush group were, on the hill, overlooking Drummuckavall. We headed off as fast as we could, listening to this heavy fire all the way. It turned out that some gunmen had sneaked or stumbled into the middle of two groups of soldiers and opened fire, wounding one soldier. Over 1,500 rounds were fired. We heard later that a van had been stopped on the border and bodies and guns were found inside. On a lighter note, a helicopter carrying a doctor flew in to the hill under fire, the doc apparently jumped out firing his pistol. The helicopter pilots were amazing guys.

We had been called out to a farmhouse north of our base, near Cullyhanna. One of the other platoons had discovered what they thought was a rifle but felt it was booby trapped. A dog handler had confirmed this and advised that no one should enter the building. We were on call in case it was a hoax and the building needed to be searched. When we arrived our search commander and an officer went into the building. After they went in there was an explosion and the farmhouse disappeared. Soldiers quickly began digging in the rubble but it was a waste of time. I had been on the radio getting other support. One body seemed to be intact apart from the combat jacket being torn, with nothing but dust on it. I still don't know what happened; whether one of them picked up the rifle butt or whether something else triggered a bomb. What was clear was how quickly life could be lost.

Members of the UDR were only part-time soldiers and did their military duties after work and on weekends. The many tentacles of the IRA's intelligence section did their homework well and they generally knew every home or work address of many, if not all members of the UDR. Private Samuel Porter (30) was a plasterer by day and a soldier by night and the IRA knew where he lived and where he worked. On the morning of 22 November, he returned home in

THE BLOODIEST YEAR: 1972

the very early hours and as he drove into his driveway masked gunmen opened fire and killed him. They had earlier poisoned his guard dog so that he would not be alerted by its barking.

Keith Williams, With 4 UDR in 1972

In 1971 following a tour in Albert Street Mill on the Falls Road as a Rifle Platoon Sergeant I returned to Osnabruck, was promoted C/Sgt, purchased a new tax-free car and went on block leave. On return I informed I was going to be attached to 4 UDR in County Fermanagh as a signals instructor and departed the following day leaving my family in BAOR to fend for themselves.

I was met at the docks in Belfast and driven to Enniskillen via the Falls Road and Sandy Row; when I complained to the driver about the dangerous route he replied he was only following the traffic signs. At Enniskillen, accommodation was not available and I was placed on the lodging list and told to make my own living arrangements. For the next twelve months I lived in two different guest houses and a caravan before finding a bunk at the newly opened St Angelo Camp. The IRA later bombed the camp, using a hijacked laundry van.

The first training priority was to convert the entire battalion from the Lee Enfield No. 4 Rifles to the 7.62 mm SLR in just one month including qualifying on the open range. Due to the shortage of ranges some of the soldiers went on duty armed with SLRs never having fired one. The issue of SLRs proved to be a great boost to unit morale and possibly the start of losing the resented 'Dad's Army' image.

The unit was equipped with vehicle-mounted civilian Pye Westminsters and portable Pye Bantam radios which were rather fragile and not suited for use in country areas. Fortunately a full time ex-regular signals instructor and a civilian radio technician were recruited and by their combined efforts established manual Pye Westminster relay stations in selected police stations, mounting the antennas on top of the police radio masts. Patrols positioned a man to operate this radio, and where possible only operated within radio range, and the link between the police station and the operations room was by civilian landline. This improvised basic concept worked but regrettably the Army, RUC and UDR radios were not compatible resulting in unacceptable confusion when an incident occurred.

Living outside the security of a military base the apprehension and anxiety I felt on returning back from duty especially on the final approach to my lodgings instilled in me nothing but the greatest respect and admiration for the UDR soldiers who lived in far more remote and vulnerable areas who overcame their own justified fears every time they left and returned to their homes. It was relatively easy for me to vary my routine or stay overnight in a UDR centre or police station but for those who had civilian occupations or livestock to feed, varying their daily routines to any meaningful extent was just not possible.

Because of the dangers to Land Rovers in the county it was decided to issue covert civilian vans for administrative tasks between the company locations and the static key points. These were delivered brand new, with consecutive numbered Belfast registration number plates (COI 1352, COI 1353 etc), painted in outlandish colours including purple and yellow and fitted with Whitewall tyres. It was rumoured they were purchased as a cheap job lot because the awful colours did not appeal to civilian purchasers. They were quickly dented, tyres changed and repainted to blend in with the rural Fermanagh countryside.

208

On one occasion, a soldier coming off duty negligently discharged a number of rounds from his SMG into the unloading bay causing a major alert and panic in his UDR centre. When he appeared before his company commander there was a heated debate when he was fined £3 for the offence, arguing he had not caused any damage because that was what the sandbags were for. Finally he accepted his punishment but requested a month to pay because he was short of money.

There were humorous moments also. A political VIP was visiting the Battalion by Wessex Helicopter and the signals of the UDR Ground Marshal instructing him where to land were disregarded by the aircrew, who opted to hover and disembark their VIP passenger about 25 metres away. The VIP jumped out straight into a bog from which he needed assistance to be extracted.

William Clarke (45) was badly wounded by gunmen late in October having been lured to the Loyalist estate at Forthriver in the mistaken belief that he was a Catholic. He was shot by two UFF members and died of his wounds in the RVH on the same day that the two Argylls were killed at Cullyhanna.

Over the course of two days, the UVF and the UFF killed two more innocent Catholics. They killed Joseph McIlroy (32) at his home in east Belfast with his wife in the next room and his four young daughters asleep upstairs. Then the Loyalists killed William Chivers (48) as he walked his dog in Castledawson, Co Londonderry late that night.

On the morning of Monday 27 November, a surgeon from Belfast's Mater Hospital, which is based just off the Crumlin Road, was taking his children to St Malachy's School. As the family car drove along Downing Street, approximately 700 yards from the Mater, gunmen from the UVF opened fire at them. *Lost Lives* speculates (p295) that the children were identified as Catholics because of their distinctive school uniform, but it is entirely feasible that, given his reputation as a surgeon, the real target was the children's father. Several rounds hit the car and Rory Gormley (14) was hit and fatally wounded and the car crashed. A local woman found the badly wounded boy crawling along the street and immediately did all she could, cradling him in her arms. Rory died at the scene, another tragic example of how callous the Loyalist terrorists could be.

On Tuesday the 28th the IRA attacked the RUC station at Belleek in Co Fermanagh with an RPG-7 and killed police reservist Robert Keys (55) a father of six children. The border town of Belleek, famous for its pottery, is one of the most westerly parts of Northern Ireland and sits just a short six-mile journey from Erne in the Republic and the waters of the Atlantic Ocean. There was then an immediate IRA machine gun attack, likely to have been mounted from the Cloghore area of the Republic.

This was the first known use of the RPG-7 and the IRA chose the RUC station there as it sits only a few yards from the Irish border. Gun fights with gunmen were an almost daily occurrence and on the day of the attack, 16/5 Lancers were manning the base. Robert Keys was caught by the full blast of the explosion which cut through the armour-plated glass like a knife through butter and the lifeless policeman's body crashed at the feet of an NCO from the 16/5. The same NCO ran to man the machine guns of his Saracen and spotted at least five gunmen in a field behind the station. The vehicle had to be first manoeuvred into a better firing position and as he did so, came under a hail of bullets.

He spotted the gunmen in a nearby wood and opened fire on them and was supported by another comrade inside the wrecked building who also fired at them. In the village, scores of frightened civilians had to dive for cover as IRA rounds came scorching through the street and houses. Eventually after an exchange of gunfire which lasted over twenty minutes, the gunmen withdrew over the safety of the border. On the same day, a soldier was shot in the back at Crossmaglen but thankfully survived, and an Army unit manning a VCP on the Londonderry-Buncrana Road were involved in a major gun battle with the IRA in which almost 800 rounds were fired.

In an incident on that same day Private John McGarry (20) was shot after a negligent discharge; no further details are known. The IRA was a formidable enemy without the added tragedy of an ND death. The day was still not over, and the IRA lost two bombers in a premature explosion at Meenan Drive in Londonderry's Bogside. IRA members John Brady (21) and James Carr (19) were killed instantly but the unsuspecting occupant and her four children were mercifully uninjured.

Before that bloody Tuesday finally ended, another soldier was killed, this time in Londonderry after a bomb warning was telephoned through to the Army. The IRA planted a bomb outside Long's Supermarket on the Strand Road which runs parallel to the River Foyle. Gunner Paul Jackson (21) from Leeds in West Yorkshire of the Royal Artillery was attached as a photographer to 321 EOD, the bomb disposal unit. He was killed when the device exploded and he was hit in the head by shrapnel. The official version of events states that the shrapnel penetrated the observation slit of the armoured vehicle in which he was sitting. However, the author has been informed from utterly impeccable sources that Paul Jackson was either asked or, more likely, ordered outside and was standing in the open when the bomb exploded. A definitive explanation cannot be offered at this stage.

At this point in time, there would be nothing to be gained in naming names or even contesting the 'official' version of events. Jackson, originally from Glasgow but with all his family in Leeds became the 21st member of the Royal Artillery to lose his life in, or as a consequence of the Troubles. With over 60 deaths of artillerymen attributable to Northern Ireland over the course of Operation *Banner*, this regiment suffered the most casualties of any mainland regiment.

GUNNER PAUL JACKSON'S DEATH

Bill 'Spanner' Jones, REME

In addition to our usual duties, the LAD [Light Aid Detachment] REME had a boat to run errands on the Derry River. The 18ft punt was usually skippered by Corporal Mat Hinds whilst the rest of us took turns to crew. HMS *Ramses* was moored at the dock and the crew would lift the punt in or out of the water for us with their derrick.

It was my turn to go out with Mat; this time two wooden boats tied together had been floated down river and become stuck on the boom that was there to prevent bombs being floated down to the road bridge. The bomb squad, consisting of a Major and two Warrant Officers, went to investigate. Steel helmets and flak jackets were not used out on the water; floatation vests and berets were the dress order. We all boarded the punt, with me in the bow, Mat at the helm and the three Felix men [Bomb Disposal] in between. Going upstream, the Major asked if we could get onto the bridge for a look, and Mat steered us to one of the piers which had iron rungs for access. I tied up and we all ascended to the lower tier which was for security personnel.

We could see nothing unusual from the bridge so went back down to the punt, going closer to the boats, and the Major used his 12 bore to put some solid shot through them to see what would happen. Nothing, so he asked Mat to give them a nudge with the bow, so I moved back near Mat, and the Major was puzzled and asked where I was going. To which I replied: 'If we are going to bump those boats to see if there is a bomb there, I am NOT sitting there to find out!' He seemed to think it better not to argue with a windy Spanner carrying a loaded sub machine gun.

Still nothing from the boats so he decided that we would tow them downstream, under an old disused wharf and sink them with the 12 bore to stop them floating out as a nuisance again; we were glad to be safely back at Fort George.

A few days later, 28 November, I got up as usual, had breakfast and prepared for work, and I chatted to Gunner Paul 'Jacko' Jackson and exchanged a bit of banter. We laughed and went our separate ways; it was the last time I ever spoke to him. Later that day, we were told that Jacko had been killed by a bomb. I could not believe it and hurried to his room; his bedding was all gone, just a bare iron bedstead, and, next to it, doors open, was his empty locker. The other HQ Battery lads sat in silence with pale faces. It was true. Gunner Paul Jackson was 21, married with two little boys.

It took us a couple of days but we managed to talk to the RCT driver who had been out with Jacko, and this is what he told us. He had been tasked to take a Saracen out with Felix to a bomb that had been left by the wall of a shop near Fort George which we sometimes used. It was the same three men we had been up the river with, and they had found that the bomb was one not seen before. They came to 'borrow' Jacko as he was our regimental photographer, and they asked the driver to back up to the bomb and when close, stop. They opened one back door and asked Jacko to lean out to get a picture but, as he did, the bomb exploded; taking off half of his head. One of the Felix crew lost an eye and all were injured, with even the RCT guy having blast injuries; despite these, he drove off and raced back to base with the wounded to get help. He did a terrific job and I pray he does not suffer from the memory. For Jacko, it was too late.

I was posted to Germany on 29 December and so with embarkation leave, I was home for Christmas; Jacko never went home and I have survivor guilt to this day.

TIME STANDS STILL!

Bob Luke, Royal Corps of Transport

I wrote earlier about the petrol bomb attack in the 'Murph and this next incident took place the same day. We had been back on base for only a short time when we got a call to get mobile as there had been two bomb alerts and not many bods available. We high-tailed it towards the city centre and wondered which way we would end up going. We approached the Unity Flats complex and were directed to an area to set up a cordon. Within a couple of minutes, we were on the go again, this time to the Europa Hotel [a favourite target for the IRA]. As before we were positioned well back from the suspect vehicle and waited, all the time wondering if this was a hoax or a definite bomb.

It must have been about 10–15 minutes when, without any warning, there was an almighty flash and bang and then I was flying through the air. You often hear stories of time slowing down when something like this happens and I can tell you it's true. I was facing the suspect vehicle when it went off, and it felt as though I had been kicked by a horse. Mind, saying that, I haven't got a clue what that would be like! For me, time had slowed down; I was inside a balloon of smoke debris and, funnily enough, tranquillity. I could see my rifle following me, due to it being fastened to my wrist, and then as quickly as it started, I hit the road surface with a sickening thud. The wind had been knocked out of me and I was struggling to breath. I recall at the same time seeing my new combat trousers with a bloody great hole ripped in the knee area. As the dust settled I could see all of our crew were alright, apart from the fact that we could hear bugger all. After a short while the medics had checked us all and gave us the ok to return to base.

On arrival back at base, we went through the usual ritual of checking and double checking and of course I headed for the stores again, just to get a lecture on how expensive military uniform was and I was lucky – yet again – not to have to pay for the damaged items! After a while we all sat in the ready room, some reading and some sleeping. I just looked around and thought: 'what a bloody shit sort of day we've had!' I finished my tab, looked at our team for the last time and nodded off; in a lot of ways that was a normal day in Belfast!

To many this would mean nothing, but to me I was proud to be a section commander with these lads and doing a good job; yes it was hard and yes we did lose mates, but deep down I doubt that I would change a thing. As time goes on I do relive these memories, in fact sometimes they are my night demons. I left NI with more than memories; I left NI as a man, just 21 years old and feeling like one of the old hands in our squadron.

The Europa Hotel stands in Great Victoria Street, close to the Dublin Road and in 1972 was a symbol of Belfast's commercial heart. As such, it was a prime target for the IRA's economic bombing campaign, designed to spread terror and at the same time, damage the British infrastructure. At one time, it was the most bombed hotel in Ulster. Soldiers, forced to evacuate guests, talk with glee about rousting US journalists and businessmen from their rooms whilst muttering at them: 'Blame the IRA; you lot support them!'

November ended with yet another senseless and random sectarian killing when a local barman was murdered by the UFF. Gerard Gearon (22) a Catholic from the Ardoyne area finished his shift and set off for home. As he walked over to a taxi, he was approached by two men who told him that they were also going to the Ardoyne. Lulled into a false sense of security, he agreed to share the ride with them. One of the gunmen asked the taxi driver to stop near to the local Mater Hospital off Crumlin Road and when he did so, the gunmen opened fire, killing Gearon and wounding the driver. Almost two years to the day, the same terrorists murdered one of the owners of the taxi firm for daring to give evidence at the inquest into the murder of Gerard Gearon.

PARTING GIFT FROM THE IRA

Jim, Argyll and Sutherland Highlanders

My final incident was on the last day of the tour. I had just gone on watch in the back sangar. Everyone else was handing in equipment and packing; we were on our final hour, handing over to the 1st Battalion, Royal Hampshire Regiment. There was a whoosh; I thought some of the guys were playing around with fire extinguishers, then a bang, whoosh, bang. I looked out of one of the slits and saw two holes in the police station roof. Then it was like an explosion in the sangar, except it was machine-gun fire. Sand from the sandbags was spraying everywhere as well as splinters of wood. It seemed like it was disintegrating around me. This was serious and there was nothing I could do except open the trap door and go out headfirst. Then it went silent; the back wall (corrugated iron) looked like a sieve. An IRA group had sneaked up to the far end of the football pitch with a heavy machine gun giving covering fire to another group with an RPG-7. They had also used a furniture truck, thus blocking the road and stopping any follow up. This was the first time RPG-7s had been used in Ireland and it was a concerted attack on a number of border police stations. We were lucky with no casualties; other police stations were not. I went home; I had survived!

November was over and a further 24 people had been killed. During the month, 9 soldiers, 10 civilians, and 3 members of the IRA lost their lives. It is worth noting that Loyalist terror gangs were responsible for nine sectarian murders.

CHAPTER TWELVE

DECEMBER

Chuck Berry's 'My Ding a Ling' started the Christmas month off as the number one single in the British music charts. In Australia, Gough Whitlam was elected Prime Minister in the first victory in 23 years for the Australian Labour Party. Christmas was a mere 25 days away but it was unlikely that any of the paramilitaries had thoughts of goodwill to all men. It was business as usual.

On the first day of December, the UVF took the war to Dublin. The government of that city was perceived by many – even in non-paramilitary quarters – to encourage the IRA's activities, and it certainly turned a blind eye. The Garda Siochana often knowingly allowed terrorists to cross the border and prevented the British Army and RUC from pursuing them. On many occasions the Irish Judiciary – nominally under the control of the Houses of the Oireachtas composed of *Dáil Éireann* (House of Deputies) and *Seanad Éireann* (Senate) – had refused to extradite IRA suspects to Northern Ireland or the mainland. The Republic was also criticised for seemingly ignoring the fact that huge quantities of explosives were being stolen from quarries and civil engineering sites in Ireland with apparent impunity; an unlocked gelignite store here, a nod and a wink about a gelignite delivery there.

There had already been an attack in Dublin, but it had been the work of the IRA in response to what many observers saw as a half-hearted crackdown by the Dublin government on 'illegal' Republican movements. On 26 November there was a bomb explosion at the Film Centre Cinema, in O'Connell Bridge House. A late film was being shown and although no one was killed, approximately 40 people required hospital treatment. The explosion happened at 1.25am and the bomb had been placed outside the rear exit door of the Film Centre Cinema in a laneway connecting Burgh Quay to Leinster Market.

At the time of the explosions the Dáil had been debating the Offences Against the State (Amendment) Bill, which would have given the Irish government much greater power against dissident movements, in particular the IRA. Suspected members could be tried and sentenced on the word of a senior police officer in front of three judges. Prior to the explosions most observers felt that the bill would not become law; the Dáil, which was comprised of some IRA sympathisers, was not considered a strong enough institution to resist the organisation. However, following the explosions there was a one-hour adjournment after which Fine Gael (FG) abstained in the vote and the amendment was passed.

At approximately 20.00 on the evening of 1 December, a UVF car bomb exploded outside Liberty Hall and the huge explosion injured dozens of civilians. Then, just before 22.30, another one detonated in Sackville Place in Dublin city centre. A passing bus was hit and both staff

It is Christmas, 1972 and the season of goodwill, but to this Scots soldier, there is none!

members were killed; George Bradshaw (30) the driver and Thomas Duffy (24) died at the scene. The UVF justified the attack by blaming the Irish for their tolerance of the IRA and for allowing their country to be used as a bolt hole for terrorists.

On the 2nd the UFF abducted, tortured and shot Patrick Benstead (32) and dumped his body in Crossley Street in Belfast. The killing – described as 'depraved, savage and sadistic' – shocked the whole community, especially since Benstead was educationally sub normal and described locally as 'slow'. He was burned by a hot iron and had a cross and the initials IRA seared into his skin. On the same day, not too far away in Flora Street, UFF gunmen targeted a Catholic man, but in the confusion succeeded in killing his Protestant wife, Sandra Meli (26) as they fired indiscriminately into the house. Bloody tit for tat followed and the IRA shot and killed a Protestant just hours later. Samuel Hamilton (50) was shot by Republicans in Comber Street in east Belfast; he was a Protestant picked purely at random.

On 5 December the Army was involved in exchanges of gunfire with the IRA in the Ardoyne and after an ambush in Woodvale Road, close to the edge of the Republican area, IRA member Bernard Fox (16) was killed. Soldiers manning a covert OP in a house on the Crumlin Road observed the teenager who was armed and shot and killed him after coming under fire themselves. There was further tragedy for the area, when the Army accidentally shot and killed a man when they mistook a metal tube that he was holding for a firearm. William Bell (30) died at the scene and there was a genuine and immediate apology from the Army to the dead man's family. Somehow, Army admissions of regret rang less hollow than the contrived ones issued by the paramilitaries.

Two more soldiers were to die that day in different parts of the Province. An Army post at Kitchen Hill, Lurgan came under a mortar attack by an IRA firing team. Two of the three mortars fired exploded and an EOD team was called in to defuse the unexploded one. Sergeant Roy Hills (28) from Lewisham was killed instantly when the bomb he was handling went off. The terrorists then targeted UDR soldier Private William Bogle (28) as he sat outside a shop with his three children in Killeter, Co Tyrone. The family lived in Gortnagross, near the Co Tyrone-Donegal border. The children were sitting in the car when several masked IRA gunmen approached and shot him three times. His wife rushed out of the shop and cradled her dying husband in her arms pleading 'Willie, don't die!' The soldier managed just a few words but had succumbed to his wounds before medical assistance arrived. When IRA gunman Stanislaus Carberry was killed a few weeks earlier, an IRA spokesman called the killing 'cowardly'; just how would he have described the murder of William Bogle?

On December 6/7, the IRA killed two civilians and Loyalists one of their own members. The first to die was Samuel White (32) a Protestant murdered for purely sectarian reasons in Lisbon Street, Belfast, near the Republican Short Strand. The following day a senior UFF figure, Ernest Elliott (28) was found in a car off Donegall Avenue in the 'Village' area. Initially thought to have been an IRA victim, it now appears that he was shot by the UDA in a dispute over a handgun.

The IRA, self proclaimed defenders of the Catholic community, then showed their true colours when they murdered Jean McConville (37). Mrs McConville was a widow and the mother of fourteen children; she was abducted by the IRA from her Divis Towers' home. She was never seen alive again and her body simply disappeared. It was rumoured that her corpse had been hidden in an oil drum and buried either on a beach or in remote countryside, but the truth came out 31 years later when, in 2003, her remains were discovered at Shelling Beach near Gyles Quay, Co Louth, in the Republic. She was finally laid to rest in November of that year.

Her killers accused McConville of comforting a wounded soldier and of being an informer. There is evidence (see Ed Moloney's *Voices From The Grave*) that the latter may have been true, specifically that she had a short wave radio transmitter and was informing on PIRA movements, seen from her vantage point high up in the Divis flats. In Moloney's interview with Brendan Hughes, the latter lays the blame for her disappearance and the decision to murder her firmly at the door of Gerry Adams. Adams has claimed that he was interned at the time of the murder, but in fact he had been free for at least six months.

A day before the murder of Jean McConville, a soldier in the Royal Green Jackets had been shot by an IRA sniper in the Ballymurphy estate. On the 8th, Rifleman Raymond Joesbury (18) from Birmingham died of his wound in hospital.

On the 10th, Colour Sergeant Henry Middlemass (33) of the King's Own Scottish Borderers (KOSB) father of three was killed instantly when examining an abandoned explosive device. He was killed inside Fort Monagh, a fortified Army position in the Turf Lodge area. It has always been understood that the device was booby-trapped by the IRA but sources close to the author state that the device – a rocket fin – might have been a piece of unsafe British Army ordinance. That the IRA had it in their possession is undoubted; the question is whether they abandoned it as unsafe or actively booby-trapped it.

The Army – who had accidentally killed William Bell six days earlier – was then involved in another killing, this time careless. A Private from the Queen's Lancashire Regiment manning a sangar outside North Queen's Street RUC station had a negligent discharge and hit Joseph Ward (58), an innocent passer by. The soldier was later jailed for manslaughter.

Above: Two Gunners from 57 Battery, 94 Locating Regiment, Royal Artillery ensure that no-one makes off with the Ford Zephyr abandoned beside Diamond's corner shop at the junction of Cyprus and Plevna Streets. Running parallel to, and just north of, Leeson Street and now long-demolished, this was one of the most dangerous places in the Lower Falls at that time, being familiar territory for men such as Brendan Hughes, John Joe Magee and Gerry Adams.

Right: Perhaps it's the presence of the housewives, but from the relaxed attitude of this 57 Battery Gunner, you wouldn't think it was a street in the same area. It is though, as confirmed by the twin spires of St Peter's Cathedral, and the next two views confirm why he should really have been more wary of his surroundings.

13 December saw the death of RUC man Constable James Nixon (49), a father of two. Nixon was leaving a hotel when an IRA gunman opened fire with an automatic weapon. Following his murder his 12-year-old daughter had a nervous breakdown, and his policeman son had to resign from the RUC after suffering from incident-related stress.

Over the course of the next three days, both the Loyalists and the IRA were involved in more blood-letting. The UVF took their revenge for the murder of UDR soldier William Bogle in Killeter by planting a car bomb outside a mainly Catholic bar in the same village; when it detonated, bride-to-be Kathleen Dolan (19) was killed instantly.

The IRA, ever desperate to outdo each previous outrage, made an opportunistic attack on the RUC in Lurgan. An RUC team had just visited the Republican Kilwilkee estate in the town following an accident between one of their cars and a local child. They had organised a whip round in order to buy toys as a gesture of both regret and goodwill. As they left, they spotted a stolen

A Humber 'Pig' had to accompany foot patrols. And the graffiti on the van leaves no doubt as to the residents' political affiliations. Is that the GPO Exchange on the Grosvenor Road just visible beyond the derelict terraces?

The motor vehicles date it as later than the early 20th century inner-city dereliction that the rag and bone man's cart suggests, but it's the presence of the two squaddies that defines this scene as not being Manchester, Leeds or Birmingham. Another part of Mulhouse Street-based 57 Battery's TAOR.

Left: Their presence is studiously ignored by the locals. There's that Zephyr again!

Below: Time to unwind in more secure surroundings.

57 Battery, Royal Artillery
's Mess Mulhouse Street

car and, fearing that it might be a Loyalist bomb, began shepherding people from nearby houses. As they did so, six IRA gunmen opened fire on them, wounding three including Constable George Chambers (44), father of six children. As he lay helpless on the ground, they stood over him and killed him. With only one officer still standing and returning fire, the cowardly killers ran off. The injured child's mother, despite knowing that the Republicans might target her for 'breaking ranks', expressed her sorrow at the death of Constable Chambers. She thanked the officers for their gesture and said that she just wished that they had posted the gifts instead.

The very same evening, an unnamed Loyalist murder gang – likely the UFF – attacked a group of youths who were standing in Dandy Street and Shore Road, Belfast just over half a mile to the east of Antrim Road and close to the docks. They approached a suspicious motor-bike and were shot at by the pillion passenger and several were wounded. James Reynolds (16) was fatally wounded and died later in a nearby hospital. It is thought that a family member had received sectarian death threats at a local college and there was tension in the air. *Lost Lives* (p305) reports that the Belfast Coroner said 'One wonders what kind of generation we are raising in Northern Ireland today.' It also reports that the machine gun used in the killing was later found in the Loyalist Shankill Road area.

Finally, in the evening of the 15th, the IRA targeted the UDR yet again and shot part-time soldier Private Fred Greeves (40) as he left work. The production manager at a dairy in Armagh City was attacked by gunmen hiding in the factory grounds. He was armed and returned fire but was hit and died shortly afterwards. His killer claimed later in court that he had only intended to rob Private Greeves.

OBSERVATIONS OF A MEDIC

Sergeant John Black, RAMC

The staff at the Military Wing, Musgrave Park Hospital were constantly under a great deal of strain. Part of this problem could have been avoided had active service conditions prevailed. For example, if the paperwork had been reduced we would have been able to admit, evacuate or discharge soldiers far more quickly and expediently. Under active service conditions, it only took one document to either admit, transfer or discharge a soldier back to his unit. [It took five documents to admit a soldier to the Military Wing Musgrave Park Hospital, seven to a civilian hospital and three to discharge him.] I still feel a little guilty about the 'Dickensian' hospital administration procedures. But may I state to the reader who had never experienced the early years of the Northern Irish campaign, that it was and still is part of the United Kingdom. Over 160 soldiers were killed in Northern Ireland in 1972, on British soil!

Equally I believe that the Ministry of Defence and the government of the day considered the 'war' as a 'jolly', a few Irish Fenians giving a little trouble. There was no training for Northern Ireland until well into the mid 1970s. Regiments were deployed to the Province from West Germany and the UK well versed in the tactics of the Cold War and were expected to keep law and order in a growing hostile environment, and all this was happening in a part of the United Kingdom.

Loyalists then killed IRA member Louis Leonard (26) while he was working at his 'day job' in Derrylin, Co Fermanagh. On the same day, Loyalists killed Joseph Blaney (41), an innocent Catholic, at his shop in York Road, Belfast.

A week before Christmas, the IRA targeted William Johnston (48), a member of the Police Authority. He was the owner of a carpet store in Armagh City and was out working close to the Irish border when he was shot several times by IRA gunmen before they skulked across the border.

CHRISTMAS IN BELFAST

Eddie Atkinson, Green Howards

We arrived in Andersonstown in late 1972; it was the only time I spent Christmas in Northern Ireland on a four-month tour. We were based in 'Silver City', and the area was very similar to any post-war housing estate. It consisted of semi detached houses, flats and terraced town houses; most with small gardens in the front and back.

On our first night we were posted to a school in the middle of the estate where we had a guard post of a sandbagged sangar. Darkness descended and some time, around 2000 hrs I was in the sangar with the late Tony Gosling. We were just passing the time when the sangar was hit by a volley of machine gun fire; we couldn't see where the fire was coming from, with the street lights on, so we just hit the deck. 'Gozzy' and I just looked at each other and said 'Welcome to Andytown.'

There was a guard post dug into the hillside opposite the camp; it was supposed to be there to stop RPG attacks on the camp from that wooded area. We used to go in for a day and we lived underground for the full 24 hours. It was like a First World War dugout; duck boards all over the floor to keep us out of the mud and water. To get to the sangar we had to scramble, stooped along a tunnel on duckboards. You couldn't stand upright in the sangar and you could hear the rats running up and down behind you. All our food was kept in Norwegian containers; it wasn't a pleasant duty.

Although you have interviewed me about 1972, the incidents swung into a New Year and I need to include this in my account. We were called out sometime in late January to East Belfast. All we had been told was that the Catholic churches were being attacked by the UDA. We were on Albertbridge Road close to Carnforth Street junction. [Albertbridge Road sweeps along the southern part of the Catholic Short Strand, before linking up with the Newtownards Road further east. The area of which Eddie writes is east of the Short Strand and is Loyalist territory.]

We had a confrontation on Templemore Street with the UDA. There was a crowd being controlled by three or four UDA men wearing camouflage jackets, scarves over their mouths and wearing dark glasses. This came to nothing and the main threat was on the main road where we took up position on the junction with Carnforth Street. We had a Saracen and a PIG in the middle of the road, and there was a crowd around the corner who were throwing everything they could lay their hands on. At this time I had a riot gun, and a gunman kept popping round the corner in Carnforth Street and firing a couple of rounds from a pistol. An Artillery soldier was laid out in the middle of the road waiting for him to try it again and he was pelted with bricks and bottles but he never flinched; I thought 'Good on you, mate.' I believe he [the gunman] came around the corner once too often and the soldier bagged him.

All of a sudden there was a volley of shots from down the road and the rounds hit the shop windows above my head. I thought to myself that this was the right time to change this useless riot gun for my SLR. I went to the Saracen for my rifle and in the back of the vehicle was a fellow soldier; it did occur to me that was a strange place for him to be, but said nothing and just got my rifle and rejoined the lads. [Eddie and I discussed naming the man but agreed that it would be inappropriate; let sleeping dogs lie.] I knelt down at the side of the Saracen and there were shots coming from down the street and I saw two puffs of smoke from further down the road and fired two rounds back. I don't know if I hit him but he stopped firing, so I have always thought I must have hit him or come very close. They used to lie down on blankets and if they were hit the dickers and supporters pulled them back, rolled them up and spirited them away.

Eventually we advanced and to my surprise, the street they were firing at us from was Skipton Street, my old town. The one sad thing to occur this day was 'Tapper' Hall was wounded in the back and he died six weeks later in hospital; he will never be forgotten.

Private Raymond 'Tapper' Hall — so named because of his habitual 'tapping' of cigarettes from comrades — died of his wounds on 5 March 1973. He was 22 and came from Hornsby-on-Sea; he died with his parents at his bedside.

On 20 December no fewer than eight people were killed, seven at the hands of Loyalists. The UFF and UVF respectively, shot David McAleese (37) a father of three in Newtownards Road, Belfast and Alphonsus McGeown (19) in Loughall, Co Armagh. McAleese was shot from a passing car as he waited for a lift to work and McGeown had just arrived home when he was killed. Later that day, UDR soldier Private George Ellis Hamilton (28) was at his job at Croppy Hill reservoir, Co Londonderry. He and his colleagues were employees of the Derry Development Commission and had been repairing a fault at the site when he was hit in the back by a single round from an IRA sniper. The 8th Battalion man died some two hours later in Altnagelvin Hospital. Private Hamilton, married with a five-year-old daughter, came from Kildoag, near Claudy. He was a brother of Ernest Hamilton, the proprietor of the Beaufort Hotel, whose wife, Mary, was seriously injured by the second bomb which had detonated outside their premises less than five months previously.

In the evening the UFF targeted the Top of the Hill bar on the Old Strabane Road in Londonderry's Waterside area, close to the Republican Gobnascale estate. Frequented mainly by Catholic drinkers, it was close to the Loyalist Fountain area – a convenient bolt-hole. Several armed men burst in and indiscriminately opened fire with what soldiers call a 'smig', a Sterling sub machinegun or SMG. The two men sprayed shots around the packed bar, causing utter carnage. Five people died and four others were wounded, some badly. The dead were Charles Moore (31) a Protestant father of two; Charles McCafferty (30) father of seven; Bernard Kelly (26); Francis McCarron (58); and Michael McGinley (37). The latter four were all Catholics.

Christmas Day was only 96 hours away and the Loyalists continued their killing, shooting dead James Mullan (25) in Bangor, Co Down as he waited for a lift to work outside his home. On Christmas Eve Lance Corporal Colin Harker (23) of REME died of wounds received on 14 September during an attack in the Bogside. The gunman had used a crowd of children to shield himself from the soldiers. Harker became the 172nd and final British soldier to die in 1972.

Christmas Day and Boxing Day passed without incident, but on the Wednesday an Army undercover patrol in Strabane was laid up in a field and observed two men carrying rifles. IRA men had taken several shots at soldiers in the area during the previous weeks, and the Army was on high alert. One soldier shot dead IRA member Eugene Devlin (22) and wounded the other man who then escaped but was captured later.

On the 28th the UVF planted car bombs in the border area inside the Republic, killing two innocent teenagers. Geraldine O'Reilly (14) and Patrick Stanley (16) were killed at Belturbet, Co Cavan, as the Loyalists again took the terrorist war to the IRA's spiritual home. Elsewhere Private Thomas Boyd (21) of the UDR died in circumstances and place unknown.

1972 was limping bloodily to an end; on the 30th an Army border patrol at Ballyarnett, Co Londonderry observed several men crossing from the Republic. The soldiers challenged the men and ordered them to stop but they ran away and one, according to the soldiers, dropped and took up a firing position. He was shot and died at the scene and the IRA later claimed that he was one of their volunteers. James McDaid (30) was a 'Captain' in the Londonderry Brigade.

In the early hours of New Year's Eve, UVF gunmen lay in wait for a night shift bakery worker, shooting and killing Hugh Martin (55), a father of five, as he left work. He was a resident of the Ardoyne and according to *Lost Lives* he was also a former PoW, having been captured by the Germans in North Africa. The New Year of 1973 was just around the corner and five children had lost their war hero father simply because he was a Catholic working in a Protestant area.

NEW YEAR'S EVE

Sergeant John Black, RAMC

In the November, we had been reinforced by a section from 24 Field Ambulance, commanded by Captain Kidd, a medical officer from Northern Ireland. Boy could those guys drink! The day was quiet, so we arranged for an impromptu New Year's Eve party in our very own cellar bar. But we had no booze as Military Wing, MPH did not have either a Sergeants' Mess or Officers' Mess, so we shared a communal bar in the cellar. Some twenty years later, a bomb was planted there in a very cowardly attack.

The whole unit chipped in and the erstwhile captain plus two good mates of mine from 24 Field Ambulance went into Dunmurry in order to resolve this difficulty. Unusually for Ireland I must say, the booze shop was closed with a notice telling customers to come back at 10.00 hours. We had arrived at 09.00 hours. Now the British soldier is renowned the world over for 'living off the land' and we noticed a café just down the street. Egg, sausage, beans and real coffee beckoned and off we went.

There were three girls serving and we sat there munching and slurping away, when about 20 RUC police officers came in and another five outside, all tooled up for some heavy duty action. All 20 officers bought coffee and almost took over the establishment. Nothing to do with us we thought and carried on with our munching and slurping. Then the RUC inspector came over with a heavily armed colleague and told us in no uncertain terms to get outside where we were spread-eagled and searched. I bleated out that we were soldiers from the military hospital and if given a chance could identify ourselves. One officer undid my coat, and lo and behold I was carrying the pistol (without any ammo of course). How very embarrassing. Nevertheless all was resolved by the production of our MOD Form 90 (military identity card), and we all piled back into the café where we had a second breakfast at the RUC's expense. The party was a success too, and we had invited the RUC 'hit squad' to join us. A pleasant way to end a nasty year!

Northern Ireland had become one of the most dangerous places on Earth, in particular Belfast and Londonderry. No-one but soldiers or police travelled at night unless they were up to no good; night was great cover for the terrorists and the murder gangs of both sides. The following account from an RAMC medic took place after 1972, but it relates to an incident which meant much to him and I have decided to include it in this chapter.

JAMES HESKETH

Starlight, RAMC

I returned to the Lower Falls in late 1973, which was again a very hard tour. But of all that happened on that tour, one incident above all is etched into my brain. We had been 'crashed out' to a shooting contact in Leeson Street, just off Grosvenor Road and not far from the Divis. On arrival we were unable to get the Saracen ambulance close to the casualty because of the risk of an RPG attack. We therefore parked in a side street, the name of which I forget. We debussed and ran to deal with the casualty who had fallen into a doorway.

I discovered that it was a Private James Hesketh whom I knew well, and he had been shot through the throat with an M16 and was clearly dying. I attempted to resuscitate him and open an airway, but his injury was so bad that I decided to carry him in a 'fireman's lift' to the Saracen and get to the RVH which was just four minutes away. We needed to get there as quickly as possible so that an emergency tracheotomy could be performed. As I lifted him, the owner of the house where James had fallen when hit, who must have been lurking just inside the door, came out and poured a kettle of hot water over the blood and mucus stain, as if it was a piece of dirt, he then started to scrub his step clean. I made eye contact with him and the look was one of pure hatred. Not one ounce of sorrow for the young soldier who had bled his last on his doorstep; he just scrubbed as if a dog had shat on it. Sadly James Hesketh was beyond resuscitation. The image of the callousness of the householder still haunts me to this day.

The following day our Pipe Major, Andy 'V' played a lament at the spot where he died. Several years later I attended an appeals court case where those found guilty of his murder, the murder of two soldiers from the Glosters in Divis Flats (bomb in a mattress) and the attempted murder of a Light Infantry Padre all had their sentences reduced and minimised through the obnoxious use of plea bargaining. There was just no justice.

James Hesketh (21) a soldier from the Queen's Own Highlanders was shot in the throat, whilst on a foot patrol at the junction of Leeson Street and Grosvenor Road on 10 December 1973. The young man, from Clydebank in Scotland was just starting what was only his second week in Northern Ireland. He was 'tail end Charlie' in the patrol and died within minutes of being hit despite the efforts of medics to save his life.

In December, a further 41 people had lost their lives in or as a direct consequence of the Troubles. These included 8 soldiers, 2 RUC and 26 civilians, no fewer than 20 of whom had been killed by Loyalist terror gangs. The IRA lost four members and the Loyalists lost one.

Over the course of 1972, the bloodiest year of the Troubles, 566 people had been killed or died as a consequence. The grim toll was 172 soldiers, 17 policemen, including one officer from the Garda Siochana, a staggering 265 innocent civilians, 86 IRA and 26 Loyalist terrorists; an average of 1.5 killings a day over the course of the leap year.

Private Eddie Atkinson, Green Howards. Eddie was involved in an incident early in 1973 near the Republican Short Strand area.

EPILOGUE

In a country of approximately 1.5 million people, 566 people had lost their lives in or as a consequence of the Troubles during 1972. There were over 10,000 separate shootings and 1,382 explosions. It was a year of bitter controversy and included the tragedy of the deaths of fourteen unarmed civilians in Londonderry on 30 January. Bloody Sunday was an IRA recruiter's dream come true and inspired a whole new generation of angry young men to avenge their community's dead. What the events of that tragic day and of subsequent self-serving justification also did, was show the double standards and hypocrisy of the Nationalist communities. They overlooked the atrocities at the Abercorn Restaurant, Donegall Street, Bloody Friday and Claudy while constantly eulogising the events at Free Derry corner. When it came to atrocities, the British Army did not have a monopoly, far from it; the PIRA visited ten-fold back upon their own community alone.

The reader should look to the following atrocities: La Mon Restaurant, Droppin' Well, Shankill Fisheries, Kingsmills, Tullyvallen Orange Hall, the M62 coach bomb, Hyde Park, Enniskillen, Darkley Mountain Lodge Pentecostal Church and many, many others. How did the deaths of seven Royal Green Jackets bandsmen in Regents' Park on 20 July 1982 advance the cause of Irish Republicanism? How did blowing up eleven Royal Marines bandsmen as they slept at Deal, Kent on 22 September 1989 bring forward the day of Irish reunification? How did killing Australian tourists Nick Spanos and Stephen Melrose because they 'resembled' British soldiers in Roermond, Holland in 1990 possibly benefit Sinn Féin/IRA's desire to be seen as a future government? No amount of airbrushing of history or hollow, pious apologies from 'respectable' Sinn Féin politicians can ever change those atrocities; the dead are still dead. The troubles lasted for almost four decades; 1972 was just the worst year. The author maintains that within the Provisional movement there was undoubtedly a genuine motivation, a single-minded determination and a desire to 'free' the North. But there was also a spirit of evil, and the psychopaths who were attracted to the movement took full advantage of the killing chances afforded to them, as indeed did their counterparts in the Loyalist killing gangs.

The Army did not beat the Provisionals in 1972, but neither did they lose. They had many successes and vastly increased their knowledge of the shadowy organisation and both intelligence and penetration methods were moderately successful. Arms finds increased and surveillance methods improved. Soldiers became less naïve, more wary. They would no longer make themselves easy targets by standing under street lamps, open ginnells or white-painted walls. No longer would a weary squaddie out on foot patrol lean his full weight against a wall; it would be the limited weight of his foot which even today marks out former soldiers. 'Hard targeting' was here to stay and it would save many uniformed lives.

1972 saw the beginning of the end for the old-style IRA leaders such as Ruairí Ó Brádaigh, Billy McKee and Dáithí Ó Conaill. The setbacks suffered by the Provisionals were seen as failures of the leadership and paved the way for the young bloods such as Adams and Hughes to remove them from positions of power. The setbacks were evidenced by the increasing number of executions of PIRA members as Adams took more control. 1972 was the bloodiest year of the Troubles because the IRA – by no means a defeated force afterwards – threw everything into their 'struggle'. In later years, whilst still an implacable force, cash and weapon-rich thanks to the NORAID coffers, they were restricted in their operations. They were hampered by defections, internal feuding and the seemingly omnipresent informers. Their foe was also more deadly; the superior urban warfare tactics and strategies of the Army and RUC and the reduction in the naivety of the earlier Operation *Banner* tours greatly reduced the IRA's killing opportunities.

Could the Army have done more to protect the Catholics and their property over a more prolonged period of time? The 'honeymoon period' was certainly over by the second summer of deployment. It was somehow inevitable – given the history of the previous 50 years – that the relationship between the Nationalist communities and the soldiers would end in acrimony. But could we as soldiers have done more? There were many fair-minded members of the British Army who felt that the Catholics were a downtrodden mass and we British have always loved an underdog. We saw that they had suffered at the hands of the Protestant/Unionist ruling class prior to the onset of the Troubles. Indeed, it was a company of British soldiers, totally outnumbered as they were by a Protestant mob, who stood firm to defend the Unity Flats on at least one occasion. Wasn't it the RRW who defended the Catholics in the Falls and lower Springfield Road right back in the first days of deployment? How quickly the sympathisers and the Irish-Americans and Sinn Féin's history writers forget that.

Was the political will there in HQNI? Did the Army's top brass, the 'bloody red tabs' want us to be seen as defenders of the Catholic communities? Or were they pressurised by the Heath government who in turn were pressurised by the Stormont government to acquiesce to the Protestant will? Had we done more for the besieged Nationalists, could we have done more to help slow down or even halt the trickle and ultimately the torrent of recruits joining the ranks of the Provisionals? There is, one feels, no doubt that once the Catholics perceived that the soldiers were siding with the Loyalists, the die was cast. The estrangement was absolute and irrevocable. There is little doubt that the behaviour of some soldiers left much to be desired. Some were overzealous during searches, raids and arrests, pushing decent people into the arms of the Provisionals. There were also unsubstantiated rumours of theft; as they say, 'mud sticks.'

The killings began again just two hours into 1973, when the UFF seized and murdered a young Catholic and his fiancée as they walked home from a night out. Oliver Boyce (25) and Briege Porter (21) were killed in Co Donegal, some four miles inside the Irish border; their deaths would be followed by almost 300 more that year.

FINAL THOUGHTS

Two ducks flying over Belfast's Black Mountain; one duck goes 'Quack, quack!' The other duck retorts 'Hie fuckin' quack d'yez want me to flay?'

Mick 'Benny' Hill, Royal Anglians

A few weeks ago I was admitted to my local hospital for a minor operation. The nurse who measured me for and fitted the DVT stockings was chatty, caring 50-ish, and with a soft Belfast accent. When she saw my collection of scars on my shins, she said: 'Sweet Jaysus, where did yez collect all those from?' A few years ago I'd have lied and muttered something about 'rugby', but I told her that some of them were a souvenir from her home town.

She told me what it was like being a young teenager in a Protestant enclave in West Belfast. In '71 and '72 her Mammy's house was a tea-stop for a Light Infantry Battalion's patrols. One evening her mum noticed a soldier laying in the gutter near her house, sheltering behind a car. Her mum went out and asked him if he would like a cup of tea. He just looked at her, and said in a broad London accent 'This ain't a good time, darlin.' Her mum then noticed the sporadic gun fire coming from the end of the road!

As the nurse said to me: 'Typical of the madness of those times.'

Sergeant John Black, RAMC

I wish to dedicate my experiences to all the guys who patrolled the streets day and night in Northern Ireland during the bloody year of 1972, who had to patrol a war zone, although it was never recognised as such by politicians both then and now. In particular my feelings go out to the soldiers of 1 RRW, 1Kings RGJ, LI, 1 Para and QLR. Most of these fine regiments no longer exist, but in 1972 these were the regiments I came across during my sojourn in Belfast. I was posted to the relative safety of the military hospital in Belfast, and our accommodation was better than the lads' on the streets, although the food was lousy.

The year 1972 was an eventful year for me but for the wrong reasons. I was posted to the permanent strength of Military Wing Musgrave Park Hospital Belfast one week after Bloody Sunday. Until then I had been a corporal at the Military Hospital Colchester, but was posted at relatively short notice in the acting rank of sergeant. The problem that the situation was not declared a war zone made the administration of our hospital very difficult. Peacetime paperwork was still the order of the day. It took five pieces of paper to admit a soldier to the Military Wing

Musgrave Park Hospital, seven if the soldier was admitted to a civilian hospital and three to discharge the soldier. All paperwork was in triplicate. The strain of this system was to become all too apparent.

James Henderson, UDR

When reading your book *Bloody Belfast* I noted a reference to Strabane and its 'black heart'. As you know this was where I lived and worked during all my service with the UDR. In normal times Strabane, as my local town, would have been logical for casual shopping or socialising. My children received the bulk of their further education in local schools there. However I never shopped in Strabane but went with my wife to various supermarkets and shopping centres in Waterside and Limavady.

Although the surrounding countryside was approximately 60% Unionist and 40% Nationalist, the town itself was dominated by strong forces of extreme nationalism. To reach certain schools the Protestant children from the country had to travel through Republican areas. This often meant a hazardous journey in buses escorted by Army or police and subject to considerable verbal and physical abuse from the local supporters of terrorism. Some of the better-off parents, Catholic and Protestant, paid to have their children attend school in safer areas. The rule for those of lower income – the majority – was that the local catchment area was the only option.

The town is, you may remember, surrounded by very beautiful countryside – which prompted Cecil Frances Alexander, the wife of Bishop Alexander the Episcopalian Bishop of Derry, to write some famous hymns when living at what is now part of Strabane Grammar School. The children's' hymn 'All Things Bright and Beautiful' is set here, from the 'purple-headed mountains' to 'the river running by'. It is the ancestral home of US President Woodrow Wilson and of John Dunlap, the printer of the American Declaration of Independence. It can claim to be the birthplace of other notables of the eighteenth and nineteenth centuries. And the rivers are full of salmon!

However, having lost a number of friends and comrades to murderers who operated from there I can concur with the description. It is the town with a black heart set in beautiful scenery. I wonder if it is better today than it was in the 1970s and 1980s?

Alex B, UDR

You talked about that most obscene of questions and there would have been many variations – 'What are yez?' 'Where are yez from?' 'Are yez Protestants or Taigs/Fenians?' Asking Protestants in that latter fashion would almost certainly elicit a truthful response in the belief that the offensive, derogatory terms used for 'Catholic' meant their interrogators were themselves Protestant. Prods would be equally devious if they suspected strangers of being Catholics. This could be an evil place for any unfortunate from either tribe who wandered into 'foreign' territory and met the likes of Lenny Murphy and his infamous Shankill Butchers. Devils incarnate.

In general, Loyalists were much more overtly sectarian than their Republican counterparts, but the bigotry was/is well-entrenched in both communities. Because of his surname, as well as the predominately nationalist area where he lives, a relative of mine is usually taken for a Catholic and thus hears the true hard-line views of the militant section of the area's Catholic population. In casual conversation, Protestants are endearingly referred to as Huns (presumably the Martin Luther connection); Nazis (similar – also in the sense of their supposed, sometimes actual, homicidal persecution of the oppressed minority); Orange b'stds & c★nts, with suggestions to the effect that, if so fond of the Brits and being 'British' they should relocate to GB. This – ironically – is the identical 'wisdom' that loyalists dispense in respect of wishing nationalist migration in a southerly, cross-border, direction if they're so keen to be 'Irish'. In my cousin's case they've no idea they're talking to a 'Hun' and I've warned him not to react in any circumstances. Discretion, etc!! With that level of peace 'n love 'n trust 'n respect can you ever see a harmonious future for this place? No, I can't either.

Pete Whittall, Staffords

I only witnessed Bloody Sunday on the telly, but such images and personal experiences would soon haunt me. Those that did were the pub bombings in Birmingham in November 1974, my home town, when by sheer coincidence I was coming to the end of my first tour of duty in Londonderry, and in May 1988 when the two Royal Corps of Signals Corporals were set upon by an IRA funeral cortege in West Belfast, beaten, stripped and killed, most of which was graphically captured by television images. Between 1974 and 1981 I undertook four tours of duty in the Province, all different, each with its own life-changing experiences and memories that will live with me forever. A number were pleasant with laughter and happiness, but sadly the majority were just awful; war is never pleasant is it? To the SF Northern Ireland was a war. The bloodiest and most repetitive part was 1972 as a whole. May true lasting peace continue to be strengthened by all who strive to retain it. The good people of Northern Ireland and mainland Britain deserve this right after too many years of bloodshed and hatred.

Mike, Royal Artillery

In late 1976, I'd caught this character with a pistol in a back street garage. He was charged and remanded in the Crumlin Jail. My tour ended in December and it was not until June 1977 that his case came up before Crown court. I was flown over from Germany and transported to Moscow camp where they had accommodation set aside for court witnesses. The next day, I was transported in civvies in an unmarked car to Crumlin Road court. I was told that the case was second on the list so I ear-wigged the first one which was a compensation claim which made the news. A pregnant woman had been caught in the crossfire during a shoot out and had been wounded, the bullet hitting both her and the unborn child. Luckily for them, they both survived and I believe the judge awarded something like £60,000 which was a huge sum in those days. The gallery was packed with this twat's relatives and friends and I got a fair bit of verbal abuse as I gave my evidence. Also, the accused didn't do the usual 'I refuse to recognise the court' bit.

My side was that I was on foot patrol in a certain area of Belfast. As we were checking some garages in an alleyway, we came across this character inside one of the garages. I saw him put a cloth over a bucket so while one of my lads searched him outside I looked inside the bucket where I found a Sauer 38H pistol, dating, apparently from the last days of the Second World War. Telling the rest of my lads to back off a fair bit, I 'persuaded' this person to use the cloth to lift the weapon out of the bucket and lay it on the ground. I felt fairly safe doing this as the Irish didn't go in for suicide bombers. I then called for 'Rucksack' who arrested him and combed the place for evidence. The pistol was loaded and later forensics proved that it had been used in the attempted murder of an off duty policeman, so naturally the RUC threw the book at him, and his finger prints were found all over the weapon.

Pat Finucane [Republican solicitor] then got stuck into me big style and his argument concerned the use of the cloth to pick up the weapon. He said that the accused had said that I threatened to kill him there and then if he didn't pick up the weapon with his bare hands. He went so far as to say that a common soldier wouldn't have the intelligence to think of taking precautions about finger prints. I felt like jumping out of the box and flooring the smarmy git but the judge bollocked him for his comments. Some of the defendant's relatives in the gallery started screaming abuse so the judge called a recess. When we resumed, Finucane gave it his best effort but I wasn't having any of it.

The bottom line was that the judge threw out the attempted murder charge, but gave him ten years for possession with intent of a loaded weapon. Nice one. I was on the first available flight back to Germany thinking that that will be the last time I visit this shit hole as I was due to leave the army the next month. However, I had been out just under two years and had settled in London working for a security company when one morning I was called upstairs to see the boss who handed me this thick registered envelope with a Northern Ireland postmark on it. Due to its origin, the company had already scanned it so it was safe to open. Inside I found a load of documents: a copy of my original police statement, an open return flight ticket to Belfast, a £20 money order and a letter from the Northern Ireland Crown Court explaining that I was required to attend as a prosecution witness at the appeal hearing of this character and to pack enough clothes for a three-day stay. I must admit at the time, I was having severe regrets about not shooting this bastard. I would have had every chance of getting away with it.

So there I was, a couple of weeks later winging my way from Heathrow. At Aldergrove, the Army actually had an office for court witnesses to report to. It was explained to me that as I was a civilian, I could not stay at Moscow Camp in case it was attacked and I might not be safe, so I would be staying at a hotel. All thoughts of a couple of nights in the Europa disappeared when I was told that the hotel was in East Belfast, just off Holywood Road, smack in the middle of a Proddie area. Nice! I thought: 'Any chance of a camp bed at Flax Street Mill?' They stuck me in a 'Q' car with an RMP escort and an RCT driver and headed for Belfast. On the way, the MP who was from the Courts Witness section, briefed me on the ins and outs of the case. It appeared that the defence had convinced the Appeals Court that some doubt could be shed on my evidence concerning the use of the cloth. In those days, an appeal hearing was almost the same as a trial so I would have to give my evidence again and then wait and see what the defence came at me with. Great!

On the way, my escort asked me if I fancied a bit of nostalgia. 'Why not?' said I and so we headed down through Glengormley passing the Carnmoney factory where I had spent several weeks. We then passed the zoo, Cliftonville and New Lodge down to Carlisle Circus. The memories came flooding back with a vengeance. I asked if we could cross the Lagan using the Albert Bridge and so we did. As we approached the end of the bridge with its junction with Short Strand, and I saw that the bullet strikes were still there from the contact my section and I had back at the end of November 1976. 40-plus shots exchanged with two fire positions all over in about 30 seconds. None of mine hit but a claim of one hit on theirs. But that's another story. I lost interest in the guided tour and we soon pulled up outside this tiny hotel.

It turned out that the hotel was run by an ex soldier, his wife and son. At least it had a bar. I was shown my room and then told a list of don'ts: 'Don't talk to strangers, don't get pissed and above all, don't leave the hotel.' With a last 'see you at 0830 hrs tomorrow' they left me to it. The people were friendly enough and after a decent meal and a couple of pints served up by the son, it was pretty pleasant. Next morning, after a brilliant Ulster fry-up breakfast, the same escort crew turned up and whisked me off to the Crumlin Road court.

Waiting in the witness room for it all to start, the prosecution guy came in for a few words. It turned out that he was a part-time UDR officer so we spoke the same language. He told me that when I got called he would take me through my statement and then it was down to me not to let the defence budge me. He also warned that Finucane was a lot more polished than he was two years earlier.

A couple of police officers were up first; I was surprised that the accused was next in the box, flanked by two prison officers. I couldn't hear too much of what was said but it went on for quite a while and the judge recessed for a short break. It was then my turn. I was a bit surprised when the clerk called for me by my former rank of bombardier and as I walked to the witness chair I could feel dozens of pairs of eyes drilling into me. The prosecution did his thing, again addressing me by my former rank; then it was over and he passed me to Finucane. His first words to me were: 'As you are no longer in the army, I will address you as Mister.' The judge jumped on him but he had already got his point over.

I answered all his questions easily and calmly denied any of his accusations. The only awkward time was when the judge himself asked me a couple of questions. The first one was why I had told the other members of my section to withdraw around the corner. I said it was for their safety just in case of a problem. The second one was in relation to the defence's accusation of me using the threat of shooting the accused if he didn't pick up the weapon. He asked if I cocked my rifle and why. I said yes and the reason was that I was taking no chances and that it wasn't done as a threatening gesture, more a reminder not to try anything. 'Fucking lying bastard' and 'We're going to get you' screamed the gallery. And that was it over. The judge retired to consider his verdict while I had sausage and chips, complements of the RUC.

The judge didn't hang about. He was back in less than an hour and he announced that the original verdict was sound. With the shouts from the gallery echoing in my ears, I was ushered out the back door, into the car and off back to the hotel. I grabbed my bag, had a quick celebration pint and then off to Aldergrove for the first available flight to Heathrow.

Soldier 'P'

I have nothing but total admiration for all the security forces – including the canine four-legged furry friends – that provided the buffer zone for the good people of Northern Ireland during the sad days of the Troubles. But I would like to dedicate this to the faceless, fearless men and women of all the Security Forces who put themselves daily into the forefront of danger every time they worked undercover on covert operations. This includes the RUC Special Branch and the many other respected but little known surveillance teams.

I know of the sheer fear and tension that every one of these operatives went through as I served with a number of these units and still have vivid memories of the missions I went on and the sleepless nights. I have never been myself since, even though my last tour of duty in Ulster was in the early 1980s. It stays with you forever, just as it would have done for the uniformed branches of our distinguished comrades at arms; any life-changing experience has that effect. My time in the province, both as a uniformed and plain-clothed British soldier, had a significant impact on me as a human being and has partly moulded me into the person I am today, both the good and the bad.

I would particularly like to pay recognition to the female operatives because typically our heroines both in uniform and civilian clothes were very seldom given the praise and recognition they deserved. I often worked with the 'Greenfinches', 'Rucksacks' and so many others whose nicknames or radio identification names confirmed which security force unit they were from; 27 years have passed since I was last on active service in the Province and I have forgotten a lot of the names by which these extremely brave women were known, but they will know who they were. Without them we would not have gained the intelligence leads that we did. The world of the undercover surveillance and intelligence squads was one of living on a knife edge, not knowing when or if your cover would be blown or if you were going to be compromised by informers. We don't have to reflect too deeply to be reminded of colleagues who lost their lives whilst on covert operations, such as Captains Robert Nairac, Grenadier Guards and Herbert Westmacott. Even to this day I still take precautions and adopt some of the safety checks and procedures we were taught and used every day of our lives during those sad times.

We often operated with two or more in a team dependent on the operation and the TAOR. There were some who took greater risks and operated in isolation; they knew the depth of danger that this brought and in some cases paid the ultimate price. We were very close-knit units and looked out for each other, knowing full well that our role tended to take us into the very heart of the paramilitaries themselves and often brought us much closer than comfort really dare allow, but that was our job and an absolute necessity to fight the war against the terrorist evil at the time, both Loyalist and Nationalist. We had to blend in with the populace; in the '70s and '80s we favoured armoured-plated Maxis, Cortinas and Zephyrs because they were popular on the Ulster scene, and wore clothes and cut our hair to fit it. We quite often worked with female colleagues in pubs and clubs as this reduced the possibility of suspicion when we walked in and sat down. We pretended to be husband and wife or boyfriend and girlfriend or pretended to be a group of friends out for a good time. The risks and adrenalin flow were equally high. We tended to use a set procedure which included communication signals and covert communication systems as necessary for each operation; we always went 'tooled up' (armed). Favoured small arms for closequarter surveillance operations were the Browning 9mm pistol, 38mm Smith & Weston or Walther PPK. We would have back up teams in close surveillance support when the operation required it and they would carry the heavy weapons just in case we were compromised.

Other operations would include stake outs for several days/weeks in covert positions; we would infiltrate the area and maintain a constant watch on known 'players' from both communities and report back on their activities and confidants. We would spend many long boring hours taking photos, recording developing situations and taking the fight to them. Many successful ambushes leading to arrests or 'contacts' took several days/weeks of surveillance work to secure. We did from time to time have informers to call on. Sometimes these were double agents working with ourselves and the paramilitaries who could set us up and a few of them did from time to time. The risks were great and we were forever on our guard; it was very nerve racking.

Luckily I didn't get married until I left the military and so had no wife or children worrying where I was, unlike some of my colleagues. All my family ever got to know was that I was being posted somewhere unknown and they understood that the unit of the Army I was in needed to operate in this way. Our covert teams frequently operated in the most volatile and dangerous areas of the province and would often be on the streets or out in the country unknown to the uniformed patrols. If we were stopped or searched we would have to quickly inform them as discreetly as possible that we were 'tooled up' and confirm our ID upon which they would swiftly do an improvised body search, treat us like everyone else and let us go on our way. This only happened to me a few times thankfully. When a big op was going down then the local area commanders of the RUC and Army would be informed and we would likely use the uniformed SF to act as a visual deterrent, deliberate decoy or be there as backup so we could go about our 'sneaky beaky patrols'. The fear of confrontation was always in the back of our minds and particularly when going on a 'hit' operation. These often needed very senior authority and were always meticulously planned and often rehearsed if time and facilities were available.

We inevitably got into firefight contacts with those we were 'watching' or 'engaging' during our operations. These were very intense moments and one was grateful for being able to hear the crack of each enemy shot or having the defence of your armoured plated car or wall. I do recall one operation where a lamp post deflected a round to the left of me during a very close quarter gun battle in which I had knelt down to return fire; the round hit the lamp post at face height and ricocheted into a wall behind me, my maker was definitely looking after me that day.

Progressive British and Stormont governments have much to answer for in letting Northern Ireland sink to the lows that it did. In the end, that which should have been put into place many, many years before, finally was. Why did it take over 38 years to achieve peace, why did 1,300 British soldiers lose their lives? Why did we have to operate within the restrictive 'yellow card' system of engagement against the petrol bomber, nail bomber and gunman? This cost many soldiers and security force colleagues their lives, and those responsible in the successive British governments should be made to account for their negligent actions in restricting our right to defend ourselves. Why did so many innocent men, women and children in Ulster and the mainland also have to lose their lives or suffer serious injury for all those years? Why were the Nationalist community not better protected and provided for by the discriminatory Stormont government, which led to the troops needing to go in on 14 August 1969, because of the civil unrest that had been created by their direct discrimination against this sector of the community?

Why were the likes of Ian Paisley, Gerry Adams and their cohorts not dealt with more severely at the time of their provocative speeches, which almost certainly encouraged the hatred and take-up of violence on both sides of the community? Even today there is no complete settled peace, and the murder of police officers by breakaway factions of the IRA continue. There are still ongoing sectarian violent actions taking place, attempts to break down the peace accord. The strength and determination of the majority of the people of Northern Ireland will not allow these few unfortunate, sad events to deter them from continuing to fight for a total peace settlement, for they are the saviours and guardian angels of this rightful legacy – a happier and better, peaceful future.

Corporal Paddy Lenaghan, King's Regiment

I talked earlier [see Chapter Five] to you about the black Kingo I was mates with, Leon Smart. Well, flash forward a few years to a different time and a different place, after my injury at Springfield Road Police Station. The battalion were in Hong Kong and we were in the Families' Club and I was there with my seven-year-old daughter and Leon was there too. My little girl, because kids of that age have no fear, asks Leon: 'Why are you that colour?' He just smiled at her and said: 'Because God made me this colour; why are you that colour?' She was half-Maltese and was an olivey shade and she just replied, so proudly: 'My daddy made me this colour.' Needless to say, this broke everyone out into big smiles and everyone around the table was laughing out loud. I am pleased to report, that in the finest traditions of the British Army, no beers were spilled; but you had to be there.

John Bradley, 23 Engineer Regiment

I was so happy to be going home I never wrote anything down for that last week or so. I did get to do a real sloppy thing though. You see I left behind my wife in Germany and she was pregnant (yes before I left, smart asses!) She was due in October and so while I was on the *Maidstone* I worked the BFPO radio with Gloria Hunniford. This meant I could send my loving messages back home. I have a photo of that somewhere. I shall have to find it. It was a tough year all round but on 6 October 1972 at BMH, Munster, my life changed forever. My wife gave birth to the cutest baby girl ever born. How lucky I was to survive.

UDR Man

Did you know that post 11 September, RUC officers here made donations to some of the NYFD stations – but pointedly refused to give to the NYPD, primarily because that police force's pipe band always attended the annual Sinn Féin parade in Ballyshannon, Co Donegal? It was the south Donegal Provo unit from the Ballyshannon/Bundoran area that was responsible for the Enniskillen Cenotaph bomb and the attempted massacre of the Cubs/Scouts/Brownies/Guides parade at Tullyhommon/Pettigo the same Remembrance Sunday morning. Some things you don't forget.

Keith Williams, RRW, Attached to the UDR

I found my time with 4 UDR to have been very rewarding and a privilege. The courage and devotion to duty was second to none. In the early days I was often saddened by the ways some of the regular units treated the UDR with distrust or even contempt when other more enlightened units used their local knowledge of the area and people to their full advantage.

Stevie, Ulster Defence Regiment

I never served in 1972 but perhaps, if I might be allowed, I'd like to offer a few reflections on the changes the Army went through in that year.

The Army in Northern Ireland had had to alter its concepts and ways of dealing with a new enemy, to which a new name was given – 'urban terrorism'. Up until 1969 the Army, in dealing with insurgent groups in Cyprus, Malaya, Borneo and Aden, had been in support of local forces and effectively defending a gradual withdrawal from its old colonies and empire. There had been a sense that this was 'real' war and therefore there was a clear separation from the realities and detail of the situation on the part of the soldiers, inasmuch as it was not 'their' land or their people so did not touch their lives, unless a comrade was killed or injured. There was a sense that the issues and conflict were 'not their business' so it was easier to keep any feelings in some sort of perspective. They were there to do a job and then leave.

In Ulster this degree of separation began to fade several months after August 1969; it began to dawn on all ranks that this was not going to be a swift settling of 'rowing natives' and then back on the boat home. In fact it became very clear that it would be a lot harder to extract the Army than it had been to commit them in the first place. As understanding grew, the senior officers in Lisburn and London realised that, rather than them being in control of how the conflict was conducted, there would be a greater degree of political control (interference?) and direction over decisions at almost every level. The eyes of not only the UK but of the world were on their every action and move.

A lot of the difference lay in the changing moods and attitudes all over the world: since the late 1960s; many countries had seen large-scale and often violent demonstrations against the established order, and the will was strong to actively try to change policy, especially foreign, by use of mass rioting and disturbance. This involved free-thinking and progressive students, politicians and union movements who felt that the use of effectively revolutionary methods to pressurise governments could bring about change.

However, where there existed both peaceful and more militant viewpoints, as the decade changed the emphasis drifted toward the use of violence in the shape of organised civil unrest and, when the means became available, the use of arms to further the 'cause'. This had been seen in Ulster with the gradual shift from peaceful organised marches and sit-down demonstrations to open warfare as in the 'Battle of the Bogside' and similar sectarian street fighting in Belfast and other towns and cities. While the move to fighting had a long history in Ireland, the change in social thinking and the influence of ideas from Ireland's past and from European movements rising more recently in France, Germany and also from the US had a significant effect that was instrumental in the rise of the Provisional IRA and the evolution of their campaign of murder and destruction.

By 1972 this basis had been built upon as both sides escalated their level of activity in a 'race' to beat the other into submission. 'Temporary' bases had become permanent; units now did tours on a regular basis that could last from four months to two years. Troop levels had risen to nearly ten times that of July 1969 (2,700) reaching more than 30,000 during Operation *Motorman* in July 1972, a major commitment of defence resources in the face of the on-going threat from the Eastern Bloc and the need to maintain both a coherent home defence capability and the garrisons abroad.

Most of this however was not at the forefront of the thoughts of the soldier on the streets or in the countryside of Ulster. He – and increasingly, she – was concerned with more basic and immediate concerns like surviving to the end of the tour. The events of that fateful year – Bloody Sunday, Bloody Friday, Claudy village, the Abercorn bombing, Direct Rule introduced, truces and secret talks – all contrived to inflame and ferment the conditions that would embroil the British Army for 38 years, the longest period of active service of any campaign.

Living conditions were a big part of the soldier's concern – that and the 'old chestnuts' like getting enough sleep, food, mail from home, R'n'R, doing guard duties and staying dry (something often hard to do in Ulster) as well as the hundred other duties like 'dixie-bashing', 'area cleaning' etc. The biggest effect however was one that was not, in most cases, noticed or understood for many years after they had left the Army. They worked often 20 or more hours at a stretch; they did mind-numbingly boring duties on guard or on checkpoints; they searched houses that were not fit for human inhabitation; they walked, ran, stood, kneeled, or lay prone in all sorts of places and in all sorts of conditions.

Most confusingly they worked in places that looked uncannily like their own home towns, among an 'enemy' that, if it were not for the strange accent and expressions, could have been the people from their own neighbourhoods and estates. Streets with the same names as ones in their towns, with the same post boxes and corner shops, the same terraced housing. And amongst all this familiarity of surroundings where they lived in police stations, schools and meeting halls that resembled castles, double-decker buses, derelict houses, lorries, even on the very pavements, they watched their friends die in front of them, day after day, night after night.

A constant grind of boredom, fear and excitement, suffering basic or worse conditions, and losing their friends began to evolve. This became 'normal', expected, and slowly ingrained itself into the minds of both soldier and public, both in Ulster and at home. The 'tradition' of doing duty abroad, and serving the country by doing what you were told without the need to understand was gradually worn away – it became personal, as the terrorists intended it to become. The mindset of not showing fear, being 'tough', never showing emotion, these were all part of being a soldier; the stiff upper lip, 'carrying-on' in the face of all adversity and in front of your mates. It was a central part of being a man in a man's job.

But this was also a time when the long-term effect of stress and loss was not known or appreciated. Soldiers were expected to simply brush emotion and fear aside and continue to do their jobs. Anything else was a sign of weakness, something no-one wanted to show or admit to feeling in front of their mates or even to their families. They had to be strong, and be seen to be so. So the wave of confusing and 'inconvenient' feelings, which often showed as anger or frustration, was often deflected toward the people outside the camp walls and sangars – the locals. It became easier to let emotions be spent out on the 'paddies' who, while many were often 'anti' Security Forces, became convenient outlets for pent-up emotions and in time became the 'enemy', being the only visible aspect of the otherwise unseen foe. This too was another facet to the campaign of violence, planned as a means to turn the community against the Security Forces.

With no respite from the roundabout of patrol, stags, sleep (minimal) and the many sundry and mundane tasks that filled the day, time to consider and arrange the feelings and emotions inspired by the madness around them was simply not available, so these uncomfortable and confusing thoughts were boxed off and put away, for many only to re-emerge many years later as sharp and vivid as if they had just happened.

By 1972 the 'honeymoon' period of earlier years was over. The realisation dawned on generals, private soldiers, terrorists, civilians and politicians alike that there was no quick end in sight. This was war in all but name.

APPENDIX ONE

THE SAVILLE INQUIRY

The findings of the Saville Inquiry into the events of Bloody Sunday were published in the UK on Tuesday 15 June 2010. However important the events of 30 January 1972 may have been, it was some 38 years ago, and whilst the findings do corroborate much of what I and others have written about the event, what did it prove? I have never felt that even those tragic events could justify the decade-plus and near £200,000,000 cost. The ten volume report was brought about by the incoming Labour Prime Minister, Tony Blair MP, back in the heady days of the first Labour government in eighteen years. Many saw it as a sop to Irish Republicans and it seemed to mark the start of Blair's antipathy to anything military. Whilst he was happy to use the blood of British soldiers in the military campaigns post-September 11, this 'euphoria' did not extend to providing them with adequate financial and logistical support, then or later.

The report may not lay the ghosts of Bloody Sunday to rest; it potentially gives succour and encouragement to Republican activists in general and in many ways might even go as far as to 'justify' – in Republican mythology – post-Bloody Sunday IRA/INLA atrocities. It is almost as though PIRA's campaign of bombing and murder can be explained away by the events of that day. Time will tell if it gives impetus to any Republican attempts to drag the tragedy into a fourth, fifth or even sixth decade, providing fresh prospects and more emotional support to what many call the MOPE (most oppressed people ever). Here, it must be emphasised that this term in no way refers to the relatives of the dead. But it is an insult that Saville effectively brands the British soldiers as criminals.

The report looked at General Sir Robert Ford, who was commander of land forces in 1972 and was and increasingly concerned that the Army had no control over a large part of Derry. He wanted to see rioters dealt with swiftly. The inquiry learnt of the existence of a memo, written by Sir Robert in January 1972, in which he suggested shooting (but not killing) some of the ringleaders of the rioting, known as the 'Derry Young Hooligans'. In the general's mind the Army was 'virtually incapable' against these gangs, because they operated under the cover of snipers.

Lord Saville's report said the panel were 'surprised' that the General should have seriously considered such a plan and did not believe it had been adopted, though I still find it improbable that, once committed to paper, the idea of 'shooting, but not killing' DYH ringleaders had no influence on the planning for the military reaction to the banned parade. Furthermore, how the General ever imagined that anyone shot with an SLR wouldn't be killed does not appear to have been addressed by the report. Dismissing the memo was probably the best means of dealing with an awkward piece of evidence that had the potential to implicate much more senior military figures than Colonel Wilford – and possibly even their political masters. But the inquiry believed General Ford could not be criticised for deploying soldiers to arrest rioters, although he had probably sent the wrong unit.

> In our view his decision to use 1 PARA as the arrest force is open to criticism, on the ground that 1 PARA was a force with a reputation for using excessive physical violence, which thus ran the risk of exacerbating the tensions between the Army and nationalists in Londonderry. However, there is to our minds a significant difference between the risk of soldiers using excessive physical violence when dispersing crowds or trying to arrest rioters and the risk that they would use lethal weapons without justification.

The inquiry concluded the General had no reason to expect the tragedy that then unfolded. It accepted his denial in evidence that he sent 1 Para in to provoke republican gunmen to confront them in the street. Paddy Lenaghan, King's Regiment who was badly injured four months later said of the report:

> I do not know how the papers or the TV are reporting the fall-out of the report in the UK, but I know that I am very pissed off with the way the report is being handled by some news outlets here in Australia. 'The British Army guilty of murder!' I am not guilty of any crime; I went to Northern Ireland because my Regiment was sent there, so why the fuck should I, or any soldier posted there have to be branded a murderer due to the actions of soldiers, who should never have been posted in a peacekeeping role at that particular time and place? And do you know what the most hurtful part is? The arseholes from the so called political wing; Adams and co, gloating that their actions were justified and we all get 'tarred by the same brush'. Was the whole of the Army of the United States responsible for the actions of Lieutenant Calley at My Lai, Vietnam [Pinkville massacre]? No, of course they weren't!

Mike from the Royal Artillery told the author:

> To quote Napoleon: 'there is no such thing as a bad soldier; only bad leaders.' I watched it on the 6pm news and could sympathise with the relatives of the dead, but my brand new telly with all the bells and whistles was in great jeopardy when Adams and company stood gloating in front of the cameras.
>
> I wonder what the chances are of us getting £200 million to take those bastards to task over their murderous activities; no need to answer that one.
>
> I promise if I ever win the Euro lotto, a very large percentage of it would go towards bringing them to justice, and to hell with the Good Friday agreement. With regular and TA service, I gave 30 years of my life to this country and at the moment, all I feel is a sharp pain between my shoulders caused by a knife sticking in my back. I now know how the American servicemen felt after Vietnam. We won the battles but lost the war; sold down the river by our politicians.

The Saville Inquiry was far too expensive and at almost twelve years took far too long to establish what we already knew; that the Paras over-reacted and that their officers totally lost control of their men on that awful day. The new British Prime Minister, David Cameron, chose not to avoid the issue – of course, if he wished, he could have laid the blame at the door of the late

Edward Heath, though that would have contradicted the report – and publicly stood up in the House of Commons and confirmed the findings and apologised for the actions of that day.

The report found that the deaths were not a part of a government-ordered plan but instead blamed the soldiers of 1 Para for being 'trigger happy' and said that they overreacted to the pressures of the day. It also found that they should have never have been ordered to 'police' the NICRA march and were clearly the wrong regiment to do so. It established that they fired the first shots – something which I do not believe – and that their response to the ugliness of the mob was not justified. The people at whom they fired were unarmed and in some cases were actually running away and a number of victims were shot whilst on the ground. The report stated that none of the dead or wounded were doing anything that justified them being shot. The report also stated that no warnings were given in direct contravention of ROE (Rules of Engagement) or the 'yellow card' and that the soldiers exercised no self-control.

The report further criticised the Paras' CO, Lieutenant Colonel Derek Wilford, who has always maintained that his soldiers were fired on first and were merely doing their duty. However, Saville criticised his actions, saying he should not have launched the incursion into the Bogside. It said he was wrong to do so because he disobeyed the orders given by his superior, Brigadier Pat McClellan, and also because his soldiers, whose job it was to arrest rioters, would have no or virtually no means of distinguishing them from those who had been involved in the march. It said he was also wrong to send soldiers into an unfamiliar area where there was risk of attack from Republican paramilitaries, in circumstances where the soldiers' response would risk people other than those engaging the soldiers with lethal force being killed or injured by army gunfire.

The report concluded that the Paras who were there that day lied to both the Widgery Tribunal and also the Saville Commission. Consequently, David Cameron said that the British government and people were deeply sorry. He further stated to MPs that Bloody Sunday was wrong and should never have happened.

Cameron's statement included the following points: no warning had been given to any civilians before the soldiers opened fire; none of the soldiers fired in response to attacks by petrol bombers or stone throwers; some of those killed or injured were clearly fleeing or going to help those injured or dying; none of the casualties was posing a threat or doing anything that would justify their shooting; many of the soldiers lied about their actions; and that the events of Bloody Sunday were not premeditated.

> The conclusions of this report are absolutely clear. There is no doubt. There is nothing equivocal, there are no ambiguities. What happened on Bloody Sunday was both unjustified and unjustifiable. It was wrong. These are shocking conclusions to read and shocking words to have to say. But you do not defend the British army by defending the indefensible.

Whilst the victims of Bloody Sunday were rightly exonerated, the report did not make comfortable reading for Republicans. It revealed that the former IRA chief Martin McGuinness, now Deputy First Minister of Northern Ireland, was carrying a submachine gun that day. 'We cannot eliminate the possibility that he fired this weapon after the soldiers had come into the Bogside.' It added that the same gun may have been used to kill two policemen in Londonderry two days before. It also rejected the received wisdom that nail bombs had been planted on Gerald Donaghy, one of the Bloody Sunday victims, after he had been shot.

Jeffrey Donaldson MP, Democratic Unionist Party for Lagan Valley added:

The difficulty is that we have the truth on one side, but not the truth on the other. We don't know the truth about what Martin McGuinness and the IRA were doing on that day. While we regret every death … we must not lose sight of the need for balance.

Lord Trimble, former Ulster Unionist leader, in a statement said that the killings were wrong, and mistakes had been made in the planning and conduct of the operation on Bloody Sunday. However, he added: 'It would be perverse if the events of Bloody Sunday were used to justify those unjustifiable events that PIRA launched in the 1970s.'

Northern Ireland's Deputy First Minister Martin McGuinness, Sinn Féin, was present at the time of the violence and 'probably armed with a sub-machine gun' but did not engage in 'any activity that provided any of the soldiers with any justification for opening fire'. The British laws of libel do not allow me to comment on the former IRA commander for the Creggan and for once in my life, I will remain quiet.

The *Guardian* newspaper reported of Cameron's words:

These were powerful, moving and fully justified words by the Prime Minister. Across the water in Derry people had been waiting long years to hear them, not least because the perfunctory 1972 Widgery tribunal had added to the original affront of Bloody Sunday itself. Yesterday, in the sunshine outside the Derry Guildhall, a crowd finally heard the words they deserved, with Mr Cameron's speech relayed on a big screen and applause greeting several of the prime minister's clear statements. A few minutes later, relatives of the victims emerged to trumpet the innocence of their loved ones. Inevitably there was some political grandstanding – both the SDLP and Sinn Féin have worked hard in their own ways for this moment. But the most striking impression from Derry was not of implacable triumphalism but of long-suffering people finally awarded the vindication and justice which they should have had years ago. The potent and emotionally charged scenes in both Westminster and Derry put most of the objections to the inquiry into proper perspective.

Irish journalist Jim Gibney had his 'two-penn'eth', writing of Saville's comments: 'media personnel from all over the world attended (and) heard him state four succinct points: the Paras were guilty of wilful murder; they shot indiscriminately, denied spiritual and medical attention to the wounded or dying and none of the dead or wounded was armed.' He also stated that a journalist from the *Irish Mail on Sunday* actually turned up on the doorstep of Lieutenant Colonel Derek Wilford and presumably tried to harass him into making a comment about Saville.

Simon Winchester, whom this author had previously admired, wrote in the *US Globe and Mail* that the events of Bloody Sunday could be directly compared with the massacre at Amritsar in India in 1939. On that occasion, British and Indian soldiers opened fire on an unarmed group of protestors with automatic weapons and killed 379 men and women. Presumably that journalist was trying to win favour with the Irish-American readership of his US employer's journal.

In the *Daily Mail* General Sir Michael Rose wrote an article titled: 'It wasn't Blair who brought peace to Ulster but brave British soldiers about to be branded as criminals.' This was written by a top soldier who was present during the events of Bloody Sunday. He stated that he was certain that 'it was the IRA who started the firing.' The article went on to say:

As I lay in the gutter, I could see bullets hitting the wall of the building above me. There was no doubt that the IRA gunmen were firing from their positions on the galleries of the flats opposite, where I was taking cover. In my view, it is entirely possible that they could have been responsible for some of the civilian deaths, shooting from on high down into the streets below where the crowd was trying to escape from the killing zone.

But it was absolutely clear that in exchanging fire with the terrorists, the British Army had fallen into the trap laid for them by the IRA, who had set out that day to commit murder and mayhem, caring nothing for the lives of their own republican supporters. Indeed it was their specific aim to get as many people killed as possible. For the deaths would serve as a ruthlessly cynical recruiting tool. As news of the dead in Londonderry that day spread around the world, the result was much the same as Irish people everywhere rallied to the nationalist cause.

Leading Ulster Unionist Jim Allister said:

My primary thoughts today are with the thousands of innocent victims of the IRA who have never had justice, nor benefitted from any inquiry into why their loved ones died. Thus today's jamboree over the Saville report throws into very sharp relief the unacceptable and perverse hierarchy of victims which the preferential treatment of Bloody Sunday has created.

A jubilant Sinn Féin spokesman said that the report put the

… lies of the Widgery Report in the dustbin of history. Today is a day for the families of those killed and those injured on Bloody Sunday. They have campaigned for 38 years for the truth and for justice. They have campaigned for the British government to end their policy of cover-up and concealment.

Whilst the author will never seek to excuse or condone the actions of the Paras on Bloody Sunday, the results of the Saville Inquiry leaves more stones which will need to be turned. When will the relatives of the 1,294 British soldiers killed in, or as a consequence of, the Troubles have their inquiry and their justice? What of the loved ones of the 300+ RUC officers; when will they have their day in court? When will the countless loved ones of those killed in IRA/INLA and UVF/UFF atrocities be accorded the same eulogies as those killed on Bloody Sunday? Will the now 'respectable' politicians of Sinn Féin and Unionism who sit in the Northern Ireland assembly admit their knowledge of the atrocities of those bloody years?

Do I believe Saville? In part, yes. I believe that the 1 Para's officers lost control on the day; I believe that pressure was put on Wilford to 'invade' the Bogside; and I believe that the fourteen people killed were all innocent and were wrongly and shamefully shot down. I also believe that McGuinness, known locally as 'the butcher of Derry' was there and was armed with a machine gun, as Saville alleges. But where I disagree with the respected Lord Saville is in his assertion that Paras fired first; I believe that the IRA fired first and thus precipitated the events of that tragic day.

On 15 June 2010, I appeared on a live show for BBC Radio Wales to discuss the Saville Inquiry and its implications. On that show was Jean Hegarty, sister of Kevin McElhinney who was killed on Bloody Sunday. She was a brave and dignified woman and although I was not afforded the opportunity to speak to her, I wanted to tell her that I shed the same tears for the loss of my mates in Northern Ireland as she did for her young brother. Perhaps those tears will unite us; only time will tell.

APPENDIX TWO

RECENT IRA 'EXECUTIONS'

Michael Madden
Pensioner was shot six times at his west Belfast home in 1980. The IRA claimed he had given information to police about an attack in which a police officer was killed. A detective told the inquest there was no truth in the claim. The coroner described him as 'a recluse causing no trouble to anyone.'

Frank Hegarty
Body was found on the border in 1986. Originally from Londonderry, he moved to England after an arms find, but later returned to the city. The Republican leader Martin McGuinness strongly denied claims by his mother that he helped persuade her son to return home, assuring him he would be safe.

Eamon Maguire
Former member of the IRA, his body was found close to the border in 1987. The IRA claimed he had worked for eight years as an informer with police in the Irish Republic, which his family denied.

Patrick Flood
IRA member from Londonderry was killed in 1990; his body found hooded and gagged on a border road. He had been missing from home for seven weeks. His mother said 'At the end of the day it's people like me, and their families, that are left to pick up the pieces.'

Christopher Harte
Shot in 1993 by the IRA, who said he was a member of the organisation and claimed he was an informer. His body was found with gunshot wounds to the head.

Caroline Moreland
Mother of three from Belfast was shot and her body left on the border in 1994. The IRA claimed she had been working as a police informer.

Dennis Donaldson
Former 'pre-sixty niner' Provisional recruited by British Intelligence in 1983; revealed as an informer in 2006. Murdered by shotgun blast at his remote cottage in Co Donegal by the Real IRA.

APPENDIX THREE

1972 ROLL OF HONOUR

14/20 KINGS HUSSARS AND 15/19 KINGS ROYAL HUSSARS
2/LT ROBERT WILLIAMS-WYNN 13/07/72   Shot by IRA sniper in West Belfast

5 REGIMENT ARMY AIR CORPS
SGT I C REID   24/06/72   IRA landmine, Glenshane Pass, Co Antrim
L/CPL D MOON   24/06/72   Killed in same incident

ARGYLL AND SUTHERLAND HIGHLANDERS
L/CPL DUNCAN McPHEE   10/09/72   IRA landmine Dungannon
PTE DOUGLAS RICHMOND   10/09/72   Killed in same incident
L/CPL WILLIAM McINTYRE   11/09/72   DoW from same incident
2nd LT STEWART GARDINER   22/09/72   Shot by IRA sniper Drummuckavall, Armagh
PTE DAVID HARPER   12/11/72   Killed by passing train whilst on patrol
CAPT WILLIAM WATSON   20/11/72   IRA booby trap Cullyhanna
C/SGT JAMES STRUTHERS   20/11/72   Killed in the same incident
PTE JOHN McGARRY   28/11/72   Friendly fire

ARMY CATERING CORPS
PTE ROGER KEALEY   18/06/72   Cause of death unknown

COLDSTREAM GUARDS
SGT ANTHONY METCALF   27/08/72   IRA sniper Creggan Heights, Londonderry

DEVON & DORSET REGIMENT
PTE CHARLES STENTIFORD   21/01/72   IRA landmine, Keady, Co Armagh
PTE DAVID CHAMP   10/02/72   IRA landmine, Cullyhanna, Co Armagh
SGT IAN HARRIS   10/02/72   Killed in same incident

DUKE OF WELLINGTON'S REGIMENT
PTE GEORGE LEE   6/06/72   IRA sniper, Ballymurphy estate, Belfast
CPL TERRENCE GRAHAM   16/07/72   Landmine attack, Crossmaglen
PTE JAMES LEE   16/07/72   Killed in same incident

GLOUCESTERSHIRE REGIMENT

PTE KEITH BRYAN	5/01/72	IRA sniper, Lower Falls area, Belfast
CPL IAN BRAMLEY	2/02/72	IRA sniper Hastings Street RUC station, Belfast

GORDON HIGHLANDERS

WO2 ARTHUR McMILLAN	18/06/72	Booby-trapped house in Lurgan, Co Down
SGT IAN MARK MUTCH	18/06/72	Killed in same incident
L/CPL COLIN LESLIE	18/06/72	Killed in same incident
L/CPL A.C. HARPER	8/08/72	RTA

KING'S OWN ROYAL BORDER REGIMENT

PRIVATE GEORGE P RIDDING	10/05/72	Died of natural causes after being taken ill.

KING'S OWN SCOTTISH BORDERERS

L/CPL PETER DEACON SIME	7/04/72	IRA sniper, Ballymurphy Est. Belfast
L/CPL BARRY GOLD	24/04/72	DoW after gun battle at VCP in Belfast
C/SGT HENRY S. MIDDLEMASS	10/12/72	IRA booby trap, Turf Lodge, Belfast

KINGS REGIMENT

CPL ALAN BUCKLEY	13/05/72	Shot on Turf Lodge, Belfast
PTE EUSTACE HANLEY	23/05/72	IRA sniper Ballymurphy estate
PTE MARCEL DOGLAY	30/05/72	IRA bomb, Springfield Road, Belfast
PTE JAMES JONES	18/07/72	IRA sniper, New Barnsley, Belfast
PTE BRIAN THOMAS	24/07/72	IRA sniper, New Barnsley, Belfast
PTE RENNIE LAYFIELD	18/08/72	IRA sniper, Falls Road, Belfast
PTE ROY CHRISTOPHER	30/08/72	DoW after bomb attack, Cupar St ,Belfast

LIGHT INFANTRY
1st Battalion

PTE RICHARD JONES	18/08/72	Shot by sniper in West Belfast
PTE R. ROWE	28/08/72	Shot accidentally in Ardoyne, Belfast
PTE T.A. STOKER	19/09/72	DoW after accidental shooting in Berwick Road, Ardoyne
PTE T. RUDMAN	30/09/72	Shot in Ardoyne, Belfast

2nd Battalion

SGT ARTHUR WHITELOCK	24/08/72	IRA sniper in Londonderry

PARACHUTE REGIMENT

FATHER GERRY WESTON, MBE	22/02/72	Killed in IRA bomb outrage, Aldershot
PTE ANTHONY KELLY	18/03/72	Killed in accident, Holywood, Co Down
PTE CHRISTOPHER STEPHENSON	24/06/72	IRA landmine, Glenshane Pass, Londonderry
PTE FRANK T. BELL	20/09/72	DoW after being shot on Ballymurphy estate

QUEENS LANCASHIRE REGIMENT
PTE STEPHEN KEATING 3/03/72 IRA sniper, Manor Street, West Belfast

QUEENS REGIMENT
PTE RICHARD SINCLAIR 31/10/72 IRA sniper New Lodge, Belfast
PTE STANLEY EVANS 14/11/72 IRA sniper Unity Flats complex, West Belfast

ROYAL ANGLIAN REGIMENT
2/LT NICHOLAS HULL 16/04/72 IRA sniper Divis Street flats, Belfast
PTE JOHN BALLARD 11/05/72 IRA sniper, Sultan St. Lower Falls, Belfast
L/CPL MARTIN ROONEY 12/07/72 IRA sniper Clonard St., Lower Falls, Belfast
CPL KENNETH MOGG 13/07/72 IRA sniper Dunville Park, Belfast
L/CPL JOHN BODDY 17/08/72 IRA sniper, Grosvenor Road area of Belfast
CPL JOHN BARRY 25/09/72 DoW after gun battle Lower Falls, Belfast
PTE IAN BURT 29/09/72 IRA sniper Albert Street, Lower Falls, Belfast
PTE ROBERT MASON 24/10/72 IRA sniper Naples St, Grosvenor Rd, Belfast

ROYAL ARMY MEDICAL CORPS
PTE DENNIS 'TAFFY' PORTER 24/04/72 Violent or unnatural causes

ROYAL ARMY PAY CORPS
PTE MICHAEL PRIME 16/02/72 Shot in ambush at Moira roundabout near Lisburn

ROYAL ARMY ORDINANCE CORPS
PTE T F McCANN 14/02/72 Abducted and murdered by the IRA, Newtownbutler
SSGT C.R. CRACKNELL 15/03/72 IRA booby trap, Grosvenor Road, Belfast
SSGT A.S. BUTCHER 15/03/72 Killed in same incident
MAJOR B.C. CALLADENE 29/03/72 IRA car bomb outside Belfast City Hall
CAPTAIN J.H. YOUNG 15/07/72 Defusing IRA bomb, Silverbridge near Forkhill
WO2. W.J. CLARK 3/08/72 Defusing IRA bomb at Strabane
SGT R.E. HILLS 5/12/72 Attempting to make live shell safe, Lurgan

ROYAL ARTILLERY
L/BDR ERIC BLACKBURN 10/04/72 Killed in bomb attack, Rosemount Avenue
L/BDR BRIAN THOMASSON 10/04/72 Killed In same incident
GNR VICTOR HUSBAND 2/06/72 IRA landmine, Rosslea, Co Fermanagh
GNR BRIAN ROBERTSON 2/06/72 Killed in the same incident
SGT CHARLES COLEMAN 7/06/72 IRA sniper, Andersonstown, Belfast

GUNNER WILLIAM RAISTRICK	11/06/72	IRA sniper Brooke Park, Londonderry
BOMBARDIER TERRENCE JONES	11/07/72	Shot by IRA, Londonderry
GNR LEROY GORDON	7/08/72	IRA landmine, Lisnaskea, Co Fermanagh
L/BDR DAVID WYNNE	7/08/72	Killed in same incident
MAJOR DAVID STORRY	14/08/72	Booby trap, Casement Park, Andersonstown
GUNNER ROBERT CUTTING	03/09/72	Killed in friendly fire incident, New Lodge
S/SGT JOHN GARDNER CRAIG	15/09/72	RTA
GNR PAUL JACKSON	28/11/72	Hit by shrapnel, Strand Road ,Londonderry

ROYAL CORPS TRANSPORT

DRIVER STEPHEN BEEDIE	26/03/72	RTA
DRIVER LAURENCE JUBB	26/04/72	Killed in vehicle crash after mob attack, Armagh
L/CPL MICHAEL BRUCE	31/05/72	IRA sniper Andersonstown, Belfast
S/SGT JOSEPH FLEMING (TA)	9/07/72	Shot dead by IRA in Grosvenor Road area of Belfast
DRIVER PETER HEPPENSTALL	14/07/72	IRA sniper Ardoyne area of Belfast
DRIVER STEPHEN COOPER	21/07/72	IRA car bomb on Bloody Friday, Belfast
DRIVER RONALD KITCHEN	10/11/72	IRA sniper at VCP in Oldpark Road, Belfast

ROYAL DRAGOON GUARDS

TROOPER GEOFFREY KNIPE	7/08/72	Armoured vehicle crashed after mob attack, Armagh

ROYAL ELECTRICAL & MECHANICAL ENGINEERS

SGT STUART C. REID	24/06/72	IRA milk churn bombs at Glenshane Pass
L/CPL D. MOON	24/06/72	Killed in same incident
CFN BRIAN HOPE	14/08/72	IRA booby trap Casement Park, Andersonstown, Belfast
L/CPL COLIN HARKER	24/12/72	DoW; was shot by IRA sniper Lecky Road, Londonderry

ROYAL ENGINEERS

SAPPER RONALD HURST	17/05/72	IRA sniper whilst working on base, Crossmaglen
S/SGT MALCOLM BANKS	28/06/72	Shot by IRA Short Strand area of Belfast
SAPPER EDWARD STUART	2/10/72	Shot whilst working undercover, Belfast

ROYAL GREEN JACKETS

MAJOR ROBIN ALERS-HANKEY	30/01/72	DoW after being shot in Bogside area
RFN JOHN TAYLOR	20/03/72	IRA sniper, William Street, Londonderry
RFN JAMES MEREDITH	26/06/72	Shot in Abercorn Road, Londonderry
L/CPL DAVID CARD	4/08/72	Killed by IRA gunman in Andersonstown, Belfast

CPL IAN MORRILL	28/08/72	IRA sniper in Beechmount Avenue, Belfast
RFN DAVID GRIFFITHS	30/08/72	IRA sniper, Clonard Street, Lower Falls, Belfast
L/CPL IAN GEORGE	10/09/72	Thought to have been shot by an IRA sniper, Belfast
RFN RAYMOND JOESBURY	8/12/72	DoW after being shot in Whiterock, Belfast

ROYAL HORSE GUARDS
| L/COH KEITH CHILLINGWORTH | 14/06/72 | RTA |

ROYAL IRISH RANGERS
| RANGER WILLIAM J. BEST | 21/05/72 | Abducted and murdered by IRA while on home leave |
| RANGER THOMAS McGANN | 26/05/72 | RTA |

ROYAL MARINE COMMANDOS
40 Cdo
| MARINE LEONARD ALLEN | 26/07/72 | Shot by IRA, Unity Flats, Belfast |
| MARINE ANTHONY DAVID | 17/10/72 | DoW after being shot by IRA on Falls Road |

ROYAL PIONEER CORPS
| PTE IRWIN BOWEN | 2/08/72 | RTA |

ROYAL REGIMENT FUSILIERS
FUSILIER K. CANHAM	14/07/72	IRA sniper in Lenadoon
FUSILIER ALAN P. TINGEY	23/08/72	IRA sniper, West Belfast
CPL. JOHN L. DAVIS	15/09/72	Shot by IRA in Bogside, Londonderry
FUS TERRY THOMAS	25/01/72	Cause of death unknown

ROYAL REGIMENT OF WALES
L/CPL JOHN HILLMAN	18/05/72	IRA sniper Flex Street Mill, Ardoyne, Belfast
L/CPL ALAN GILES	12/06/72	Shot in gun battle with IRA, Ardoyne, Belfast
PTE BRIAN SODEN	19/06/72	IRA sniper in Ardoyne, Belfast
PTE DAVID MEEKE	13/07/72	IRA sniper, Hooker Street, Ardoyne, Belfast
PTE JOHN WILLIAMS	14/07/72	Killed in gun battle with IRA, Ardoyne

ROYAL SCOTS DRAGOON GUARDS
| TROOPER IAN CAIE | 24/08/72 | IRA landmine attack at Crossmaglen |

ROYAL WELSH FUSILIERS
| CPL GERALD BRISTOW | 16/04/72 | IRA sniper Bishops Street, Londonderry |
| FUSILIER KERRY MCCARTHY | 21/06/72 | IRA sniper Victoria RUC station, Londonderry |

SCOTS GUARDS

GUARDSMAN JOHN VAN BECK	18/09/72	DoW after being shot by IRA, Lecky Road, Derry
GUARDSMAN GEORGE LOCKHART	26/09/72	DoW after being shot by IRA, Bogside
L/SGT THOMAS MCKAY	28/10/72	IRA sniper, Bishop Street, Londonderry

STAFFORDSHIRE REGIMENT

S/SGT JOHN MORRELL	24/10/72	DoW after IRA booby trap, Drumargh, Armagh

ULSTER DEFENCE REGIMENT

2nd Battalion

SERGEANT HARRY D. DICKSON	27/02/72	Murdered by the IRA at his home

3rd Battalion

L/CPL JOE JARDINE	8/03/72	Shot by IRA whilst working
CPL JIM D. ELLIOTT	19/04/72	Abducted and murdered by IRA
C/SGT JOHN RUDDY	10/10/72	Shot by IRA on his way to work

4th Battalion

PTE JOHNNY FLETCHER	1/03/72	Abducted and murdered by IRA
L/CPL HARRY CREIGHTON	7/08/72	Murdered by IRA at his house near Monaghan
PTE JIMMY E. EAMES	25/08/72	IRA booby trapped car at Enniskillen
L/CPL ALFIE JOHNSTON	25/08/72	Killed in same incident
PTE TOMMY R. BULLOCK	21/09/72	Murdered along with his wife at their home
PTE J. ROBIN BELL	22/10/72	Shot by IRA whilst with his father

5th Battalion

PTE THOMAS CALLAGHAN	16/02/72	Abducted and murdered in the Creggan, Londonderry
PTE SAMUEL PORTER	22/11/72	Shot and killed by the IRA as he walked home
PTE GEORGE E. HAMILTON	20/12/72	Shot by the IRA as he worked on repairs at a reservoir

6th Battalion

PTE TED MEGAHEY	9/06/72	DoW after IRA shooting
PTE WILLIAM J. BOGLE	5/12/72	Murdered in his car as he sat with his children

8th Battalion

L/CPL HENRY GILLESPIE	20/05/72	Shot by IRA patrolling near Dungannon
PTE FRED D. GREEVES	15/12/72	Shot by IRA as he left work in Armagh

9th Battalion

SGT MAYNARD CRAWFORD	13/01/72	Shot as he waited in a car at Newtownabbey
CPL ROY STANTON	9/06/72	Shot by IRA as he drove home
PTE HENRY J. RUSSELL	13/07/72	Abducted, tortured and shot by IRA

10th Battalion

PTE SAMUEL TRAINOR	20/03/72	IRA bomb, Belfast city centre
PTE ROBERT McCOMB	23/07/72	Abducted and murdered by IRA in Belfast
PTE TERENCE MAGUIRE	14/10/72	Abducted and murdered in Belfast

11th Battalion

L/CPL VICTOR SMYTH	6/09/72	IRA bomb underneath his car, in Portadown

Battalion Unknown

PTE THOMAS MOFFETT	26/02/72	Cause of death unknown
PTE GEORGE CURRAN	12/03/72	Cause of death unknown
PTE DONALD KANE	4/04/72	Cause of death unknown
CPL BRIAN HERON	18/05/72	Cause of death unknown
CPL SIDNEY HUSSEY	20/05/72	Cause of death unknown
SGT WILLIAM REID	28/05/72	Cause of death unknown
WO2 BERNARD ADAMSON	31/05/72	Accident, place unknown
PTE GEORGE ELLIOTT	26/06/72	Accident, place unknown
PTE WILLIAM WILKINSON	12/07/72	Cause of death unknown
MAJOR ERIC BEAUMONT	25/07/72	Cause of death unknown
CPL ALBERT JOHNSTON	1/08/72	Cause of death unknown
PTE WILLIAM HAMILTON	4/08/72	Accident, place unknown
PTE KENNETH TWADDELL	5/08/72	Accident, place unknown
PTE ANDREW SIMPSON	18/09/72	RTA
PTE THOMAS OLPHERT	6/10/72	Cause of death unknown
PTE EDMUND SIMPSON	10/10/72	Cause of death unknown
PTE ROBERT McKEOWN	13/10/72	RTA
SGT WILLIAM CALDERWOOD	15/10/72	Cause of death unknown
MAJ JOHN MUNNIS	16/10/72	RTA
PTE THOMAS BOYD	28/12/72	Cause of death unknown

WELSH GUARDS

SGT PHILIP PRICE	21/07/72	IRA car bomb on Bloody Friday

WORCESTER & SHERWOOD FORESTERS

PTE MARTIN ROBINSON	16/04/72	Killed by IRA, Brandywell base, Londonderry

ARMY CIVILIAN PERSONNEL KILLED IN ALDERSHOT IRA BOMB OUTRAGE 22/02/72

THELMA BOSLEY	JILL MANSFIELD
JOAN LUNN	JOHN HASLAR
MARGARET GRANT	CHERIE MUNTON

ARMY WOMEN AND CHILDREN KILLED AS A RESULT OF TERRORISM

MRS EMILY BULLOCK	21/09/72	Murdered by IRA, Aghalane

I gratefully and wholeheartedly acknowledge the incredible services of Emma Beaumont, without whom the compiling of this comprehensive Roll of Honour could never have been done. Great assistance by individual Regimental Associations was also given and I would like to mention Norman Brown of the Royal Pioneer Corps, Kevin Gorman of the Scots Guards, Kevin Stevens, Royal Green Jackets, Pete Whittall, Staffords, Richard Nettleton, Grenadier Guards and Robert Osborne, QLR. I gratefully acknowledge the Armed Forces Memorial Roll of Honour and the Northern Ireland Veterans' Association for the ability to cross-reference between these two excellent sites.

SELECT BIBLIOGRAPHY

Barzilay, David, *The British Army in Ulster Volume 1* (Century Books, 1973)

Bradley, Gerry & Brian Feeney, *Insider: Gerry Bradley's Life in the IRA* (O'Brian Press, 2008)

Clarke, A.F.N., *Contact* (Secker & Warburg, 1983)

Clarke, George, *Border Crossing* (Gill & MacMillan, 2009)

Dillon, Martin, *The Shankill Butchers* (Arrow Books, 1991)

Hamill, Desmond, *Pig In The Middle* (Methuen Books, 1985)

Harnden, Toby, *Bandit Country* (Hodder & Stoughton, 1999)

Moloney, Ed, *Voices From The Grave* (Faber & Faber, 2010)

McGartland, Marty, *Fifty Dead Men Walking* (Blake Publishing, 1997)

McKittrick *et al*, *Lost Lives: The Stories of the Men, Women and Children Who Died Through the Northern Ireland Troubles* (Mainstream, 2007)

Myers, Kevin, *Watching the Door: Cheating Death in 1970s Belfast* (Atlantic Books, 2008)

O'Callaghan, Sean, *The Informer* (Corgi Books, 1999)

Potter, John, *A Testimony To Courage* (Pen & Sword, 2001)

Pringle, Peter & Philip Jacobson, *Those Are Real Bullets Aren't They?* (Fourth Estate Books, 2000)

Urban, Mark, *Big Boys' Rules* (Faber & Faber, 1993)

Van der Bilj, Nick, *Operation Banner* (Pen & Sword, 2009)

Wharton, Ken, *A Long Long War; Voices From the British Army in Northern Ireland, 1969–98* (Helion Books, 2008)

Wharton, Ken, *Bloody Belfast: An Oral History of the British Army's War Against the IRA* (The History Press, 2010)

Wharton, Ken, *Bullets, Bombs and Cups of Tea; Further Voices of the British Army in Northern Ireland* (Helion Books, 2009)

INDEX